I See Men as Trees, Walking

I See Men as Trees, Walking

The Crowd in Untruth, the Single Individual, and Becoming a Self
Volume 2—Mark 5:1 to 8:38

A KIERKEGAARDIAN READING OF THE GOSPEL OF MARK

BRYAN M. CHRISTMAN

RESOURCE *Publications* • Eugene, Oregon

I SEE MEN AS TREES, WALKING
The Crowd in Untruth, the Single Individual, and Becoming a Self
Volume 2—Mark 5:1 to 8:38

A Kierkegaardian Reading of Mark

Copyright © 2024 Bryan M. Christman. All rights reserved. Except for brief quotations in critical publications or reviews, no part of this book may be reproduced in any manner without prior written permission from the publisher. Write: Permissions, Wipf and Stock Publishers, 199 W. 8th Ave., Suite 3, Eugene, OR 97401.

Resource Publications
An Imprint of Wipf and Stock Publishers
199 W. 8th Ave., Suite 3
Eugene, OR 97401

www.wipfandstock.com

PAPERBACK ISBN: 979-8-3852-0329-1
HARDCOVER ISBN: 979-8-3852-0330-7
EBOOK ISBN: 979-8-3852-0331-4

Scripture quotations marked ESV are taken from The ESV® Bible (The Holy Bible, English Standard Version®), copyright © 2001 by Crossway, a publishing ministry of Good News Publishers. Used by permission. All rights reserved.

Scripture quotations marked KJV are from the King James Version, Public Domain.

Scripture quotations marked NIV are taken from the Holy Bible, New International Version®, NIV® Copyright ©1973, 1978, 1984, 2011 by Biblica Inc.® Used by permission. All rights reserved.

Contents

Abbreviations | *vii*

Introduction to Volume 2 | *xi*

1 The Defiant Man of the Tombs: *The Sickness Unto Death*, "The Publican," and the Modern Demonic Age | 1

2 The Little Daughter of Jairus: "To Need God is a Human Being's Highest Perfection" | 34

3 The Unnamed "Daughter" Who Touched the Hem of Jesus' Garment: "The Single Individual" as "The Category through which the Human Race Must Go" | 46

4 "The Un-miracle Story" in Jesus' Hometown: Reflective Envy as the Social Ethos of the Age of Reflection | 60

5 The Gospel of the Terrible Inversion: The Loftiness of God in the Solidarity of Lowliness | 73

6 John the Baptist, King Herod, and *Two Ages*: "The Idea for Which I Can Live and Die" | 81

7 Jesus, "Son of Man" on the Mountain and Theophany on the Sea: Historical and "Philosophical" Fragments | 101

8 "Corban" and the "Christian" Bourgeoise Settlement: God's Eternal "Like for Like" | 116

9 The Syrophoenician Woman and Fragments from the Children's Table: The Parable of the Offensive Invitation | 130

10 Sighing to Heaven, Spitting and Restoring on Earth: The Gospel of Groaning, Hearing, and Speaking | 146

11 Beware the Leaven . . . Welcome the Gadfly: "Socratic" Gadflies and the Established Order | 162

12 "I See Men as Trees, Walking": The "Radical Cure" of the Second Touch | 177

13 The "Disciple" Who Rejected the Way of Jesus' Death: The Crowd in Untruth, "The Single Individual," and Becoming a Self | 197

Conclusion to Volume 2 | 215

Bibliography | 219

Index | 227

Abbreviations

Bible Versions

ESV	English Standard Version
KJV	King James Version
NIV	New International Version

Kierkegaard's Writings

ALSC	A Leper's Self-Contemplation
AC	Attack Upon Christendom (Lowrie)
CA	The Concept of Anxiety
CD	Christian Discourses
CI	The Concept of Irony
COR	The Corsair Affair
CUP1	Concluding Unscientific Postscript Vol. 1
CUP2	Concluding Unscientific Postscript Vol. 2
EO1	Either/Or Vol. 1
EO2	Either/Or Vol. 2
EUD	Eighteen Upbuilding Discourses
FSE/JFY	For Self-Examination/Judge For Yourself
FT	Fear and Trembling
GNG	"Guilty?"/ "Not Guilty?"
JP	Journals and Papers

LTK	The Living Thoughts of Kierkegaard (Auden)
MLW	The Moment and Late Writings
PC	Practice in Christianity
PH	Purity of Heart is to Will One Thing
PF	Philosophical Fragments
PSW	Provocations: Spiritual Writings of Kierkegaard (Moore)
PV	The Point of View
SK	The Soul of Kierkegaard (Dru)
SLW	Stages on Life's Way
SD	The Sickness Unto Death
SWK	Spiritual Writings: Gift, Creation, Love (Pattison)
TA	Two Ages
TDIO	Three Discourses on Imagined Occasions
UDVS	Upbuilding Discourses in Various Spirits
WL	Works of Love

Scripture

Col	Colossians
Cor	Corinthians
Dan	Daniel
Eccl	Ecclesiastes
Eph	Ephesians
Exod	Exodus
Ezek	Ezekiel
Gal	Galatians
Gen	Genesis
Hab	Habakkuk
Hag	Haggai
Heb	Hebrews

Isa	Isaiah
Jas	James
Jer	Jeremiah
Kgs	Kings
Lev	Leviticus
LXX	The Septuagint
Matt	Matthew
Mic	Micah
Nah	Nahum
NT	New Testament
OT	Old Testament
Pet	Peter
Phil	Philippians
Ps	Psalms
Rev	Revelation
Rom	Romans
Thess	Thessalonians
Tim	Timothy
Zech	Zechariah

Introduction to Volume 2

This volume is about seeing the real, becoming real, and the crowd constraining us from "becoming a self." This is the challenge and promise of the place we're thrown, wherein "we live, and move, and have our being."[1] Most live a love/hate relationship with the crowd, wishing to escape or petulantly forming some "identity" in relation to it, for better or for the worse, till death do we part. We also live and die in a love/hate relationship with ourselves. Who are we now? Who should we become? Are we created by God, our self, or the crowd? This volume shows that these were the concerns of first-century Mark and nineteenth-century Kierkegaard.

In Mark's gospel the crowd is ever-present, ambiguous and needy, demanding and ominous. He demonstrates *the single individual* emerging from it. Kierkegaard called the crowd the mass-men. The crowd is never one's *home* in Mark. The crowd itself is ever-seeking but never-finding. The self, the home, cannot be found *in, through,* or *by the* crowd. Nevertheless, Mark's crowd is *on the road.* Yet looking at it one sees ambiguity—men, as trees—walking.

The witty, wise, and adventurous G. K. Chesterton once said "there are two ways of getting home; and one of them is to stay there. The other is to walk round the whole world till we come back to the same place."[2] Our problem is *seeing* home. So, the latter way is what most of us travel. Our spiritual blindness requires seeing the world anew. That view is gained on the return approach as we come home from the around the world trek. Coming from the distance we see as *"for the first time"* through restored eyes. "Men as trees, walking" signifies the crowd to Mark. In his gospel story a blind man appears just before the anti-climactic mid-point. He had become blind and could no longer see "home." Lack of sight makes life difficult and dangerous. But he's brought to Jesus, the one known to heal the blind. Obligingly, Jesus spat in his eyes, placed his hands on them, and asked what

1. Acts 17:48.
2. Chesterton, *The Everlasting Man,* 9.

he saw. He answered, "I see men *as trees, walking*." So, Jesus touched his eyes *again*, fully "restoring" his eyes. Mark exhibits the divine *process* that heals spiritual blindness.

We are all spiritually blind, and *stubbornly* so. We're unable to see the possibility in which we nevertheless live. Mark's gospel-narrative aims to lead its readers "*round the whole world till we come back to the same place.*" The new view also presents something else. A decision we missed previously, for there was none to be made from *that* place. Soren Kierkegaard's writings provoked the same place of decision. He aimed to lead his readers "*out on 70,000 fathoms*" in a risky *inward* and *outward* journey from the pseudo-comforts of the home that is not *home*.[3] For there are no *individuals* there. The crowd is never home, because the crowd has no individuals. Staying in that "home" is the way to remain a non-self. For Kierkegaard, and we think for Mark also, *salvation—was to become—*"the single individual" through *the gospel*. That was what Kierkegaard dedicated his life to: "*the idea for which I am willing to live and die.*"[4] Mark shows that the idea Kierkegaard searched for requires one's life and death, the reception of the gospel-way of Jesus, the paradoxical way of life via "the cross."

The greatest obstacle to true existence is the allurement of the "comfortable home" in which we are already living—and dying—whether we know it or not. That is why, from the beginning, the gospel birthed new communities that were "a home for the homeless." The homeless already know they are not *home*. But those "at home" in the crowd, are not *home* but think they are. Mark and Kierkegaard both saw the crowd as of special interest to "the established order." For that order promises the crowd a "home." But Mark and Kierkegaard reveal the skeletons in the closets of that "home" which builds and maintains its established order through its propaganda, "bread and games," and the old stand-by, force. As "masters of suspicion" they deconstruct the "sacred canopy" every established order fastidiously builds and maintains, to provide the "home" that is no home.

Mark and Kierkegaard both prescribed the risk of boldly venturing from "the crowd" to a new and unknown life outside. They called forth this new, previously absent decision. But this is no momentary decision. It requires the resolve of a lifetime. Nevertheless, both writers called for a "*leap of faith.*" When our building is burning what can be done but leap? But "there's the rub" for the crowd. Is *our* building really burning? Are there truly *no individuals* here by choice?

---

3. "Out on 70,000 fathoms" was a favorite term of Kierkegaard's to describe the "perilous" situation of life where faith is not merely helpful, but *always* necessary.

4. Dru, *The Soul of Kierkegaard*, 44.

Jesus warned his disciples about "leaven." The *safe and reasonable way* of building human-all-too-human sacred canopies and clamoring to live beneath their self-protection. Our stubborn blindness lends a hand to that great and humanly perennial construct. For at least we see something, men with sacred (tree) canopies walking! But we need Jesus' "second touch" to see the reality of the walking crowd. But alas, that second touch also reveals the way of the cross from which we shrink back. Yet paradoxically, that is the only way of life, of becoming a self, apart from *ego*. Jamie Lorentzen writes:

> The ethical development of a human being begins and ends with the suicide of the I . . . the psychological self-murder of various false selves of an individual that have been malformed externally by culture, with at least tacit consent by the individual . . . Suicide of the I creates a true self by the self-murder of false selves.[5]

This book attempts to provide insight into Mark's and Kierkegaard's uncannily collaborative deconstructions and reconstructions of their host worlds and of ours. Perhaps they can help us "walk round the whole world," discovering upon our return approach a strangely *new* home in which we can see more than "*men as trees, walking.*" And in that process, with the help of the God who is not the *product* of any established order, we will discover that *we ourselves* have been deconstructed and reconstructed as *the single individual* walking in *a new world* of possibility. More specifically, volume 2 depicts Mark's interesting and colorful characters struggling in and through the various Kierkegaardian "stages of life" to become true selves through the person-forming gospel. The more this Kierkegaardian reading of Mark proceeds, the more I think that Mark would fully endorse Kierkegaard's statement:

> There is a view of life that holds that truth is where the crowd is, that truth itself needs to have the crowd on its side. There is another view of life that holds that wherever the crowd is, untruth is . . . What Paul says is eternally, divinely, Christianly valid: 'Only one reaches the goal' . . . this means that everyone can be this one; God will help him in that—but only one reaches the goal.[6]

---

5. Lorentzen, *Sober Cannibals, Drunken Christians*, 17. Mark and Kierkegaard specialized in revealing the false selves in the "optical illusion" the false society creates. See Mark 11:12–14; Kierkegaard, MLW, 34.

6. Kierkegaard, PV, 105–6. See UDVS, 4.

1

The Defiant Man of the Tombs

The Sickness Unto Death, "The Publican," and the Modern Demonic Age

Mark 5:1–20 (ESV)

They came to the other side of the sea, to the country of the Gerasenes. 2 And when Jesus had stepped out of the boat, immediately there met him out of the tombs a man with an unclean spirit. 3 He lived among the tombs. And no one could bind him anymore, not even with a chain, 4 for he had often been bound with shackles and chains, but he wrenched the chains apart, and he broke the shackles in pieces. No one had the strength to subdue him. 5 Night and day among the tombs and on the mountains he was always crying out and cutting himself with stones. 6 And when he saw Jesus from afar, he ran and fell down before him. 7 And crying out with a loud voice, he said, "What have you to do with me, Jesus, Son of the Most High God? I adjure you by God, do not torment me." 8 For he was saying to him, "Come out of the man, you unclean spirit!" 9 And Jesus asked him, "What is your name?" He replied, "My name is Legion, for we are many." 10 And he begged him earnestly not to send them out of the country. 11 Now a great herd of pigs was feeding there on the hillside, 12 and they begged him, saying, "Send us to the pigs; let us enter them." 13 So he gave them permission. And the unclean spirits came out and entered the pigs; and the herd, numbering about two thousand, rushed down the steep bank into the sea and drowned in the sea.

14 The herdsmen fled and told it in the city and in the country. And people came to see what it was that had happened. 15 And they came to Jesus and saw the demon-possessed man, the one who had had the legion, sitting there, clothed and in his right mind, and they were afraid. 16 And those who had seen it described to them what had happened to the demon-possessed man and to the pigs. 17 And they began to beg Jesus to depart from their region. 18 As he was getting into the boat, the man who had been possessed with demons begged him that he might be with him. 19 And he did not permit him but said to him, "Go home to your friends and tell them how much the Lord has done for you, and how he has had mercy on you." 20 And he went away and began to proclaim in the Decapolis how much Jesus had done for him, and everyone marveled.

For the first time I examined myself with a seriously practical purpose. And there I found what appalled me; a zoo of lusts, a bedlam of ambitions, a nursery of fears, a harem of fondled hatreds. My name was legion.[1]
—C. S. Lewis

Which way I fly is hell, myself am hell.[2] —Satan

What demonic madness—the thought that most infuriates him is that eternity could get the notion to deprive him of his misery.[3] —Anti-Climacus

The basic concept of man is spirit, and one should not be confused by the fact that he is also able to walk on two feet. The basic concept of language is thought, and one should not be confused by the fact that a few emotional people are of the opinion that the greatest importance of language is the production of inarticulate sounds.[4]—A

---

1. Lewis, *Surprised by Joy*, 226.
2. From John Milton's Paradise Lost, as cited in Tanner, *Anxiety in Eden*, 145.
3. Kierkegaard, SD, 72. "*Anti-Climacus*" was Kierkegaard's pseudonymous author of the book.
4. Kierkegaard, EO1, 65. "A" was the pseudonymous author of the "Papers" in *Either/Or Part 1*.

In this chapter we begin by situating the context in Mark, adding some thoughts on Mark's purposes, and then providing three different "Kierkegaardian readings" of the account. Kierkegaard often presented differently nuanced discourses on the same Biblical texts and subjects. Ultimately, it is in that spirit that we present the following three readings of Mark's account of the demoniac.

Here Mark's fast-cutting chaos cinema turns to veritable horror cinema introduced with the hell-sent storm of destruction and followed by the grisly details of a man possessed by a demonic army. As if to greet Jesus, the demoniac had emerged from his lair among the tombs, possibly "decorated" with the broken shackles and chains to commemorate his defiant strength against his unsuccessful restrainers. The region was itself, according to Jewish purity laws, *teeming* with horrible uncleanness since *unclean* swine, raised by *unclean* Gentiles lived there. Add *unclean* tombs and *unclean spirits* and you have perhaps the "ideal" scene of *uncleanness*. Apart from all that "horror," the demoniac himself provided the macabre soundtrack wherein *"night and day among the tombs and on the mountains he was always crying out and cutting himself with stones."*

Of course, Jesus had directed this little missionary trip. And as had been already seen, his prior contacts with the unclean bought *their* cleansing, instead of his uncleanness. Mark takes great interest in what transpired here and didn't seem to spare details in this account. In fact, this encounter with the demoniac contains one of the longest descriptions of any individual in all of the gospels. Moreover, the care of Jesus for this shunned demoniac cost the ultimate owner of the cattle on a thousand hills a valuable herd of swine in the "bargaining" for his deliverance.[5]

Mark describes what transpired as the man drew near to Jesus. *"And when he saw Jesus from afar, he ran and fell down before him. And crying out with a loud voice, he said, "What have you to do with me, Jesus, Son of the Most High God? I adjure you by God, do not torment me."* In order to begin to see what Mark intends to convey in this account, we begin by looking closely at this tormented man. Of course, we will also see thereby Kierkegaard's view of the process by which "demonically defiant" persons become individuals through Christ and faith.

---

5. Boring addresses how the destruction of this costly herd has bothered both ancient and modern interpreters of Mark. Boring, *Mark,* 269–70.

MARK'S VIEW OF THE DEMONIAC AND THE OPPRESSIVE LEGION

It seems likely that Mark intended the parabolic interlude of chapter 4, demonstrating the broad scope of human response to the gospel, to be contrasted by narrowly focused episodes of receptivity to the gospel. Thus, Mark presents three individual encounters with Jesus in a fairly detailed way. Mark had previously and very briefly shown several individuals in distinction to the crowds, whereas these three are considered with much more fullness. The demoniac of the Gerasene region, a ruler of the synagogue named Jairus, and an unnamed woman with a physical affliction, are each given a sort of "vignette" demonstrating faith-response to God's Son, the Christ. Through these three Mark presents individuals emerging from the ambiguous crowd because of their faith in Jesus.

The demoniac, under the influence of the demonic Legion, is quite striking in this regard, given that "his" initial "response" is to beg Jesus to leave "us" alone. The perverse conception of freedom the "buried" demoniac seems to embrace drips with irony. "He" could not bear the shackles and chains of his society but could bear the merciless unfreedom brought by the oppressive Legion of demons. "Together" he/they counted Jesus, who could deliver humans from the darkness of defiance, as the tormentor to be feared above all for that reason. This perversity may seem difficult to relate to, seemingly far from most of us. But the "modern" testimony of C. S. Lewis may help us here. In this chapter's first epigram above, we see that Lewis lamented the fact that his "name was Legion." Thus, he was "a zoo of lusts, a bedlam of ambitions, a nursery of fears, a harem of fondled hatreds." But what was the terrible source of this "Legion" that oppressed him? He revealed that it was *himself*, in hyper-allergic reaction to *God*, the one who interferes.

> Remember, I had always wanted, above all things, not to be "interfered with." I had always wanted (mad wish) "to call my soul my own." I had been far more anxious to avoid suffering than to achieve delight. I had always aimed at limited liabilities . . . Not the slightest assurance on that score was offered me . . . Total surrender, the absolute leap in the dark were demanded.[6]

The demoniac thus illustrates the genealogy of the modern quest of Lewis for a "safe" autonomy, although it is valid to ask whether the modern Lewis accurately illustrates the ancient oppression the demoniac suffered. We must admit that our initial comparison of the ancient demoniac with the

---

6. Lewis, *Surprised by Joy*, 228.

modern Lewis and the following comparisons with Kierkegaard's "Christian psychology" both labor under the question of the correlation between these ancient and modern oppressions. For *surely* Lewis was (and we are) *defiantly* sinful and *surely* the demoniac was (and some are) oppressed by *defiant* demons. How "direct" is the correlation between human and demonic defiance? Perhaps quite direct, since the "mad wish" of the victimized demoniac and/or his oppressive Legion, is later paralleled by the oppressive "community" of the region, as "they" also beg Jesus to leave their region.[7] It seems that all "mad wishes" of the creature against its Creator must labor under *some* manner of significant spiritual connection, as the Bible generally testifies.

Mark's account of the demonic Legion and demonized community may be saying that this initial response signifies the basic primal response to Jesus when he is known as "the Son of the highest God" and thus corroborating Kierkegaard's view that Jesus must *first* become "the possibility of offense" in order that people can *subsequently* come to faith in him.[8] Mark's account certainly seems to be showing that Jesus is invading territory held by the enemy of God and of humans. But humans, due to their "native" enculturation, ignorantly and initially prefer their allegiant captivity.[9]

The idea of the demonic Legion representing *us*, the hearers/readers of Mark, may be offensive and shocking. But if Mark and Kierkegaard are right, we need to be shocked by the gospel. And of course, Jesus was the shock. Perhaps "Legion" can represent the collective of Mark's *ideal sinners,* an idea that would cohere with Kierkegaard's A*ttack upon "Christendom."* This "collective" of sinners means that its members exist in different places in the spectrum of sinfulness. We need to keep this spectrum in mind as we look closer at Kierkegaard's view of demonic despair, which he saw as the highest form of despair and sin.

---

7. Garland writes "It is a community that beats, chains, and dehumanizes other human beings. It knows how to use force, how to crack down on madmen, and how to protect its property . . . Societies are no less possessed in their angry punishment of poor wretches who are discarded on the waste heap of humanity for interfering with normal society." Garland, *Mark*, 213.

8. See Christman, *Behold*, 22–25.

9. On the pre-existent *native* "gospel of culture" see Christman, *Gospel*, 146–48.

READING 1: DEMONIC DESPAIR AND THE SICKNESS UNTO DEATH

In his book "Anxiety in Eden – A Kierkegaardian Reading of Paradise Lost," John S. Tanner says he "has found no evidence that Kierkegaard ever read Milton," but nevertheless finds "affinities between their interpretations of the Edenic myth" that were due to "similar backgrounds and temperaments, common ideological commitments, and (no doubt) shared genius."[10] Thus, Tanner says,

> Yet despite all that has been written about Milton's Satan, significant new insights into his malaise are available from Kierkegaard, whose analysis of "demonic despair" in *Sickness unto Death* (*SD*, 42; cf. 72–75) often seems as if it were penned specifically with the existential position of Milton's Satan in mind.[11]

Just as Kierkegaard was an aid to understanding "Paradise Lost," so also the Kierkegaardian reading of that book can inform our purposes here by bringing the thought of Kierkegaard and Milton to bear on Mark's demoniac and thus shed light on the nature of "demonic" despair.[12]

Inclosing Reserve[13]

The demoniac's life in isolation seems to have affinities with what Kierkegaard called "inclosing reserve." Life among the tombs certainly implies an "inclosed" life essentially lived apart from others.[14] Thus the demoniac's hurried approach to Jesus did not signal natural loneliness but rather an aggressive guarding of demonic inclosing reserve. But loneliness can pave the way for inclosing reserve. Thus, Kierkegaard saw *inclosing reserve* as cultivated *from* loneliness to produce "*inwardness with a jammed lock . . . the more spiritual despair becomes, the more attention it pays with demonic*

---

10. Tanner, *Anxiety in Eden*, 4.

11. Tanner, *Anxiety in Eden*, 146. In the rest of this chapter references to Tanner's book will be cited above.

12. Kierkegaard characterized despair as characterized by either weakness or by defiance, with the latter being what he considered "demonic despair." See Christman, *Behold*, 80–91 for a discussion of both types.

13. We mention in passing what seems a definite correlation between Kierkegaard's "inclosing reserve" and Luther's basic idea of human sinfulness as causing humans to "'turn in on themselves" (*homo incurvatus in se*). See Janz, *Martin Luther*, 127.

14. Our extensive reading of Kierkegaard's "A Leper's Self-Contemplation," which was also set in a graveyard, presented in Christman, *Behold*, 74–97, in many ways overlaps with the readings here.

cleverness to keeping despair closed up in inclosing reserve, and the more attention it pays to neutralizing the externalities, making them as insignificant and inconsequential as possible."[15]

The demoniac's approach to Jesus was to keep external threats to his reserve quite literally *at bay* by turning Jesus back to the sea from where he came. Inclosing reserve carefully guards the perverse self-pleasure the demonic "self" gains through defiance against all that is outside itself. By his repellent nakedness and dwelling among the tombs he guards against *the outside*. Thereby he also guards *his inside* sense of inclosure since contact with others and the beauty of nature might threaten or remedy his self-existence. His self-isolation, achieved and maintained through strategies of distance, nakedness, uncleanness, and self-harm (cutting his own flesh with stones) cultivated a pervasive atmosphere of death among the tombs. In sum he lived to defy the "existential" threat that natural and normal human life posed against him.

Tanner explains the inner workings of this perverse self-defense by considering Milton's Satan guarding himself against Eve's natural beauty which signified the "coercive power" that normal external factors *ought* to press upon beings *knowing* they were created by God.

> Milton attributes both strength and autonomy to beauty. Eve's beauty commands Satan's grudging admiration as tribute due to an imperious sovereign power. Milton's diction lays particular stress upon beauty's coercive power: Eve "overawes," "abstracts," "disarms," and strips Satan of fierceness with "rapine sweet" and "sweet compulsion." She immobilizes and enervates her adversary, momentarily mesmerizing him with wonder at her irresistible grace. Having been thrown off balance, the Devil must willfully reassert control over his mind, which he proclaimed to be its own place . . . Satan, whose mode of existence is defined by absolute self-control, thrills to beauty like the rest of us. But he trembles in terror at the loss of control attending to his rapture (Tanner, 160).

The self-inclosed demoniac was thus greatly conflicted as he moved from his tomb-life and approached Jesus. As *demonized* and *human* he was both repulsed and attracted by the creational reality of "the glory of being human" which now stood before him *divinized* in Jesus the God-man.[16] Such is the nature of the demonic "lifestyle" in the constant *unrest* of struggle to

---

15. Kierkegaard, SD, 72, 73.

16. Given that the demons knew that Jesus was God's *holy* "Son of the Highest God." We allude to Christman, *Behold*, 63–73.

maintain defiance against the "temptations" of the good and the beautiful, and the remaining reminders of the "image of God" in humankind.

The Rejection of Creaturehood

To broaden the scope of the demoniac's life, we might say that his inclosing reserve brings him to reject creaturely existence. Kierkegaard saw human beings as a synthesis of two different categories of existence. Humans exist as *body* in relation to finiteness, temporality, and necessity, and humans exist as *soul* in relation to infinity, eternity, and freedom (Tanner, 148). The demoniac self-consciously seeks to defy creaturely existence as a categorical synthesis by rejecting the "body" factors and accepting only the "soul" factors. Tanner explains:

> From the perspective of the "factors," Satan's sickness springs from his choice to embrace only the infinite, eternal, and free potentialities of his being, while denying their corollaries: the finite, the temporal, and the necessary. Or, from the perspective of self-consciousness, Satan's despair arises from his absolute defiance. In defiance, the demonic attempts to detach himself from contingency and arrogate to himself the power of self-existence (*SD*, 68); that is (to adopt Kierkegaardian language), the demonic wills to be himself by himself, without reference to the power that constituted the self; he is the self-made man manifested in "demonic ideality" (*SD*, 72). "With all his power, however, the self-made demonic cannot "break the despair by himself and by himself alone—he is still in despair and with all his presumed effort only works all the deeper into deeper despair" (*SD*, 14) (Tanner, 150–51).

Therefore, the bitter core of the demonic defiance against creature-hood consists in ever-increasing despair. The only "positive" in life is the negative stance against God. "For all practical purposes," as God's creature this amounts to a denial of one's true existence. Kierkegaard describes this ethos of the demonic person that "in despair wills to be oneself in defiance":

> Rebelling against all existence, it feels that it has obtained evidence against it, against its goodness. The person in despair believes that he himself is the evidence, and that is what he wants to be, and therefore he wants to be himself, himself in his torment, in order to protest against all existence with this torment. Just as the weak, despairing person is unwilling to hear anything about any consolation eternity has for him, so a person

in such despair does not want to hear anything about it, either, but for a different reason: this very consolation would be his undoing—as a denunciation of all existence. Figuratively speaking, it is as if an error slipped into an author's writing and the error became conscious of itself as an error—perhaps it actually was not a mistake but in a much higher sense an essential part of the whole production—and now this error wants to mutiny against the author, out of hatred toward him, forbidding him to correct it and in maniacal defiance saying to him: No, I refuse to be erased; I will stand as a witness against you, a witness that you are a second-rate author.[17]

This ironic (and conceptually challenging) snapshot of defiant despair perhaps serves to illustrate the puzzling "worship" of the demoniac, showing it to be a mocking defiance of the "second-rate author" who wrote the error the demoniac became and now embraces. It also shows what the demons themselves reluctantly confessed: their defiance made the presence of Jesus a "torment" to them, thus exhibiting Kierkegaard's observation that theirs is a defiant despair "*at the good*" because it is to them *an evil*. God's higher creatures "ought" to despair "*over the good*," namely in their lack of conformity to it, because they are thereby at least recognizing it *as the good*. Despair "at" versus despair "over" makes all the difference.

The Cultivation of the Sudden against Boredom

The demonic rejection of creaturehood leads to several despairing and desperate activities. One is the cultivation of "the sudden."[18] Of course, the sudden is an activity chosen to alleviate the condition of *boredom*. Thus, Kierkegaard notes that "the demonic is the contentless, the boring," which leads to the despairing activities.[19] Mark's demoniac seems to exhibit terrible boredom that leads to the horrible activities already mentioned. Tanner confirms Kierkegaard's idea of "the sudden" and relates it the inclosed demoniac's rejection of the "boring continuity" of creaturehood:

> In *Paradise Lost*, as we have seen, Satan is isolated, cut off, disintegrated from others by his close reserve; this is how Satan looks if we reflect on the content of his personality. If we reflect upon how his character manifests itself in time and space, Satan's actions look dis-integrated; his movements are sudden,

---

17. Kierkegaard, SD, 73–74.
18. "*The demonic is the sudden.*" Kierkegaard, CA, 129.
19. Kierkegaard, CA, 132.

discontinuous, shifting, and unstable. Similarly, Milton's hell pulsates with erratic energy, while his heaven stands stately and serene.

This difference conforms to Kierkegaard's observations that "sin comes into the world as the sudden," and likewise "the demonic is the sudden," while "the good signifies continuity, for the first expression of salvation is continuity" (*CA,* 32, 129, 130). It follows from Kierkegaard's definition of the demonic as anxiety of the good that the devil would dread continuity, for continuity expressed salvation. The demonic, therefore, expresses itself by means of the "negation of continuity [which] is the sudden" (*CA,* 129). (Tanner, 135).

In addition to what has already been noted of the demoniac's desire to escape the continuity of bodily finitude, we note several other aspects of Mark's narrative that support Tanner's explanation. Suddenness seems to be presented as his foremost ability as he immediately meets Jesus just off the boat. His sporadic activities of howling and cutting himself disrupted any *normal* continuity of existence. His "night and day" routine sought "demonic continuity" through *discontinuity* with normal human existence. Tanner's Kierkegaardian reading of Milton describes one other aspect of "the sudden" that we find in Mark:

> The well-known Satanic degradation into cormorant, toad, and serpent recount only a few of his abrupt Protean metamorphoses . . . Satan's readiness to adapt his appearance to any shape whatsoever, no matter how degrading, argues for a certain emptiness in his self (Tanner, 136, 137).

The Legion's desire to enter the pigs demonstrates Milton's Satan: willing, able, and apparently well-practiced in possessing various and lower bodily forms.

The Cultivation of Pandemonium against Despair

Another desperate demonic activity is the cultivation of pandemonium. Tanner notes the significance of the ironic cultivation of pandemonium against demonic *despair*.

> Milton populates hell in *Paradise Lost* with many minor demons who share their leader's demonic anxiety. The last section on Kierkegaard's chapter on anxiety about good discusses the way the demonic attempts to evade the good by repressing "inwardness";

this section catches the ambiance of Milton's minor demons in Pandemonium. For example, consider the following "general observations"; these remarks could easily have been written with the likes of Mulciber, Mammon, and (especially) Belial in mind: "The demonic is able to express itself as indolence that postpones thinking, as curiosity that never becomes more than curiosity, as dishonest self-deception, as effeminate weakness that constantly relies on others, as superior negligence, as stupid busyness, etc." (*CA*, 138). Milton's demons also variously exhibit indolence, curiosity, self-deception, mindless bustle, and so forth. What is more, the purpose of either demonic indolence or bustle, indeed of every seemingly serious enterprise in Milton's hell, is to insulate its inhabitants from the painful reality of their God-relationship . . . all are designed to take their mind off the point of hell: damnation (Tanner, 137–38).

It seems that the demonic "Legion" sought to evade the torment of the "painful reality of their God-relationship" by cultivating pandemonium. The demoniac's actions, like cutting himself and howling, may have ironically been drastic measures to cut the *despair* that was even more painful. In sum, Mark's demoniac certainly exhibited characteristics that can cohere with Milton's Satan and Kierkegaard's defiant demoniac. Through those readings, the puzzle pieces of Mark's demoniac come together as a person who through some unexplained history became a living "prototype" of the demonic despair of defiance. Yet, and further to the point, all these aspects of the demoniac are dramatically contrasted by the man's "*sitting there, clothed and in his right mind*" following the exorcism. It seems that he has once again found continuity as a normal human being, in contrast to the discontinuities he experienced while demon-possessed.

The Demonized Crowd in Untruth

In Tanner's description of the boredom and despair evading activities of Milton's demons in hell's "Pandemonium," one may see Kierkegaard's nemesis, the "crowd in untruth." In fact, that "crowd" was never far from Kierkegaard's mind but was the ever-present backdrop of his authorship. Similarly, the crowds serve a similar purpose for Mark as the context from which individuals emerge and come into specific relation to Jesus. In the following brief narrative, we seek to point out the Kierkegaardian "crowd" in Mark 5:1–20.

Jesus permits the *Legion/crowd* of demons to enter a *herd/crowd* of swine, driving them down the steep slope to their watery demise in the sea. Thus, the demons' begging to inhabit the *swine/crowd*, though granted, was in a sense denied by being such a short-lived "existence." The demons' subsequent fate was undisclosed.[20] But the *herdsmen/crowd* informed the people "in the city and country" of the loss of their *herd/crowd*. Their ultimate concern was more for their loss of livelihood in cultivating the *crowd* than to gain a *single individual*.[21] And so, the *people/crowd* begged Jesus to depart from their region.

There is a theme of "begging" in this episode which carries into the next scene. The theme was previously seen in the leper whom we consider as Mark's "first individual" (1:40–45). But the contrasts in "begging" in all these accounts is evident. The leper demonstrates a proper begging. The demoniac (before his deliverance), the demons, and the Gerasene "crowd" demonstrate otherwise. It seems that everyone in Mark is begging Jesus for something, and for most their desire is for him to not be who he is and to leave them alone. Mark probably intends that the people of the Gerasene "crowd" are to be seen as themselves demonized, due to their repetition of the "demonic" begging for Jesus to leave them alone. In Mark, Jesus certainly brings disruption, as seen especially in the encounter with the Scribes and the "Holy Sabbath controversy," and now with the Gerasenes and the "unclean swine controversy." In both cases, those resisting the deliverance Jesus provided for the needy and oppressed were content to see lives remain dehumanized and demonized for the sake of preserving the status quo. It seems that the message is that each of these respective "crowds" was the truly dehumanized and demonized.

Thus, Kierkegaard helps us see that Mark's crowd is *demonic* untruth. Tanner aptly brings out the correlation between Milton's "Pandemonium," Kierkegaard's "Crowd is Untruth," and the demonized crowd of our own time:

> The escapism of Milton's lesser demons, of course, mirrors that of countless demonic denizens of our modern wasteland, the personality-types Kierkegaard no doubt had most in mind when

20. Possibly representing several Marcan eschatological "crowd-trails" that we cannot here pursue, namely the ultimate fates of demons and the crowd that in Kierkegaard's thought was ultimately an unreality.

21. Representing another "crowd-trail" we cannot pursue but mention as connected to the idea of Kierkegaard's "unclean" (unreal) crowd. We are simply pointing out this analogy in our brief "allegorical" paragraph, and do not believe or intend to imply that God's creaturely pigs are unreal or without value. We do imply that "the crowd" is an economic boon to the modern-day equivalent of "the herdsmen," and the capitalistic valuing of the ultimately unreal crowd (or public) is a devaluing of the single individual. (Kierkegaard saw the crowd, also called "the public," as "a chimera . . . a sum of negative ones . . . a package of envelopes." See Moore, PSW, 236–37; cf. JP 3, 2952.)

he described the demonic. Kierkegaard saw the modern age as everywhere conspiring to avoid consciousness of the anxious possibility of salvation by losing itself in trivial pursuits; that a game by this name should have become so popular would have amused, but scarcely surprised, the author of *The Present Age*. Demonic strategies for avoiding "inwardness" (roughly meaning consciousness of one's existential predicament before God) are manifold (Tanner, 138).

But Jesus aims to overcome the untruth of the crowd. Therefore, he touches the unclean, heals on the Sabbath, delivers the demoniacs, raises the dead, and allows demonic destruction to follow, perhaps if only so the previously unseen evil becomes manifestly revealed as evil. His positive truth and creative power disrupt the crowd and dislodge potential individuals therein, perhaps enabling ears to hear and eyes to see *"the secret of the Kingdom of God"* (Mark 4:10).[22] In contrast, the "secret" of the demoniac, the Legion, and the crowd, is the hidden power to destroy.

Deliverance and Restoration

What is of immense interest is the demoniac's complete lack of an *expressed* desire for deliverance. Jesus simply proceeds to cast the demons out of him. He seems entirely passive in this process, and in fact as has been seen, was actively resistant to salvation. Kierkegaard stressed that sin was a position against God and therefore not a passive state. This raises the problem of how a self actively positioned against God can come to *"rest transparently in God."* That definition of Kierkegaard's is given in several versions, one of which replaces "in God" with the words *"in the power that established it."*[23] This seems to emphasize that any activity whatsoever, on the part of the one "resting transparently in God" only does so through God's power. But we still need to try to ascertain what was meant by that phrase, because he certainly meant something specific. Merold Westphal says that Kierkegaard's "Anti-Climacus" never really explains what "resting transparently" means, but finds what he considers an adequate answer:

> Paul Cruysberghs makes the illuminating suggestion that transparency is the opposite of inclosing reserve. Just as inclosing reserve is the cutting off of the self from others, both human (*Works of Love*) and divine (*Sickness unto Death*), so

---

22. Mark's gospel reveals many "secrets" as we will see.
23. Kierkegaard, SD, 49.

> transparency is an essential openness to the other, an awareness of oneself as essentially related to others so that the health of the self depends on healthy relations with God and neighbor . . . Cruysberghs adds, Being transparent to God is identical with purity of heart, with willing just one thing, the good. But, taking into consideration that we are double-minded, transparency before God means as well to understand ourselves in our unclarity. Transparency indeed is a question of self-knowledge, which includes knowing that we are unclear about ourselves."[24]

Thus, it seems that coming to faith in God presupposes and parallels coming to a knowledge of sin before God (as one's criterion) even to the depths of one's double-mindedness.[25] This seems to imply that faith is not coming to a resolute single-mindedness but is rather becoming repentant concerning the state of duplicity.[26] Whether, or exactly how, this might apply to Mark's demoniac nevertheless remains an undisclosed mystery, since there is no hint of any such pre-deliverance repentance on his part. Moreover, in *Sickness unto Death* the despair in defiance is the more intensive form of despair and thus "*is further from salvation than the lesser form.*"[27] This is because it is the more willful and spirited form of despair. In any case, Jesus simply delivered the man from the demonic despair he was oppressed by and gave him a restored human spirit so that he sat "*clothed and in his right mind.*"

Perhaps this only demonstrates that *faith*, when viewed as necessary to the *reception* of the gift of life/salvation, is itself wholly gift and life (Eph 2:8; Rom 5:6–10). And the only adequate response to God's sheer deliverance is offered or even prescribed for us in Mark's description of those seeing the restored demoniac: "*and they were afraid.*" Similarly, Mark's emphasis in the previous account of Jesus' deliverance of the disciples from the demonic storm was "*and they were filled with great fear.*" Mark's overall message seems to be that the only truly proper response to Jesus' power over demonic winds, legions of demons, and hopeless demoniacs, is reverential fear before the mystery of God. It is not for us to understand but rather to be filled with awe and humility before the God man's merciful deliverances and indeed such an attitude accompanies faith. But his deliverance is also open to the faith-less possibility of offense, demonstrated here by the Gerasenes and earlier by the scribes.

---

24. Westphal, *Kierkegaard's Concept of Faith*, 253.
25. See Christman, *Behold*, 6–10.
26. See Christman, *Behold*, 193–94.
27. Kierkegaard, SD, 101.

The demoniac's restoration was shown to include his desire to go with Jesus, probably as a disciple. Here is yet another instance of "begging." Perhaps this is presented as an advance from those positive instances seen earlier and portrays a more fully developed or developing faith. The deeper faith of the demoniac exhibits a previously impossible selflessness that contentedly "rested" in Jesus' denial of his wish. But was his desire actually denied? For in essence, his desire was to be a *disciple*, and that would be fulfilled by *following the directions of Jesus*:

> Go home to your friends and tell them how much the Lord has done for you, and how he has had mercy on you. And he went away and began to proclaim in the Decapolis how much Jesus had done for him, and everyone marveled (Mark 5:19–20, ESV).

And we must not overlook that this prohibition provided an integral part of his restoration. For the directions of Jesus set in motion the reestablishment of the creaturely bonds of finitude, temporality, and necessity, in relation to the human society and which the demonic Legion denied him. Thus, Mark's gospel shows that salvation is not world-denying or ascetical regarding bodily existence, but world and body-affirming as the Kingdom of God holistically restores persons in community through the power of "*the gospel of Jesus Christ, the Son of God*."²⁸ There is essentially no true restoration of humans other than restoration to the world itself, for they inhabit the world just as the world inhabits them in a mutual indwelling that, for believers, participates in the "cosmic perichoresis" as "all things are summed up in Christ . . . things in the heavens and things on the earth."²⁹

READING 2: DEMONIC DESPAIR AND "THE PUBLICAN"

Our first "Kierkegaardian reading" of Mark's demoniac drew from several pseudonymous writings of Kierkegaard whereas this second reading will draw from one of his signed writings, a sermon called "The Publican."³⁰ We

---

28. Leithart writes that "The 'thinking thing' . . . that Cartesian self is a fantasy, like the Hobbesian natural man . . . We are beings-in-society, or, as Heidegger puts it, 'Being-with.' It's a gnostic heresy to assume that humanity is mainly a 'spiritual Thing' that is somehow 'misplaced' in the world . . . Individuals never exist except as beings who indwell some particular social reality." Leithart, *Traces of the Trinity*, 25–26.

29. Leithart, *Traces of the Trinity*, 143; cf. 5–16; 129–45.

30. Kierkegaard, CD, 371–77. The pseudonymous author of *The Concept of Anxiety* was "Vigilius Haufniensis," a watchman/psychologist who was trying "to make people understand for themselves the situation they are in . . . applying his psychological

turn to that sermon to draw a Kierkegaardian parallel between Luke's Publican (tax collector) and Mark's demoniac. The reason for this parallel is because the Pharisee can be seen as representative of an oppressive *pharisaical* "Legion" which Jesus "exorcises" from the tax collector. We are not aiming at a complete harmonization of Luke's Publican and Mark's demoniac but are simply pointing out similarities regarding the oppressive *demonic* anxiety that seems to be revealed through each gospel.

Luke's Pharisee as Signifying the Demonic

Kierkegaard's text for his sermon was Luke 18:13. "And the publican stood afar off and would not even lift up his eyes unto heaven, but smote upon his breast, saying, God be merciful to me a sinner."[31] This text of Luke's draws a contrast between the comparing self-righteous Pharisee, and the non-comparing sincere publican who returns home justified from his sin.[32] Obviously, Kierkegaard does not draw an analogy between the *justified* publican and Mark's *delivered* demoniac. But since both were in desperate need of God's *deliverance* such a comparison can be drawn. This will hopefully become more evident as we proceed. The thesis for this reading is that the *saving* "separation" of the publican from the Pharisee can be "drawn out" as analogous to the *exorcising* separation of Mark's demoniac from his *Pharisaical* "Legion" of demons. Thus, in this second reading *the demoniac publican* comes to kneel (and stand) before God in distinction from the *Pharisaical Legion*, emerging as a humble penitent before God and returning home "justified" before God.

We saw in the previous reading that defiant demonic despair was a willful position that justified itself before God. As such the Pharisee in Luke's parable similarly portrays that position. The Pharisee's problem is that his position "before God" is only "achieved" through prideful comparison to

---

insights to the concept of anxiety, guilt, and sin." Watkin, *Historical Dictionary*, 407; The author of *The Sickness Unto Death* was "Anti-Climacus," who "views himself as being exceptionally religious." Watkin, *Historical Dictionary*, 401.

31. Kierkegaard, CD, 371. Throughout this section we will cite the references to the discourse in the text.

32. Paul Martens demonstrates that throughout Kierkegaard's writings, including his sermon *The Publican*, he presents the Pharisees' "sophistry and legal externalism" (94) as embodying a demonic "polyphonic personification of a univocal idea . . . the counterpart to Jesus, the antithesis of Jesus, the anti-Christ" (103), while Timothy Polk contrastively presents the Publican as the "model of inwardness" (107). Thus, both support the reading we will pursue here. See respectively: Martens, "The Pharisee," 93–103; and Polk, "The Tax Collector," 107–120.

others. This is akin to the demonic defiance wherein one sees oneself as innately superior to the crowd, in distinction from it as "self-made." This was the "anti-social" demonic ethos we saw in the first reading that inhabited the demoniac, overtook his person, and led to his need for deliverance.

The Far-off Place Where the Publican Stood

Following some "introductory" preliminaries, Kierkegaard begins the sermon by noting the *place* of the publican. This is the first sign that he was capable of receiving grace. He "stood afar off." Asking what this meant, Kierkegaard answers saying,

> It means to stand by himself, alone with himself and God—thus thou art far off, far from men, and far from God, with whom nevertheless thou art alone . . . he was alone before God—ah, that is to be afar off. For what is farther from guilt and sin than God's holiness? —and so, for one who is himself a sinner to be alone with this, is it not to be endlessly far off? (372, 373)

As the publican stood far off from all and thus alone before God, so also Mark's outcast demoniac, his demons excepted, "stood" (fell) before God. This is where separation from the demons could begin for him. Previously, inasmuch as the demoniac had adopted the demonic and "pharisaical" attitude toward others and God, he had still never stood *before Jesus*, the God-man. Even the demons had not done so previously. Though the demons were nonetheless defiant, perhaps the buried and oppressed *humanity* of the demoniac experienced a contradiction in himself: a demonic repulsion *away* from the Holy Christ, *and* a brotherly drawing *toward* the human Jesus. Did the mere pervasive presence of Jesus draw from his buried depths great contradiction and anxiety, and longing long since forgotten but now rekindled by the compassionate face of the "Son of man" come for "lost" persons such as he? We also note that Jesus does not address or combat "the man." He *distinguishes* him from the demonic power, saying "Come out of the man, you unclean spirit!" (5:8; ESV).

The Posture of the Publican

The next point in Kierkegaard's sermon calls attention to the *posture* of the publican. He continues,

> *He would not even lift up his eyes unto heaven;* so then, he cast them down. Yes and what a wonder! Oh, even physically there is

> something in the endless space which overwhelms a man for the fact that the eye has nothing to fix itself upon, this effect is called dizziness—so that one has to shut one's eyes. And he who, alone with his guilt and sin, knows that were he to cast his eyes up he would behold God's holiness and nothing else, he surely learns to cast his eyes down; or perhaps he looked up and beheld God's holiness—and cast down his eyes. (373–74)

For the demons the presence of Jesus was a torment, but what of the demoniac? Did he dare cast even a moment's glance at the Holy? Perhaps he felt the "dizziness of freedom" that Kierkegaard held was the anxiety produced by the opposite magnetic pulls of repulsion from and desire toward God.[33] That dizziness is to experience God's most essential gift to humans, the freedom of choice. Was the demoniac being awakened to free choice? Was he becoming willing to choose "the Good" that stood before him in the restored humanity *named* Jesus?[34] Was his demonically-inspired posture of mock worship in danger of becoming *true* worship because of the buried-but-awakening humanity Jesus was "creating" within him? Would he venture forth in internal answer with the "leap of faith" when freed from his demonic oppression? It seems quite possible that such awesome capabilities and choices were being given as the demoniac *himself,* demons notwithstanding, knelt before the altar that *was* Jesus "the Savior of all people" (1 Tim 4:10, ESV). Must the demoniac *himself* confess anything before Jesus? (Rom 10:9). Kierkegaard says something that may answer the question:

> To make confession is precisely *to cast down the eyes,* not to wish to look up to heaven, not to wish to see any one else; the more sincere thy confession is, all the more wilt thou cast down thine eyes, all the less wilt thou see any one else—and all the more true is this for the fact that thou dost kneel there at the altar, since to kneel down is even a stronger expression for what is implied by casting down the eyes, for he who merely casts down his eyes stands nevertheless comparatively erect. (377–78)

As the demoniac knelt before Jesus, while Jesus addressed the demons, their spiritual/psychological/physical grip on him was already breaking.[35] This

---

33. Kierkegaard, CA, 61. We draw upon this section of *The Concept of Anxiety* in this paragraph.

34. Lewis seems to corroborate this idea of free choice, writing "The odd thing was that before God closed in on me, I was in fact offered what now appears a moment of wholly free choice . . . You could argue that I was not a free agent, but I am inclined to think that this came nearer to being a perfectly free act than most that I had ever done." Lewis, *Surprised by Joy,* 224.

35. Although the exact relation between the demoniac and the demons is beyond

was evidenced by their immediate concern regarding their next habitation. They knew they were "on the way out." And therefore, the man buried under their domination began to "come to himself" so that a bit later he is "*sitting there, clothed and in his right mind.*"

The Penitence of the Publican

Kierkegaard then considers the publican's *actions, attitude, and expression* before God. He "*smote upon his breast and said God, be merciful to me a sinner.*" (374) In some of his statements Kierkegaard uses imagery that is quite appropriate to the scene in Mark. Kierkegaard says,

> Oh my hearer, when in the solitude of the desert a man is attacked by a ferocious beast, the cry verily issues of itself; and when in an unfrequented path thou dost fall amongst robbers, fright itself invents the cry. So it is in the case of that which is infinitely more dreadful. When thou art alone, alone in the place which is more lonesome than the desert—for even in the loneliest desert it would still be possible that another man might come there; alone in the place which is more lonesome than the most unfrequented path, where it still would be possible that another might come along; alone in individuality, or as a single individual, and face to face with God's holiness—then the crisis of itself. And if thou, alone before God's holiness, hast learnt that it avails thee nothing though the cry would call upon some one else to help, that *there* where thou art as the single individual there is literally no one else but thee, that is the most impossible of all things that *there* might be or come any one else but thee—then terror discovers, as need discovered prayer, it discovers this cry, "God be merciful to me a sinner." And the cry, the sigh, is so sincere in thee—yea, how could it but be that! What hypocrisy could there be in the fact that a man cries out when the abyss opens in peril at sea? Even though he knows that the storm mocks his weak voice, and that the birds out there listen to him with indifference, he cries out nevertheless, to such a degree is the cry true and the truth. (374–75)

The demons certainly experienced terror, before "*Jesus, Son of the Most High God*" to such an extent that they actually "prayed" to Jesus saying "*I adjure*

---

comprehension, a distinguishing between them seems necessary given that the demoniac is, after all, *human*. Tracy Groot provides an interesting narrative in which she poignantly distinguishes between Mark's demoniac and the demons. See Groot, *Madman*, 284–90.

you by God, do not torment me." It seems quite possible that the demoniac himself also experienced such terror. But was his terror of torment transformed into the true "fear of God" by which he became transformed? The *"fright"* that *was Jesus*, before whom he knelt, perhaps called forth the cry: *"The cry verily issues of itself."* He had been "attacked by a ferocious beast" (*Satan*); "fallen amongst robbers" (*Legion*) who had stolen his previous life and humanity; experienced the "abyss opening in peril" into which he had well-nigh eternally fallen. Thus, *the fright* before Jesus, the "mysterium et tremendum fascinans" called forth *the cry*.

The Justification of the Publican

Kierkegaard concluded his sermon focusing on the *justification* of the publican: *"he went down to his house justified"* (377). Neither the publican, nor the demoniac, was self-transformed. We saw in the previous reading that being "self-made" is what made Lucifer into Satan, what makes the demons the demons, and what makes those humans in the despair of defiance demonic. The publican and the demoniac were delivered from self-making. Their salvation was all the work of God's deliverance. Justification does not require "religious" preparations. A humble transparency regarding utter need before God received justification. Kierkegaard writes,

> In relation to God, no change has taken place: to be exalted to God is possible only by descending. As little as water changes its nature so as to run uphill, so little can a man succeed in lifting himself up to God . . . by pride. —He went to his house justified, For self-accusation is the possibility of *justification*. And the publican accused himself. There was no one that accused him. (376)

Kierkegaard's Publican and Mark's Demoniac

It seems that these Kierkegaardian readings cohere together in that Mark's *Pharisaical* "Legion" of demons are separated from the demoniac much as Luke's publican is separated from the self-righteous Pharisaical "spirit" that oppressed him. (It is not hard to imagine that the Publican "stood afar off" from God because of the censuring oppressive spirit of the Pharisees.) Mark's record of Jesus' directions to the ex-demoniac to "Go home to your friends and tell them how much the Lord has done for you and how he has had mercy on you" certainly apply just as well to the publican.

Despite the similarities this reading has drawn out between Mark and Luke, this does not mean that Mark's demoniac serves the same "gospel" purpose Luke had for the publican. Relating both readings to Mark's specific purposes, each displays his emphases on the power of Jesus to bind the strong man, plunder his house, and free people from demonic captivity to become followers of Christ. The demons may be the Devil's supernatural "legions" or his all too worldly agents of oppression, namely the Pharisees with their *demonic* "leaven" (Mark 8:15, 33). We could summarize that the chief similarity is simply the deliverance from *demonic agencies* and the despair they bring. The main difference is that the first reading concentrated on the *demonization* of the man and the second upon the *humanity* of the man. Together, the first two readings help to portray a spectrum in human response in a fallen world where the principalities and powers against the redemption of humanity take different forms and therefore require different and multi-layered responses. The following reading expands that scope in more ways than one.

READING 3: A COMMENTARY ON MARK'S PROPHETIC NARRATIVE OF JESUS' EXORCISM OF THE MODERN AGE

In this third reading we imagine the transposition of Mark's narrative into a *prophetic* account of Jesus' exorcism of the modern age. We will see "Mark" presenting two "world-pictures" with quite different characteristics and results.[36] The entire reading is based on Ronald Hall's explication of Kierkegaard's critique of the modern age.[37] To provide clarity amidst a near-torrent of concepts in our "commentary" below we:

- Bold words from Mark.

---

36. Hall derives his use of "world-picture" from Ludwig Wittgenstein, saying "world pictures are frameworks that we both use and inhabit, that we both have and live in and from . . . a kind of world-story that we find ourselves in when we come to ourselves, and that we are called on either to appropriate as our own or to reject for some other picture." Hall, *Word & Spirit*, 6.

37. Hall, *Word & Spirit*. Of course, what we will present of Hall's lengthy and densely packed book in this brief reading can at best only be a sort of introduction to his "tour de force" which in itself serves the same for Kierkegaard's own "tour de force" attack on the modern age. In the footnotes following we will cite references to Hall without the book's title. A considerably "condensed" version of *Word & Spirit* is found in Ronald L. Hall, "Spirit and Presence: A Kierkegaardian Analysis," in *Either/Or, I* of The International Kierkegaard Commentary, volume 3.

- Italicize the Kierkegaardian vocabulary Hall has used in his "reading" of Kierkegaard.
- Quote lengthier phrases and sentences from Hall and Kierkegaard.
- Footnote these sources to further clarify the concepts and provide the source references.

We presented the "torrent" as a narrative-commentary because it seemed the best way to contrast the actual form of "life" somewhat briefly in the two world-pictures depicted and revealed therein. We note two other things regarding this reading:

- It may be best to read it twice, once with the footnotes to gain familiarity with the concepts, and once without them to better follow its "narrative" of the modern age.
- Hall has primarily drawn Kierkegaard's critique from *Either/Or, Part 1,* his earliest pseudonymous book that was concerned with the aesthetic stage (or sphere) of life. He sees Kierkegaard's general purpose therein as to "wound aestheticism from behind" and also "assert that the advent of Christianity radically changed human consciousness."[38]

1 They came to the other side of the sea, to the country of the Gerasenes.[39]

The Son of God (Mark 1:1) had come to restore man to *spirit* and *spirit* to man. For "the basic concept of man is spirit . . . identical to self . . . But even though spirit is self . . . it is possible for us to be spirit-*less,* to lack a self, or more precisely to fail to be the self each of us already is."[40] Here Mark provides a prophetic account of Jesus' mission into the modern age. Thus, Jesus and his disciples **came** from ancient Galilee, where his mission began, **to the other side of the sea,** to the modern age, **the country of the Gerasenes.** He came to give *spirit* to the spirit-less, to deliver the modern man from the *demonic spirituality* of the modern age.

2 And when Jesus had stepped out of the boat, immediately there met him out of the tombs a man with an unclean spirit.

---

38. Hall, 5.
39. The text of Mark is from the ESV.
40. Hall, 3. See Kierkegaard, EO1, 65; SD, 13.

As Jesus **stepped** into the modern age he was **immediately met** by **a man with an unclean spirit,** the demonic spirit of the modern age. This signified a meeting of the second and third stages of human consciousness that exist after the first stage in paganism. That first stage was "the most perfect expression of paganism, namely Greek consciousness" where *spirit* was "psychically qualified . . . resting in a *static* harmony and accord with the sensuous world."[41] In the second stage, "the Christian understanding of spirit . . . is understood as existing in a *dynamic* opposition, strife, and discord with the sensuous."[42] But then, a third stage became possible. For "when Christianity introduced spirit into the world it also introduced the potential for the demonic. Modernity . . . is the illegitimate child of Christianity. Brought forth as a possibility by the advent of the spirit, the modern age has turned spirit against itself; it has become demonic through and through."[43]

3 He lived among the tombs. And no one could bind him anymore, not even with a chain.

The modern man had freed himself from the old "pagan" **chain**, the *psychical* soul that had previously restrained all human spirit. It couldn't restrain the new *demonic spirit* of the modern age which possesses modern man.[44] Ironically, the new demonic *spirit* renders lessness to those it possesses. The possessed become "faithless, selfless . . . spiritless . . . restless, rootless, and placeless people."[45]

Thus, Mark reveals what modern man's vaunted freedom brought him. For the real picture of the life of modern man is **among the tombs.** Mark's exorcism account relentlessly unclothes the *world-picture* of the modern age as essentially another lessness, an ironic world-lessness. And to be worldless is to live in relation to nihilism and death. For the third stage of spirit/world relation, the *demonic stage* mentioned just above, has not become *bonded* back to the world following the *sundering* from the world in the

---

41. Hall, 5.

42. Hall, 5. The Christian stage *sunders* the spirit/soul "static harmony and accord with the sensuous world" only to then *bond* them in a "dynamic" relation, albeit with "discord." In other words, the Christian's sundering from an *absolute relation* to the "sensuous world" is followed by a bonding to the world in a *relative relation*. See Hall, 99.

43. Hall, 5, cf. 4. See EO1, 61, 89.

44. Nor could the old age confine or restrain the new human spirit of the Christian age.

45. Hall, 4. Hall credits the first triad of "less" words to Soren Kierkegaard and the second triad to Blaise Pascal.

Christian stage. The result of this is the loss of the world and perhaps the ultimate irony of the *world-picture* of the modern age. "If the bonds of a pneumatically sundered spirit are not reestablished to the world, there can be no full appearance of the self. Without a world there is no place for a human being to become fully human, to appear as spirit, as the self that relates itself to itself, as the self it is called to be."[46]

Thus, all the lessness of the modern man in the modern age is due to the *pneumatic* (spiritual) *qualification of spirit*, brought by Christianity but then become *demonic*. The new world-picture Jesus brought *sunders* our *absolute relation* to the world, *bonds* us to God in an *absolute relation*, and then *bonds* us back to the world in a *relative relation*.[47] The result is a "new self/world relation" . . . what "The New Testament characterizes as . . . one in which the self is *in, but not of,* the world."[48]

4 For he had often been bound with shackles and chains, but he wrenched the chains apart, and he broke the shackles in pieces. No one had the strength to subdue him.

Mark provides more detail regarding what appears to be the main activity of the modern demoniac. He exhibits superhuman **strength** to **wrench** and **break** anything that would restrain him. His demonic power seems to render him "in, but not of, the world," but not in the Christian sense. For as we just saw above, by not being *rebonded to the world,* his demonic spirituality renders him inversely to be "of, but not in, the world." In other words, his demonic sensuality renders him to be *of the world* in a negative sense, but his demonic wordlessness renders him to not be *in the world* in a positive sense.

In modern-era literature and art, we find varied personifications (though perhaps an oxymoron) of "spiritually qualified spiritlessness" in Don *Giovanni, Faust, and Johannes the Seducer*.[49] There is some variation in these personages, but they are united in the fact that their existence is wholly within "the aesthetic immediacy of the fleeting moment . . . the

46. Hall, 99. See Kierkegaard, SD, 13.

47. In the absolute faith-relation to God "to exist in faith is to exist in a radical covenantal bonding to God *and* to exist within a dialectical sundered/bonded relation to the world." Hall, 3, cf. 90–93. See Kierkegaard, EO1, 89.

48. Hall, 3.

49. Quote from Hall, 4. On these personages in Hall: Don Giovanni, 90–117; Faust, 118–163; Johannes, 109, 115–17, 120, 139. Giovanni and Faust are extensively referenced in *Either/Or 1*, and Kierkegaard's own Johannes is given "his own voice" in "The Seducers Diary," in EO1, 303–445.

fleeting moment of restlessness and tumult."⁵⁰ That restlessness and tumult are the cause for his activity, and **no one had the strength to subdue him.**

5 Night and day among the tombs and on the mountains he was always crying out and cutting himself with stones.

The modern age would whitewash itself as the picture of perpetual *development* and *progress*. But Mark's vision sees through Faust's "Archimedean point" whereby he would move the world.⁵¹ The continual progress of Faust's new Genesis, formulated by his "In the beginning was the act," ironically only leads to the external reduplication of his internal wasteland.⁵² Whether **among the tombs** or **on the mountains** he finds no world, all is in flux. His **crying out and cutting himself with stones** signify that "Faust is pure frenzied activity, perpetual dissatisfaction, constant renewal; he is restless, frenetic, hyper, mad."⁵³ For the deal Faust made with the world and himself was in fact with Mephistopheles at the cost of his soul, or spirit, to be more precise.⁵⁴

6 And when he saw Jesus from afar, he ran and fell down before him.

This account places the primary drive for the encounter on Jesus intentionally crossing the sea and coming to the demoniac, to deliver him. But **he, seeing Jesus from afar** aggressively **ran** at *and* humbly **fell down before him.** The aggression becomes clearly revealed in verse 7, and the humility in verse 8. This indicates at least two things. The first is the aggressive "antitheism" of the modern age which is against its deliverance because of its "tragicomic attempt to conceal an infinite emptiness and a demonic anxiety

---

50. Hall, 13. Hall writes "for Kierkegaard this perpetually vanishing presence is the farthest removed from the human; it is, we could say, inhuman, what Kierkegaard calls the demonic. It is the demonic presence of Don Giovanni and Faust, a presence that is perpetually absenting itself, a presence without reflexivity, a presence without a trace of continuity, a worldless flux of disconnected immediate moments, a perpetual disengaging without a center of gravity." Hall, "Spirit and Presence." 278–79.

51. Hall, 141. See Kierkegaard, EO1, 37.

52. Hall, 120–21, 142–43, 156. Bernard Williams demonstrates that this idea of "Faust" is still a "live" question. See Williams, *In the Beginning*, xvi, 18–28.

53. Hall, 132.

54. Hall, 136. Kierkegaard locates Faust's fall in his sickness of "'romantic irony' . . . a sickness of the spirit, a demonic, nihilistic madness; it is the sickness at the heart of the modern age; it is a sickness unto death." Hall, 117.

about the good."⁵⁵ The second is the basically human need of true *spirit* by the one possessed by the demonic spirituality of the modern age. The man's acts toward Jesus, who is both exorcist of the demonic and deliver of the human, reveals modern man's ultimately conflicted existence. Thus, Mark reveals that the modern demoniac is not quite univocal, though **he** would like all, including himself, to think otherwise. His conflictedness expresses the "secret warfare" between the would-be human individual and the demonic spirit of the age.

7 And crying out with a loud voice, he said, "What have you to do with me, Jesus, Son of the Most High God? I adjure you by God, do not torment me."

Truth is, Jesus has nothing **to do with** demons other than to **torment** them (to cast them out), and everything to do with the demoniac he has come to deliver by giving him "spirit, self, personal existence."⁵⁶ The "monosyllabic," demonic, **loud voice**, of the modern/postmodern age is all "sound and fury, signifying nothing," a **crying** from "a world that is perpetually vanishing."⁵⁷ Nevertheless, the **voice**, as did Faust's Mephistopheles, desired to make a deal, boldly pressing a treaty with **Jesus** whom he **adjured** to God. When push comes to shove, the *postmodernist* man must deny his demonic avoidance of *felicitous speech* and appeal to the very thing he *lives* to deny and use such speech to make something happen in the world. "To utter a sentence is not only to make a world appear; it is at the same time to place oneself in that world as one in a community of speakers who in the covenants they mutually establish become the responsible agents in and through whom the world's continuity and stability are grounded. For the demonic individual, this is just too fragile, just too heavy; he must avoid felicitous speech at all costs."⁵⁸

8 For he was saying to him, "Come out of the man, you unclean spirit!"

---

55. Hall, 114, Kierkegaard, CA, 135–36.
56. Hall, 18.
57. The quoted phrases in order: Hall, 167, 14, 116.
58. Hall, 107–8. See Kierkegaard, CA, 129–30. Concerning the postmodern "avoidance of felicitous speech" Hall adds, "The most staggering irony plaguing the modern age is the fact that our basic understanding of ourselves is radically discrepant with the way we live our lives, with our existence." Hall, 164.

For what Jesus **was saying to him** was a *speech act*, the authoritative *"spoken word (dabhar) of Yahweh at the very center of reality."*⁵⁹ For **Jesus, Son of the Most High God** was come to give *felicitous* and *world-making* speech to humanity, even to modern and especially to postmodern man, to overcome his *demonic, twisted and deranged dabhar.*⁶⁰

Jesus, differentiating between spiritual realities, saw **the man** meant to become a self by becoming spirit with world-making speech as suppressed by his own *demonic spirituality,* the **unclean spirit**. For that **unclean spirit** says, "we, in our essential selfhood, are outside of the world . . . essentially *sundered* from the world, as essentially hovering in an aesthetic *musical* flux above the given historical actuality of the world and above our own embodiment in it . . . as essentially god-like 'spiritual' beings . . . absolutely free."⁶¹ And that essentially god-like and absolutely free being is what Jesus aims to cast out. For that *demonic speech* is *the lie* that sows the wind and reaps the whirlwind of the selfless, spiritless, and world-less modern age that Mark reveals.⁶²

9 And Jesus asked him, "What is your name?" He replied, "My name is Legion, for we are many."

Jesus **asked** the "one" crying out with a loud voice its **name,** to reveal that it had no name. For it was not human. It had no real, true, positive, human relations to self, others, the world, and God. It had no true relation to its own

---

59. Hall, 29, cf. 55. Hall's *Word & Spirit* applies Kierkegaard's (aesthetic/ethical/religious) "spheres of existence" to their expressive *mediums* of *speech* (as ethical/religious) or *music* (as aesthetic). These mediums cohere with and are revelatory of *spiritual* existence as either *Christian* or *demonic*. Hall derives Kierkegaard's thought largely from the lengthy "paper" of "A" called "The Immediate Erotic Stages or The Musical-Erotic" in *Either/Or Part 1.* Due to its complexity, Hall's explicit Kierkegaardian foundation can only be mentioned, and its significance implied in this reading. Several of Hall's most concentrated "textual" presentations of Kierkegaard's thought in this regard can be found in these pages of *Word & Spirit*: Hall, 26 / EO1, 67–68; Hall, 37 / EO1, 70–71; Hall, 43, 45 / EO1, 57, 70–71, 102; Hall, 76 / CI, 14; Hall 105–6 / CA 123–26; Hall 107–8 / CA, 129–30. This listing is a brief attempt to provide references by which the reader can retrace Hall's use of Kierkegaard regarding Christian "word and spirit" and the demonic spirituality of the modern age.

60. Hall, 7, 32, 130. The world-making Hall refers to is not physical creation ex-nihilo but more accurately the "thematization" (or reception) of "that place that we have already been given." Hall, 3. It is part of the rebonding of the Christian to the world in relations to others wherein felicitous speech-acts cohere with, and "create" the world-picture "we both have and live in and from" (Hall, 6).

61. Hall, 164.

62. Hall, 113–14.

words but spoke as two do under one cloak in a child's game.⁶³ Its words did not originate in *freedom* from a self, speaking in a *mutual relation* to another self for *covenanting* together through "word-as-bond" that is not "word-as-bondage."⁶⁴ It spoke truly that it was **Legion** for it was **many**. But it spoke falsely because Legion spoke words without *spirit* from namelessness.⁶⁵

Thus, "Legion" is the spiritless *crowd, the herd, the public*. The term evokes the Roman military unit of a legion and therefore Mark reveals the demonic will to power. But its force is without an authoritative world-creating *dabhar*. The univocal unhuman demonic voice speaks from untruth and unfreedom and brings destruction.⁶⁶ The speech of **Legion** *is the lie*. It cannot "create" a world through its speech-act. Its **many** is *demonic spirituality* in the place called "utopia." It is no self in no place mimicking true existence in the "sudden" stationary leap it considers as act: "The horror that seizes one upon seeing Mephistopheles leap in through the window and remain stationary in the position of the leap!"⁶⁷

10 And he begged him earnestly not to send them out of the country. 11 Now a great herd of pigs was feeding there on the hillside, 12 and they begged him, saying, "Send us to the pigs; let us enter them." 13 So he gave them permission. And the unclean spirits came out and entered the pigs; and the herd, numbering about two thousand, rushed down the steep bank into the sea and drowned in the sea.

True to "himself" only, **"Legion" earnestly begged** to remain in **the country** of the Gerasenes where he had fabricated together the modern place-less wasteland. His non-humanity is demonstrated by his desire to **enter** the less-than-human **pigs**. The end-result of Jesus' **permission** was seemingly to reveal the destruction that follows the *infelicitous speech* of the modern age. This is an ironic lesson since Faust sought to tame the sea with development

---

63. Hall, 103. Kierkegaard, CA, 118–19.

64. Hall, 107–8, 201–2,

65. In contrast, "Language is the perfect medium [for expressing spirit] precisely when everything sensuous in it is negated." Kierkegaard, EO1, 68, as cited by Hall with added parenthetic clarification in Hall, "Spirit and Presence," 278. Moreover, *spirit* enables speaking "in my own name." Hall, "Spirit and Presence," 285.

66. "Action in its demonic form is a transmutation of the positive power of the speech-act into a nihilistic power of destruction." Hall, 131.

67. Kierkegaard, CA, 131.

and continual progress only to *replicate externally his internal wasteland*.⁶⁸ Another irony is that the demonic spirit of the modern age, though preferring to hide its true nature as an "ascendancy of the bestial," when found out is unashamed to inhabit the unclean **pigs**.⁶⁹ Mark reveals that Faust's *spirituality* and Don Giovanni's *sensuality* run together in the modern age, and graphically demonstrates the exponentially destructive potential of spirituality and sensuality when they become *demonic*.⁷⁰

14 The herdsmen fled and told it in the city and in the country. And people came to see what it was that had happened.

The **people** are perhaps meant to signify neutral persons who can be like Mark's outsiders who often see and hear more clearly than the insiders who in this case seem to be the "in the know" **herdsmen** who fled the scene, told others what they saw, and blamed **what happened** regarding the **herd** on Jesus, as we shall see below (5:17).⁷¹ Perhaps the **herdsmen** signify the pre-Christian time which Jesus' invasion with *word and spirit* upset, to put it mildly. In contrast, the **people** may signify those pagans that will subsequently hear the *speech* of the delivered man (5:19).

Of course, it can't be denied that Christianity not only brought spirit into the world but enabled the demonic spirit also, along with the death and destruction that has devastated the modern age.⁷². The Faustian modern age was born into Faust's motto "in the beginning was the deed," and the sickness of "pure frenzied activity, perpetual dissatisfaction, constant renewal; he is restless, frenetic, hyper, mad." Mark reveals that the *nihilistic* project called the modern age is indeed *the sickness unto death*.⁷³

---

68. Hall, 142–43.
69. Hall, 103. Kierkegaard, CA, 118–19.
70. Hall, 118–19. "
71. "Throughout the book, as the insiders 'stumble on' Jesus and take offense at him, outsiders also stumble on him and respond with faith." Burdon, *Stumbling on God*, 37.
72. "As spirit, qualified only as spirit, renounces this world, feels that the world not only is not its world but is even not its stage, and withdraws into the higher realms, it leaves the worldly behind as the playground for the power with which it has always been in conflict and to which it now yields ground. Then, as spirit disengages itself from the earth, the sensuous shows itself in all its power." Kierkegaard, EO1, 89. Kierkegaard seems to be expressing that the demonic spirituality of the modern age makes those it possesses "of the world, but not in it."
73. Hall, 156.

15 And they came to Jesus and saw the demon-possessed man, the one who had had the legion, sitting there, clothed and in his right mind, and they were afraid.

The **people** from the city came and saw the results of the exorcism. It had become a simple and even serene scene in contrast to the prior scene of chaotic and constant *flux*. This was in fact to glimpse a new world spoken into existence by the *dabhar* of **Jesus**. Thus, Mark continues to portray and contrast the two *world-pictures* in and by which their respective populaces *thematize* their existence, for good or ill.[74] But we will see that not all appreciated the new world.

The **demon-possessed man**, newly delivered from the **legion**, was quietly **sitting there, clothed and in his right mind**. He had found *himself* and the *world* in which he now lived. "He remains himself, exactly the same as he was before, down to the most insignificant feature, and yet he becomes another, for the choice penetrates everything and changes it."[75] In **Jesus** the man had encountered the *absolute* to which he could now be absolutely related. He had been delivered from *absolute relation* to the world, *sundered* from it, but only to be *rebonded* to it, as shown by his **sitting** with **Jesus** who, after all was fully human and fully "in the world, though not of the world."[76] The delivered modern man could now also live in the same way rather than follow the impossible task of the modern age of being "of the world, but not in it."[77]

Seeing this, the **people . . . were afraid**. Their reaction was the same as the women at the empty tomb of Jesus. In both instances this signifies arriving at a climactic moment where possibility, faith, and "free" advance stand face to face with impossibility, unbelief, and "unfree" retreat. The free advance follows reverential fear in relation to the free God, while the unfree

---

74. Hall writes, "In order to come to ourselves in faith, we must consciously choose not only to be absolutely related to God, we must also choose our place in the world, that place that we have already been given prior to our thematized self-understanding . . . As Kierkegaard puts it, when the individual chooses himself, be 'becomes conscious as this specific individual with these capacities, these inclinations, these drives, these passions, influenced by this specific social milieu, as this specific product of a specific environment. But as he becomes aware of all this, he takes upon himself responsibility for it all' (E/O II, 251)." Hall, 3–4.

75. Kierkegaard, EO2, 223.

76. Hall, 2–3.

77. "Of the world but not in the world" seems an apt way to picture Hall's modern demoniac as a "radically sundered self" which Hall saw as applicable to Descartes as "Faust in his first stage . . . as scholar, as intellectual." See Hall, 144–45.

retreat follows servile fear based in relation to the old unfree self.[78] Ultimately, the former signals a new *self/God/world relation* while the latter the old *self/world/God relation*.

16 And those who had seen it described to them what had happened to the demon-possessed man and to the pigs. 17 And they began to beg Jesus to depart from their region.

We see the general pattern of retreat from **Jesus** that Mark records throughout his gospel. For their **begging** Jesus to **depart from their region** signals retreat from the advance God has made toward them. This parallels the stated desire of the demoniac in v 7, but possibly also presents a significant and possibly ironic contrast since the demoniac had run toward Jesus.

We also note the irony of the fact that Jesus is blamed for the destruction that demonic spirituality was responsible for. And that is doubly-ironic since God's restoration of *spirit* to humanity can be perverted toward the destruction of humanity. The positive speech-act power of *dabhar* can become a *demonically twisted dabhar* bringing nihilistic destruction. But Mark's account shows that the destruction was caused by man's *twisted dabhar*, not God's pure *dabhar*. Jesus is not blameworthy for the wholly positive *dabhar* given first in Galilee, nor the same wholly positive *dabhar* given later in the country of the Gerasenes.

**18 As he was getting into the boat, the man who had been possessed with demons begged him that he might be with him.
19 And he did not permit him but said to him, "Go home to your friends and tell them how much the Lord has done for you, and how he has had mercy on you."**

The departure of Jesus demonstrated that God's new world, created through his *dabhar*, is without coercion, unlike the false *dabhar* of world-less and spirit-less modern and postmodern men. But as he **was getting into the boat,** he would not permit **the man** to go **with him.** This was not merely for the man's becoming *rebonded* to his world. It was also for the man's own *dabhar* to be spoken to the **people** of the region and his **friends.** Jesus would not leave them without witness of God's salvation from the modern age, seen in the man **the Lord . . . had mercy on.** Some may think it sad or harsh that Jesus denied the pleas of the man to go with him. Of course, we have

---

78. Hall, 202.

already seen the mercy in the *rebonding* that would follow. But we need to note that the words of the man, his *dabhar*, were not unanswered. For his **begging** was now with words spoken by a new self in relation to God and from *freedom*. And Jesus' seeming prohibition was a divine commissioning that only sealed the man's *absolute bonding* to Jesus that is not *bondage*.

20 And he went away and began to proclaim in the Decapolis how much Jesus had done for him, and everyone marveled.

Thus, the ongoing *dabhar* mission of Jesus coincided with the beginning *dabhar* mission of the man. His mission was merely the **proclamation** of **how much Jesus had done for him**. Throughout this commentary we have in a sense merely attempted to point out some main aspects of how much was in this **how much**.[79] Mark's narrative of the exorcism of the modern age in its *sickness unto death* ought to be something that brings about the reaction of those in **the Decapolis: everyone marveled.**

FINAL REMARKS ON THE THREE READINGS OF MARK'S DEMONIAC

In sum, this three-fold reading suggests that Mark strongly presented what Kierkegaard called the "infinite qualitative distinction" between God and man, *demonized* man, in fact, and the ability of Jesus the God-man to "overcome" that distinction and deliver resistant ancient, modern, and postmodern men. We thus assume that Mark sees all humans as to some measure demonized, and in agreement with the crowd "begging" Jesus to depart. But emerging from "the strong man's house," where Jesus bound the strong man, are the demonized disciples whose demonization Mark explicitly reveals in Mark 8, but through *exorcism* signify God's new family and the furtherance of the kingdom of God's *new speech-act,* creating a new humanity and a new world.

But the cost of disruption for the sake of a new "single individual" and a new family is too high for the status quo bourgeoise which "always skips over one part of life" which is in fact the restoration of the main part.[80] Yet Kierkegaard saw the request of the Gerasenes as more honest

---

79. All the while knowing "how much" we left out from the fulness of Mark's depiction of the deliverance Christ provides and from Ronald Hall's deep explication of Kierkegaard's own critique of the modern age presented for its exorcism and subsequent upbuilding in true humanity.

80. Kierkegaard, JP 1, 219.

than the Christian bourgeoise which, rather than begging Christ "to leave the neighborhood," "received him" albeit with a "philistine" mentality and spoke from "nauseating, hypocritical preacher-prattle about life being worthless to us without this priceless good, which is Christianity."[81] Mark and Kierkegaard seem to be in agreement that the demonized crowd of every time, whether rejecting or "receiving" Jesus, is the farthest from the kingdom, because it does not know that its bourgeoise philistine mentality is demonic. The crowd does not seek the exorcist it needs, and Kierkegaard explains why:

> They have never caught a glimpse of the idea which lies underneath when we are pushed through the hidden mysterious door, open in all its terror only to presentiment, into this dark realm of sighs—when we see the crushed sacrifices of seduction and deception and the coldness of the tempter.[82]

---

81. Kierkegaard, JP 1, 216.
82. Kierkegaard, JP 1, 219.

2

The Little Daughter of Jairus

"To Need God is a Human Being's Highest Perfection"

Mark 5:21–24a; 35–43 (ESV)

21 And when Jesus had crossed again in the boat to the other side, a great crowd gathered about him, and he was beside the sea. 22 Then came one of the rulers of the synagogue, Jairus by name, and seeing him, he fell at his feet 23 and implored him earnestly, saying, "My little daughter is at the point of death. Come and lay your hands on her, so that she may be made well and live." 24 And he went with him . . .

35 While he was still speaking, there came from the ruler's house some who said, "Your daughter is dead. Why trouble the Teacher any further?" 36 But overhearing what they said, Jesus said to the ruler of the synagogue, "Do not fear, only believe." 37 And he allowed no one to follow him except Peter and James and John the brother of James. 38 They came to the house of the ruler of the synagogue, and Jesus saw a commotion, people weeping and wailing loudly. 39 And when he had entered, he said to them, "Why are you making a commotion and weeping? The child is not dead but sleeping." 40 And they laughed at him. But he put them all outside and took the child's father and mother and those who were with him and went in where the child was. 41 Taking her by the hand he said to her, "Talitha cumi," which means, "Little

girl, I say to you, arise." 42 And immediately the girl got up and began walking (for she was twelve years of age), and they were immediately overcome with amazement. 43 And he strictly charged them that no one should know this, and told them to give her something to eat.

He thinks he is despairing over something earthly and talks constantly of that over which he despairs, and yet he is despairing of the eternal.[1]—Anti-Climacus

How, then, should we face the future? When the sailor is out on the ocean, when everything is changing all around him, when the waves are born and die, he does not stare down into the waves, because they are changing. He looks up at the stars. Why? Because they are faithful; they have the same location now that they had for our ancestors and will have for generations to come. By what means does he conquer the changeable? By the eternal . . . What, then, is the eternal power in a human being? It is faith.[2]
—S. Kierkegaard

To Need God Is a Human Being's Highest Perfection is the title of one of Soren Kierkegaard's "Upbuilding Discourses" published in 1844. As Mark introduces several people with dire needs, Kierkegaard's title helps to "ground" the common earthly concerns of human beings upon eternal solutions. Kierkegaard shows how the gospel "makes all things new" regarding what humans need most:

> See, now everything has become new, everything has been changed. With respect to the earthly, one needs little, and to the degree that one needs less, the more perfect one is. A pagan who knew how to speak of only the earthly has said that the deity is blessed because he needs nothing, and next to him the wise man, because he needs little. In a human being's relationship to God, it is inverted: the more he needs God, the more deeply he comprehends that he is in need of God, and then the more he in his need presses forward to God, the more perfect he is. Therefore the words "to be contented with the grace of God" will not only comfort a person, and then comfort him again every time earthly want and distress make him, to speak mundanely, needful of comfort, but when he really has become attentive to

---

1. Kierkegaard, SD, 61.
2. Kierkegaard, EUD, 19.

the words they will call him aside, where he no longer hears the secular mentality's earthly mother tongue, the speech of human beings, the noise of the shopkeepers, but where the words explain themselves to him, confide to him the secret of perfection: that to need God is nothing to be ashamed of but is perfection itself, and that it is the saddest thing of all if a human being goes through life without discovering that he needs God.[3]

In this section of Mark, he shows two more individuals, because of their acute earthly needs, come out in distinction from the crowds, partly for Mark's purposes of exhibiting various circumstances through which people came to faith in Jesus. Of course, universally difficult circumstances of humankind perennially served Mark's purpose of portraying Jesus' compassionate miracle-working power so that people will be encouraged to believe and follow him. So, we see in Mark, on the one hand, *objective* narrations of salvific encounters that began with Jesus and continued to Mark's present, and on the other hand the *subjective* dynamics that contributed to the faith birthed and portrayed therein.

HUMAN AFFLICTIONS ARE THE TEMPORAL SCAFFOLDING FOR ETERNAL UPBUILDING

Of course, this "reading" of Mark is more interested in the latter since *subjectivity* was what Kierkegaard's "*upbuilding*" labors were oriented toward. "Upbuilding" was a favorite term Kierkegaard used in titles and subtitles, demonstrating that it was the goal of his authorial labors.[4] The truth of needing God as one's highest perfection demonstrates that earthly afflictions are not merely the platform for God to become some automatic miracle-machine for believers but are rather the revelation of the perennially human *need* for God that the gospel *always* answers.[5] In other words, the

---

3. Kierkegaard, EUD, 303

4. See Roberts, *Recovering Christian Character,* 14–15. Roberts writes "The self of his readers is the edifice to whose architecture he means them (his edifying or upbuilding discourses) to contribute. They are devices in aid of the construction and renovation of human beings." (Parenthesis mine.)

5. This view of faith may seem to be the construction of a human "system" of theology and contrary to Kierkegaard's largely anti-systematic theology. But it is more simply Kierkegaard's acceptance of the uncertainty of life "under the sun" through faith, the faith that "overcomes the world," including humanity's rationalistic systems of "certainty" (1 John 5:4). Kierkegaard (Anti-Climacus) writes, "When a person lives in such a way that he knows no higher criterion for life than that of the understanding, then his whole life is relativity, working only for relative goals; he does nothing unless

earthly needs of humans are *meant* to be scaffolding provided by God's for the upbuilding work of *eternal* "perfection." One of Paul's statements demonstrates that God's "miraculous" care aims to produce faith-acceptance of the *Christian* perspective that can bear every "affliction" rather than to think that God will change the *present* character of life "under the sun" which is like mist or vapor (Eccl 1:2, 15). Thus, Paul writes:

> So we do not lose heart. Though our outer self is wasting away, our inner self is being renewed day by day. For this light momentary affliction is preparing for us an eternal weight of glory beyond all comparison, as we look not to the things that are seen but to the things that are unseen. For the things that are seen are transient, but the things that are unseen are eternal (2 Cor 4:16–18, ESV).

It seems therefore that Mark's gospel, and the other gospels, were not written for the purpose of causing the followers of Jesus to continually expect Jesus' miracles for the "outer self" which is "transient." Instead, they teach that all earthly needs provide God's scaffolding for the highest perfection of humans, the *upbuilding* of the "inner self" that is not transient but "eternal."

JAIRUS AND HIS "LITTLE DAUGHTER"

Mark begins the story of Jairus and his "little daughter" by narrating that Jesus again crossed the sea back to the other side whereupon "a great crowd gathered about him . . . beside the sea." Jairus, "one of the rulers of the synagogue" sees Jesus, falls at his feet, "and implored him earnestly, saying 'My little daughter is at the point of death. Come and lay your hands on her, so that she may be made well and live.'" It is notable that Jairus was a ruler of the synagogue, demonstrating that Mark did not create impermeable borders separating stereotyped "heroes and villains" in his Gospel.[6] In fact, the relation between Jesus and the Pharisees, and early Christianity and Rabbinic Judaism may have been more positive than is often thought.[7]

---

the understanding with some help from probability can make more or less clear the advantages and disadvantages, can answer his question 'why and to what end.' It is different with the absolute." Kierkegaard, PC, 116.

6. Nor were there *any* criteria regarding what persons were of value before God and Jesus, as we move from a demoniac of little or no value to anyone, including himself, to a father and daughter of much value to others and one another.

7. Daniel-Rops presents an informative discussion of this matter. See Daniel-Rops, *Jesus and His Times*, 418–19, n8.

We again see a person in a posture of begging before Jesus and doing so earnestly with complete faith that Jesus can achieve the desired miracle. Obviously, Jairus had heard of Jesus and his miracles. This was undoubtedly big but not necessarily "good news" in the synagogues. So, Jesus went with him and after an "interruption" on the way by another "daughter" in desperate need, the story resumes with a report from Jairus' house that she had died.[8] Jesus tells Jairus "Do not fear, only believe" as they proceed the rest of the way. Jesus thus encourages Jairus' faith which had now waned. As they arrived at his house, they were met by a commotion of people loudly "weeping and wailing," to which Jesus says "Why are you making a commotion and weeping? The child is not dead but sleeping." His statement was met by obvious unbelief and derisive laughter. So, Jesus took Jairus, his wife, and three of his disciples apart from this wailing "crowd" to where she lay. He took her hand, saying "Little girl, I say to you, arise" upon which she immediately got up and began walking. All were "immediately overcome with amazement."

Kierkegaard's words that we saw above, "See, now everything has become new, everything has been changed" were certainly true, because Jesus brought the unfathomable possibility of God to the hopeless situation. The initial assurance of faith exhibited by Jairus was severely tested but rewarded in the end. The tenderness and encouragement Jesus communicated to Jairus by telling him not to fear but to believe, and his declaration that she was not dead but sleeping are touching aspects in this story. Jairus seems to be an example of Mark's "*one who has*" and therefore one to whom "*more will be given*".[9] It is interesting and instructive to note *how* this "*more*" is given by Jesus, namely, through his compassionate encouragement. Certainly, the audience of Mark's gospel would be more encouraged to faith by seeing this facet of Jesus' person, than by learning some abstract doctrine regarding hidden decrees or human epistemology. Similarly, Kierkegaard's emphasis that "truth is subjectivity" was based in the relational potentialities between the loving/seeking God and the needy/receptive person. Regarding Kierkegaard's view of objective and subjective truth Julia Watkin says,

> Especially in religious matters it is absurd to speak of proving objective truth—for example that God exists—since one is moving in the realm of metaphysical assumption. One thus has to choose whether to make a religious faith commitment. Subjective truth for Kierkegaard is therefore the sphere of personal commitment to an ethical-religious way of life, to the living of

---

8. The "interruption" is the subject of the following chapter of our reading of Mark.
9. See on Mark 4:25 in Christman, *Behold*, 183–90.

that life. The individual actualizes objective ideals and values in his or her personal existence. Since the subjective has to do with the personal, and the Christian God is viewed as personal, the relation between the individual and God is one of subject to subject and not subject to object.[10]

Kierkegaard was therefore in line with Mark and Jesus, by seeking to promote *subjective faith* in God. Of course, the age-old question is why God allows calamities in the lives of those he cares for. A short and adequate answer is that God's "governance," as Kierkegaard called it, brings people to recognize their dire need for God to "change" the situation, to change "everything" in fact. That humans are extremely needy in the face of human existence in the world is an incontrovertible fact, no matter the explanation. But humans generally want the immediate situation changed, not everything.[11] But ultimately, Mark and Kierkegaard demonstrated that the real need is not a change of situation, but the *changed relation to God*. Thus, Kierkegaard said "it is the saddest thing of all if a human being goes through life without discovering that he needs God."[12] For that need is for the God who changes everything.

Seeking the "answer" to the problems of life in continual "Jesus-type" situational miracles misses that the gospel of God's kingdom is that "everything has become new" as Kierkegaard, quoting Paul, said (2 Cor 5:17). Faith is what "connects" us to that reality, so that faith is "the eternal power in a human being."[13] The *gospel-miracle* has relativized the transient so that through faith, life can be lived within the gospel-truth of Paul. The human being's highest perfection is not to be given a new miracle at every turn, but rather to live in the reality of the already-given gospel-miracle. Perfection is to continually *need God* so that life is always lived in subjective *existential* relation to the living God. Therefore, Kierkegaard viewed Christianity as an "*existence communication*."[14] In order to dig a bit deeper into the dynamics of the faith-response God is "upbuilding" in our "existence," we will consider, as did Kierkegaard, the account of Job in the Old Testament.

---

10. Watkin, *Historical Dictionary*, 251.

11. Robert C. Roberts writes, "People are typically ambivalent about God. They do yearn to trust and obey, to yield themselves to the Maker in happy love. But they also resist, fearing to let God get too close, anxious about changes He may require and concerning the light He may shed on their soul." Roberts, "Passion and Reflection," 93.

12. Kierkegaard, EUD, 303.

13. Kierkegaard, EUD, 19.

14. See Christman, *Behold*, 1–10.

JOB'S RELATION TO THE EARTHLY AND THE ETERNAL

Job was exceedingly blessed and God-fearing in his earthly state. Because of this, Satan (the accuser) asked God: *"Does Job fear God for no reason? Have you not put a hedge around him and his house and all that he has, on every side? You have blessed the work of his hands, and his possessions have increased in the land. But stretch out your hand and touch all that he has, and he will curse you to your face"* (Job 1:9–11, ESV). Consequently, God allowed Satan to test Job. So, one day Job received a series of knocks on the door with reports of the terrible losses of all his livestock, servants, and children. Certainly, one cannot necessarily compare Jairus "little daughter" to Job's larger losses, though perhaps she was Jairus' only child or in some sense his whole world.

Despair is the temptation that next knocks on the door in such trials. Kierkegaard saw despair as wearing several faces along a sort of "continuum" of despair and identified several "forms" thereof. But, given overlap and dialectical qualities in the forms, actual life resists exact correlations.[15] Nevertheless, he thought it helpful to outline the various forms of despair that humans can experience. One of the most concise summaries of Kierkegaard's broad outline is the following:

> First comes despair over the earthly or over something earthly, then despair of the eternal, over oneself. Then comes defiance, which is really despair through the aid of the eternal, the despairing misuse of the eternal within the self to will in despair to be oneself.[16]

Regarding the temptation to despair over the "earthly" losses of Job, which Jairus might have experienced if Jesus had not intervened, we consider Kierkegaard's further explanation:

> Despair over the earthly or over something earthly is in reality also despair of the eternal and over oneself, insofar as it is despair, for this is indeed the formula for all despair ... He thinks he is despairing over something earthly and talks constantly of that over which he despairs, and yet despairing of the eternal, for the fact that he attributes such great worth to something

---

15. *"Actual life is too complex merely to point out abstract contrasts such as that between a despair that is completely unaware of being so and a despair that is completely aware of being so."* Kierkegaard, SD, 48.

16. Kierkegaard, SD, 67. Of course we have just considered the defiant form of despair in our readings on the demoniac, and previously in Christman, *Behold*, 74–97.

earthly—or, to carry this further, that he attributes to something earthly such great worth, or that he first makes something earthly into the whole world and then attributes such great worth to the earthly—this is in fact to despair of the eternal.[17]

Job may have been initially safeguarded by this earthly despair because he did not make the earthly his entire world. He attributed "everything" to God, saying "the Lord gave, and the Lord took away; blessed be the name of the Lord." God was *over* but therefore also *in Job's world* and thus Job couldn't lose *his whole world*. Thus, the gospel-miracle *in* Job's God is magnified when Kierkegaard says,

> But the one who sees God has overcome the world, and therefore Job in his devout words had overcome the world, in those devout words was greater and stronger and more powerful than the whole world, which here certainly did not want to lead him to temptation but to overcome him by its power and bring him to his knees before its boundless might. Indeed, how weak, almost childishly so, is the blustering of the storm when it wants to make a person tremble before it by tearing everything away from him, but he answers: It is not you who are doing it; it is the Lord who takes away! How powerless is the assailant's arm, how worthless the schemer's cleverness; how pitiable is all human power when it wants to plunge the weak person into despairing submission by wrenching everything from him and in his faith he says: It is not you, you can do nothing; it is the Lord who takes away.[18]

Certainly, Job's overcoming of the world did not preclude his heart-rending grief and sorrow. Rather he overcame not by denial or refusal of such natural human emotions, but by recognizing God's relativizing of the temporal in relation to the eternal. Otherwise, one not only loses their "whole world" but also their very self. But Job kept his self, by not forgetting God *in* his

---

17. Kierkegaard, SD, 61. In Kierkegaard's book "*Repetition*," one of the "Letters from a Young Man" that was "published" by "Constantin Constantius" contains a comparison of Job to Abraham, that can be analogous to Job and Jairus by equating Isaac to Jairus' "little daughter." It reads, "*I have not owned the world, have not had seven sons and three daughters. But one who has owned very little may indeed also have lost everything; one who lost the beloved has in a sense lost sons and daughters, and the one who has lost honor and pride and along with it the vitality and meaning of life—he, too, has in a sense been stricken with malignant sores.*" Kierkegaard, FT, 198–99. Many Kierkegaard scholars also detect in the reference to "the beloved" an autobiographical note regarding Kierkegaard's ex-fiancée Regine Olsen in whom he "lost everything."

18. Kierkegaard, EUD, 121.

sorrow. Kierkegaard explains how Job avoided losing his soul by allowing both sorrow and worship to cast him to the ground *before God*:[19]

> Having surrendered to sorrow, not in despair but with human emotions, he was quick to judge between God and himself, and these are the words of judgment: "Naked I came from my mother's womb, and naked I shall return." With these very words, the dispute was settled, and in his soul every demand was silenced that would claim from the Lord something he was unwilling to give or would desire to keep something as if it had not been given. Then comes the confession from the man whom not sorrow alone but also worship cast to the ground: "The Lord gave, and the Lord took away; blessed be the name of the Lord!"[20]

Christopher Barnett summarizes what Job provides for disciples in their relating the earthly to the eternal, saying,

> Job is a prototype who shines forth a wisdom that cannot be reduced to human concepts or bromides. It must be *encountered* ... Job countenances a kind of balance, exhibiting the concrete emotions of human grief, even as he discriminates between mutable earthly life and the eternal ways of God.[21]

Job demonstrates *the upbuilding encounter* with "the eternal" that *existentially* answers why earthly "crosses" are consistent with, rather than contrary to, God's redemptive purposes for humankind. But to fill out the answer more substantially it is necessary to consider more deeply the "objective" ground for this saving subjectivity.

"EVERYTHING HAS BECOME NEW, EVERYTHING HAS CHANGED."[22]

Kierkegaard's recognition of Job subjectively "overcoming the world," the achievement of the "highest perfection" of needing God, also recognizes that it was based upon God's *prior* activity: that "*everything has become new, everything has been changed.*" For Job, who was apparently not an Israelite looking from this age toward God's age to come, God's activity was in the

---

19. George Stroup explains why even social, political, and economic restoration on the human scene would fall short of Biblical salvation if it were not primarily "before God." Stroup, *Before God*, 139.

20. Kierkegaard, EUD, 115.

21. Barnett, *From Despair to Faith*, 149–50.

22. Kierkegaard, EUD, 303.

realm of "governance."[23] Kierkegaard often spoke of governance and recognized it as no less operative under the New Covenant.[24] But on this side of the "coming forth" of Jesus "in the fullness of time" there is a deeper relativizing of the earthly in relation to the eternal.

To look at this through the question of why many fathers like Jairus, this side of Jesus' earthly miracles, have had to bury their "little daughter" is to rephrase the question: *What* changed when *"everything changed."* Of course, the easiest way to answer that is to ask what did not change. It seems that following the earthly life of Jesus and the "Acts of the Apostles," life basically "returned to normal." The miraculous acts of those days, for the most part, seem to have been a foretaste of the final restoration of all things, a "tasting of the powers of the age to come" (see Hebrews 6:5). "Normal life" seems to continue as it is portrayed in Ecclesiastes: "what is crooked cannot be made straight" (Eccl 1:15). The book of James, possibly the earliest writing of the New Testament, is also the most like Ecclesiastes, as if to signify the return to "normalcy." This is evident in James 4:13–15:

> Now listen, you who say, "Today or tomorrow we will go to this or that city, spend a year there, carry on business and make money." Why, you do not even know what will happen tomorrow. What is your life? You are a mist that appears for a little while and then vanishes. Instead, you ought to say, "If it is the Lord's will, we will live and do this or that" (NIV).[25]

Peter Leithart writes that Ecclesiastes' meditation on the vaporousness of existence makes "The Preacher" (1:1) a sort of "postmodern" of the ancient world. But he differs from them because he recognizes God's intentions for "vapor." Leithart writes,

> But he speaks the language of postmodernism not, finally, to affirm it; not, finally, because vapor is all there is. Solomon talks like a postmodern to emphasize that the world is built to force us to live by faith and not by sight. This too is something of a postmodern move. Moderns aspired to live without faith. They could see nearly everything, and anything they couldn't see either was not worth seeing or would come clearly into view in

---

23. See Dumbrell, *Faith of Israel*, 215–16.

24. Jack Mulder presents a helpful overview of Kierkegaard's simultaneously traditional and characteristically unsystematic thought on divine governance, summarizing that "Kierkegaard's full position on the doctrine of providence may be as difficult to discern as the doctrine itself." Mulder, "Governance/Providence," 116.

25. Yet James 5:13–18 holds forth the hope for "miraculous" prayers of faith which is why we somewhat qualified the sense above.

short order. But they didn't see everything, and the best knew it . . . "Vapor" pictures the world as impossible to control. But vapor is also a veil, a screen . . . To say that all is vapor is to say that it's hiding something, and Solomon is suggesting that the vapor of the world screens us from God himself, who for the time being, "under the sun," modestly remains behind the veil of the vaporous world.[26]

Therefore, even looking at what has seemingly *not* changed on the other hand seems to show that "everything has changed." Pursuing this further, from the view of Ecclesiastes to the view this side of the cross, "everything has changed." Writing of G. K. Chesterton, Eugen Rosenstock-Huessy says,

> Chesterton expressed the paradoxical nature of the Christian time concept inimitably when he wrote, in *The Ballad of the White Horse,* "And the end of the world was long ago." The Christian has the end of the world, his world, behind him; beginning and end have changed places. Pagan natural man begins with birth and lives forward through time toward death; the Christian lives in the opposite direction, from the end of life into a new beginning. In surviving death he finds the first day of the new creation again before him. He emerges from the grave of his old self into the openness of the real future.[27]

Kierkegaard's determinative thought in this regard was simply that Christianity was *"essentially related to eternity."*[28] This essential relation to eternity is what Christ definitively established through his life, death, and resurrection. Therefore, when he said to Jairus, "The child is not dead but sleeping," he not only denies the ultimacy of temporal death but signified the newness wherein "everything" would change such that even the death of Christians became known as "sleeping" in the post-Easter experience of Mark's readers and hearers.[29]

In sum, the struggles and even despair over the earthly are intended by God's governance to teach a Job, a Jairus, and all of us, that *"To Need God is a Human Being's Highest Perfection."* Consciousness of our need of God, who changes circumstances by changing everything through the gospel-miracle of Christ, creates the faith which is "the eternal power of the

---

26. Leithart, *Solomon Among the Postmoderns,* 165–66.

27. Rosenstock-Huessy, *The Christian Future,* 67. We note that Rosenstock-Huessy is only stating the truth of the death and resurrection that every Christian baptism signifies, according to Rom 6:3–10; cf., Gal 2:20 & John 5:24; 11:26.

28. Kierkegaard, PC, 221.

29. See Boring, *Mark,* 284–85.

human being that conquers the changeable." And thus, the difficult temporal things become the scaffolding by which God upbuilds the eternal in us and us for eternity. It must be stressed that the literal work of upbuilding, namely building up, cannot take place apart from the scaffolding that enables it. Therefore, the temporal "scaffold" that is continually necessary for life, *the need of God,* upbuilds our "highest perfection." And this means that the problems (and pleasures) of earthly transience are not to be despised in an ascetic other-worldliness. Rather, they are seen as the scaffolding that "works all things together for good" in the eternal upbuilding beginning in the present and enduring to the ages (Rom 8:28). Thus, *faith* is "the eternal power in a human." The relation of the transient to the eternal creates in us a proper *this-worldliness.* Kierkegaard provides the ultimate summary of all these things in the *Upbuilding Discourse* called "The Expectancy of Faith," saying,

> "What is the expectancy of faith? Victory—or as Scripture so earnestly and so movingly teaches us, that all things must serve for good to those who love God."[30]

---

30. Kierkegaard, EUD, 19, quoting Paul in Romans 8:28.

3

The "Daughter" Who Touched the Hem of Jesus' Garment

"The Single Individual" as "The Category through which the Human Race Must Go"

Mark 5:24b-34 (ESV)

And a great crowd followed him and thronged about him. 25 And there was a woman who had had a discharge of blood for twelve years, 26 and who had suffered much under many physicians, and had spent all that she had, and was no better but rather grew worse. 27 She had heard the reports about Jesus and came up behind him in the crowd and touched his garment. 28 For she said, "If I touch even his garments, I will be made well." 29 And immediately the flow of blood dried up, and she felt in her body that she was healed of her disease. 30 And Jesus, perceiving in himself that power had gone out from him, immediately turned about in the crowd and said, "Who touched my garments?" 31 And his disciples said to him, "You see the crowd pressing around you, and yet you say, 'Who touched me?'" 32 And he looked around to see who had done it. 33 But the woman, knowing what had happened to her, came in fear and trembling and fell down before him and told him the whole truth. 34 And he said to her, "Daughter, your faith has made you well; go in peace, and be healed of your disease."

THE "DAUGHTER" WHO TOUCHED THE HEM OF JESUS' GARMENT

But this is also a form of the despair, to be unwilling to hope in the possibility that an earthly need, a temporal cross, can come to an end.[1]—Anti-Climacus

Few are they who by faith touch him; multitudes are they who throng about him.[2]—Augustine

Longing is the umbilical cord of the higher life.[3]—Soren Kierkegaard

During Jairus' commandeering Jesus for the sake of his daughter's life, and from the midst of the thronging crowd, an unnamed "daughter" of Israel emerged in a "secret" venture for the healing she longed for and had all but given up hope for. Mark gives more space to her account than other gospel writers to demonstrate the faith that drove her from the milling crowd toward the man that miracles flowed from. Perhaps a "secret" touch of his garment would receive the flow of life from God that would stop the flow of "life" from her. This needful "daughter" provides another look at the relation of earthly concerns to eternal ones. Her twelve-year affliction is contrasted to the sudden trial of Jairus. If Jairus' story exhibited the momentary yet calamitous bumps in life's road, her's told the tale of lasting travail.

GOD'S GOVERNANCE AND HUMAN RESPONSE

Her story aptly illustrates that God's grace to us is that *"the world is built to force us to live by faith and not by sight."*[4] That particular grace creates *longing*, meant to serve as what Kierkegaard called *"the umbilical cord of the higher life."* Kierkegaard's following remark well applies to Mark's unnamed woman:

> There was a time when "the woman" related herself to herself in her conception of her feelings. One sorrow was sufficient to decide her life for a whole lifetime.[5]

That statement seems to mean that sorrow was once received as contributory toward a *life* of passionate response. But in modern Christendom's passionless state, that "use" of sorrow is evaded and replaced by the frivolous. He continues,

---

1. Kierkegaard, SD, 70.
2. Oden & Hall, *Mark*, 75.
3. Kierkegaard, PSW, 328. (JP 4, 282.)
4. Leithart, *Solomon Among the Postmoderns*, 166.
5. Kierkegaard, MLW, 318.

> She understood it as her task to be lost to this life, which when it is consistently carried out makes for long, long inner battles and spiritual trials, occasions many a painful collision with the surrounding world—in short, makes life difficult. Therefore, to what end all these difficulties—be a blatherskite, and you will see, all difficulties vanish! . . . So, you see, all difficulties vanish; life becomes enjoyable, cheerful, jolly, easy—in short, it is a glorious world in which to live if one just knows how to conduct oneself properly in it—by being a blatherskite.[6]

It seems this *technique* of being a blatherskite—being frivolous—was increasingly "mastered" as the modern era progressed.[7] Kierkegaard seemed to think that such manifest *unreality* was a *modern* phenomenon largely absent in earlier times, like those of this woman.

The woman's undeniable sufferings, unlike the *deniable* yet nonetheless present despair of modern times, had not been helped by the remedies of many physicians. She had spent her livelihood only to grow worse. Mark was alluding to "cures" people relied on in his day, whether they be from the religious, mystical, philosophical, or medical "professionals" of the day. Kierkegaard certainly saw the "physicians" of his day as of small practical use. For the deeper problems were the "eternal" soul-consequences of misrelation to the transient "earthly" problems. We noted in the previous chapter that the problem is not merely with the potential setbacks of life, but with the *despair* that accompanies them. Kierkegaard writes,

> In our day—this is the truth and it is indicative of the Christianity of our day—in our day the physician is the spiritual advisor. People even have a perhaps groundless anxiety about calling the pastor, who quite possibly in our day would talk somewhat like a physician anyway—so that one calls the physician. He also knows a way out. "You must go to a health resort; you ought to keep a riding horse, because you can ride away from morbid fancies; and then diversion, diversion, much diversion! See to it that you have a lively game of *L'hombre* every night, but don't eat much in the evening just before going to bed, and finally see to it that you have fresh air in your bedroom—that should help all right." "For an anguished conscience? "Oh, stop that silly talk! An anguished conscience—such a thing doesn't exist anymore, is a reminiscence of the childhood of the race.[8]

---

6. Kierkegaard, MLW, 318–19.
7. Walter Lowrie translates blatherskite as frivolous. Kierkegaard, AC, 265.
8. Kierkegaard, FSE/JFY 201–02.

HOW THE WOMAN OVERCAME DEFIANT DESPAIR

"An anguished conscience" in Kierkegaard's day notwithstanding, conscious *anxiety and despair* have had quite the comeback in our day despite the popular "technologies" of denial and diversion. The woman in Mark was in undeniable, nearly overwhelming despair. For despondency—like sin—is always *"crouching at the door"* to overtake us when our lives are *crossed*, especially if there no end in sight (Gen 4:7).[9] Kierkegaard speaks quite bone-chillingly of the *defiant despair* that may develop:

> The form of despair that despairs over the earthly or something earthly . . . also manifests itself as being—despair of the eternal, that is, an unwillingness to be comforted by and healed by the eternal, an overestimation of the things of this world to the extent that the eternal can be no consolation. But this is also a form of the despair, to be unwilling to hope in the possibility that an earthly need, a temporal cross, can come to an end. The despairing person who in despair wills to be himself is unwilling to do that. He has convinced himself that his thorn in the flesh gnaws so deeply that he cannot abstract himself from it . . . and therefore he might as well accept it forever so to speak. He is offended by it, or, more correctly, he takes it as an occasion to be offended at all existence; he defiantly wills to be himself, to be himself not in spite of it or without it . . . no, in spite of or in defiance of all existence, he wills to be himself with it, takes it along, almost flouting his agony. Hope in the possibility of help, especially by virtue of the absurd, that for God everything is possible—no, that he does not want. And to seek help from someone else—no, not for all the world does he want that. Rather than to seek help, he prefers, if necessary, to be himself with all the agonies of hell.[10]

Considering Kierkegaard's expose of the winding path toward defiant despair, it seems this woman could have easily been tempted down it. Though her faith and resolve "that speak better things" are plainly evident, her need to preserve anonymity, due to the social laws regarding her flow of blood causing ritual uncleanness, reveals a temptation toward "inclosing reserve" that settles for and even chooses despair.[11] For the law become a societal barrier would prevent her touching even the holy hem of Christ and could

---

9. We allude to the fact that life invariably meets "the cross" as God's gracious "governance" invitation. See GD, 263–65; 307–10.

10. Kierkegaard, SD, 70–71.

11. See Boring, *Mark*, 278–81. We allude to Heb 6:9.

have led her to the bitterness that hardens one's soul in despair (Heb 12:15). An ancient commentator shows her as instead choosing the way of humility, a tonic preventative against the despair of defiance. Nevertheless, she had to overcome much inner tension merely to conceive the only solution that presented itself to her as the one whom she had heard about, and thought of as perhaps her only eternal possibility, approached. This commentator writes,

> No seas were ever so troubled by the ebb and flow of the tide, as the mind of this woman, pulled to and fro by the sway of her thoughts. After all the hopeless strivings of physicians, after all her outlay on useless remedies, after all the usual but useless treatment, when skill and experience had so failed, all her substance was gone. This was not by chance, but divinely ordered, that she might be healed solely through faith and humility, whom human knowledge had failed through so many years. At a little distance apart from him stood this woman, whom nature had filled with modesty, whom the law had declared unclean, saying of her: She shall be unclean and shall touch no holy thing . . . Through many years her body has been an arena of suffering. Everyday, unceasing pain she can endure no more. The Lord is passing by so quickly. The time is short to think what she must do, aware that healing is not given to the silent, nor to the one who hides her pain. In the midst of her conflicting thoughts, she sees a way, her sole way of salvation. She would secure her healing by stealth, take in silence what she dares not ask for, guarding her respect and modesty. She who feels unworthy in body, draws near in heart to the physician. In faith she touches God. With her hand she touches his garment, knowing that healing and forgiveness may be bestowed on this stratagem, undertaken due to the demands of modesty, and not as she otherwise would have preferred.[12]

The touching account of Chrysologus portrays the pains of her affliction, those in her very body, and those of her lonely separation from God and society. He also shows her as humble, God-fearing, and therefore emerging from the crowd a fitting example of faith for Mark.

Though, to our knowledge, Kierkegaard did not comment on this woman, many things he said are applicable to Mark's story of her faith. In the next sections we will consider some of Kierkegaard's statements to draw out all that was required for her to overcome despair and find "complete" healing.

---

12. Chrysologus, as cited in Oden & Hall, *Mark*, 74.

THE "DAUGHTER" WHO TOUCHED THE HEM OF JESUS' GARMENT 51

HOW THE WOMAN WAS "INVITED" TO TOUCH JESUS

The first thing that can be mentioned in this narrative of her faith is the "invitation" she was given by Jesus. Obviously, she was given no personal, verbal invitation, and their encounter was due to her boldness to come to him *uninvited*. Nevertheless, she was "invited" in at least several ways. To begin with, the "outward" governance of affliction invited her to the "inward" upbuilding of eternity. Kierkegaard writes,

> To be made well with the aid of Christianity is not the difficulty; the difficulty is in becoming sick to some purpose.[13]

We considered earlier that her "one sorrow" could determine her life and God's purpose therein so that her sorrow, and more importantly, *her healing*, might not be in vain. Kierkegaard was always concerned that Christianity be believed in "Christianly." Otherwise, it is believed in vain. Jesus didn't want her to just go *on her own way* as "healed." He wanted her *healing* to be the *transformation* of her way, not merely the enablement of *her way*. To Kierkegaard, "Christianity" has made many "well" but what they really needed was to "become sick to some purpose." Thus, Kierkegaard held that Christ's invitation was *to sickness*, rather than *from it*.

> Come here now, all you who labor and are burdened, that is, if you feel the need, even if you are of all who suffer the most miserable, if you feel the need to be helped in this way, that is, helped into even greater misery—then come here, he will help you.[14]

Kierkegaard's conception of the invitation of Christ to those in need stresses the idea that that need must be felt, acutely! He writes,

> "Come here!" He assumes that those who labor and are burdened feel the burden to be ever so heavy, feel the labor to be heavy, and now are standing there irresolute and sighing, one person looking in all directions for help, another with downcast eyes because he discerned no comfort, a third staring upward as if it might still come from heaven—but all of them searching. Therefore he says, "Come here." The one who ceased to seek and to sorrow, he does not invite.[15]

---

13. Kierkegaard, PSW, 333. (JP 2, 18.)
14. Kierkegaard, PC, 56.
15. Kierkegaard, PC, 20–21.

Jesus didn't want the woman to "cease to seek" following the healing, as if the temporal healing was all she needed. She needed the continual need of God that is the highest perfection, the *purpose* part of "sick to some purpose." Thus, her invitation through the "outward" governance of affliction was an "inward" call of *need* toward *the highest perfection*, and of *longing* toward *eternal transformation*. Altogether, this is "the upbuilding of eternity."

Of course, another more obvious and "outward" way she was invited was through the "publicity" that preceded Jesus' coming to her region. Like Jairus, she had heard the "news" that kindled in her the possibility of a real hope beyond the failed efforts of her "physicians." For this was news of amazing miracles done through the very power of God. And again, that outward news is not merely to repair the "impediments" of outward life, but for complete transformation. And below, we will consider how Jesus' "investigation" of her potentially "incomplete" touch further "invited" her to *complete* transformation.

HOW THE WOMAN VENTURED IN FAITH

The next thing we may consider is what the invitation called forth, namely her passionate response of venturing in faith. Kierkegaard believed that "passion" was lacking in modern Christendom. He thought that people were spiritless. And passion was the expression of "spirit." Conformity to the human herd removed the need for passion and spirit. So as this woman ventured forth, though desiring anonymity, she nevertheless exhibited comparatively great passion and spirit. Kierkegaard writes,

> Spirit is fire, Christianity is fire-setting. And by nature we shrink more from this fire than from any other, The fire Christianity wants to light is not intended to burn a few houses but to burn up the *human zest* for life—burn it out into spirit, Spirit is fire. From this comes the frequent expression: As gold is purified in fire, so the Christian is purified, But spirit-fire must not be regarded merely as the fire of "tribulations"—that is, something coming from outside. No, a fire is kindled within the Christian, in this burning comes the purification.[16]

It seems warranted to imagine that the woman's perseverance in her lengthy affliction seems to portray a natural "human zest" for life. It is not difficult to see her perseverance as rooted in a deeper "longing" for the life that life itself seems to promise all that live, whether that promise is "heard" or not.

---

16. Kierkegaard, PSW, 328. (JP 4, 4355.)

And as Kierkegaard wrote and himself exemplified, such longing "*is the umbilical cord of higher life.*"[17] But her reaching forth to Jesus was also a crucial beginning of the burning process that purifies that longing. Kierkegaard said that "*the self must be broken in order to become itself.*"[18] He seems to be describing a two-faceted process wherein God brings a self to birth by incinerating the old non-self and inciting passionate response in the new-self. It is as though he is setting fire to a house in which one simply exists, to bring to passionate life the one sleeping therein. In fact, Kierkegaard kindles the "fire" metaphor, saying,

> It is not always water that is used to put out a fire. To keep the metaphor, sometimes one uses, for example, featherbeds, blankets, mattresses, and the like to smother a fire. In this sense, if you want Christianity again, fire again, then do all you can to get rid of the featherbeds, blankets, and mattresses, the grossly bulky stuff—and there will be fire.[19]

It may seem that Kierkegaard contradicts himself when he says on the one hand that people need passion but on the other that their "natural zest" needs to be burned out. For "natural zest" could seem to be passion. But what is passion before God and the natural passion of man are two different things. Kierkegaard knew that merely human passions too easily settle for the transient "comforts" and fall short of the eternal. This seems to be clarified when he boldly says that what people generally consider to be "sin"— namely sins of passion—are generally too "spiritless" to even be called sin.

> Most men are characterized by a dialectic of indifference and live a life so far from the good (faith) that it is almost too spiritless to be called sin—indeed, almost too spiritless to be called despair.[20]

It seems that Kierkegaard simply wanted to promote self-awareness, given that we humans to easily over-estimate our "passion" which barely rise to the quality the word signifies. Remember that the sacrifice of Christ is called his "passion." It also seems that Kierkegaard thought that faith needed to be "passionate." Therefore, to Kierkegaard, faith, even though not meritorious for salvation, was nevertheless the passioned "exercise" of spirit that is

---

17. Kierkegaard, PSW, 328. (JP 4, 4409.) See Christman, "Lewis and Kierkegaard," 126–27, regarding the element of longing in all Kierkegaard's writings.

18. Kierkegaard, SD, 65.

19. Kierkegaard, PSW, 329. (JP 6, 6932.) Note that "grossly bulky stuff" signifies things that provide the "normal" comforts.

20. Kierkegaard, SD, 101.

inherent in true response to God. This is much different that the modern rationalistic and reductionistic notion of faith as mental assent. Kierkegaard's understanding of human faith is very aptly illustrated by Mark's unclean yet "spirited" woman passionately reaching to Jesus. And *that* touch, *drew* power from him that got hold of her (5:30). Kierkegaard writes,

> And yet it surely is Christianity's intention that a person use this life to venture out in such a way that God can get hold of him.[21]

It seems at first that she almost inverts this as she "ventured out in such a way" that *she* got hold of *God!* (It is important to note that touching the garment was considered touching the person.)[22] But these two getting holds are not mutually exclusive, and we have already seen that God's invitations were his getting hold. And that her getting hold of God was "reciprocated" will be considered below.

A final aspect of "venturing" in faith that is exhibited by the woman is that she had to seize the moment. Though Chrysologus showed that there was some "calculation" on her part, that was subservient to her life-cause. For "cold" calculation is often the enemy of *the moment,* the enemy of "*today*" as "*the day of salvation*."[23] Thus, Mark presents the despair and faith driven woman as knowing she had to *immediately* venture forth to seize her possibility.[24] She ventured forth knowing the risk against what could only become her lost opportunity. Speaking to these things, Kierkegaard says,

> To venture the truth is what gives human life and the human situation pith and meaning. To venture is the fountainhead of inspiration. Calculation is the sworn enemy of enthusiasm, the mirage whereby the earthly person drags out time and keeps the eternal away, whereby one cheats God, himself, and his generation . . . A bold venture is not a high-flown phrase, not an exclamatory outburst, but arduous work. A bold venture, no matter how rash, is not a boisterous proclamation but a

---

21. Kierkegaard, JP 3, 3350.
22. See Boring, *Mark*, 280–81; 500–501.
23. "But you say, 'Before I do this, however, before I risk such a decisive step, I must consult with others.' Insolent, disobedient one, you are cheeky! You know very well that it is nothing but blasphemy, for you, you cheat, you are looking for a way out, an excuse, since you know very well that every human being will recommend whatever indulges you and advise you to follow what best pleases flesh and blood, and will say: For God's sake, spare yourself." Kierkegaard, JP 3, 2865.
24. Remembering that "immediately" is one of Mark's favorite words, and not only for describing the acts of Jesus.

quiet dedication that receives nothing in advance but stakes everything.[25]

THE WOMAN AS KIERKEGAARD'S "SINGLE INDIVIDUAL"

The "unclean" woman risked reprimand from the Pharisees (or even Jesus—being a teacher) if she had been discovered, and the public shame that would follow. Her "stake" of secrecy was risked in her bold venture and was lost due to the "investigation" of Jesus. He had "perceived" that "power had gone out from him" and sought "the single individual" who had drawn it forth. She serves to illustrate "*the* category" in Kierkegaard's thought:

> *The single individual* is the category through which, in a religious sense, the age, history, the human race must go . . . *the single individual* is the category of spirit, of spiritual awakening, as diametrically opposed to politics as possible . . . from the Christian point of view, this is the decisive category for the future of Christianity . . . the submission of *obedience under God's majesty* shall *be believed*.[26]

We should easily note how readily she fits and even epitomizes this category. We should also note the correlation of the "*obedience*" Jesus drew from her at this juncture in her story in Mark, and the apostolic impulse of the gospel as related by Paul in Romans 1:5. Jesus wants obedience, not anonymous people drawing from his power to suit their own ends. Not that she had that design. Her secrecy seems "purely" required by the difficulties of her situation of "uncleanness." We should marvel at the paradox this "unclean" woman presents as we ponder her illustrating the category of "spirit" and "spiritual awakening." What Jesus *required* of her, that she "**shall**" submit "under God's majesty" to "obedience," fully illustrates her as fulfilling *the category of response* to the gospel—in which God's saving purpose for the world is realized "through the obedience of faith for the sake of his name among the nations" (Rom 1:5, ESV).

It is immensely important at this point to realize what has transpired here: this "single individual" of Mark and Kierkegaard has demonstrated "the category" in and through which "the age, history, the human race must go." We see in the venture of this "unclean woman" *how* God accomplishes the redemption of humanity by inviting all, through the stages of governance,

---

25. Kierkegaard, PSW, 392. (EUD, 382; CUP1, 149.)
26. Kierkegaard, PV, 118, 121.

gospel invitation, and Jesus' "investigational invitation," to become "the single individual." And ultimately, as Paul's theology revealed, *Christ* became "that single individual" in and through whom all "**shall**" become "the single individual" as they learn and "put on" the character of the new man which is "true righteousness and holiness" (Eph 4:24).[27] We therefore see that the "individualism" of Kierkegaard, Mark, Paul, and even Jesus, is not an end in itself, but merely, or rather, magnificently, "*the category through which . . . the human race must go.*"

HOW THE WOMAN BECAME WHOLE THROUGH THE "INVESTIGATION" OF JESUS

Why Jesus drew the woman from her anonymity reveals something further about the gospel's redemption. Redemption includes the reintegration of the individual to society at large. Salvation is not merely about individuals "going to heaven" after this life's vale of tears.[28] Jesus didn't want the woman to anonymously receive healing, because individuality qua individuality is not salvation. Jesus continually presses the "single individual" toward integration in a new earthly "society." This ultimately pictures the new family of God being created in Christ, which Jesus revealed when he proclaimed "Behold, my mother and my brethren!" (Mark 3:34, KJV). Obviously, a "secret salvation," biblically speaking, is no salvation at all in regard to the "more abundant life" the gospel brings. The way Jesus brought her to this needs to be considered next.

When Jesus began searching for the anonymous "perpetrator" who had "responded" to him as already discussed, she exhibited *fear and trembling* by "falling down before him."[29] Her *second* response to Jesus was brought forth because of her "anonymous" healing and Jesus' subsequent search of her.[30]

---

27. Robert C. Roberts defends Kierkegaard against the charge of individualism, explaining that "the single individual . . . is in fact a way of speaking about a person's character" which we further note is *Christian* in all that entails for the individual and corporate redemption of humanity. Roberts, *Recovering Christian Character*, 56.

28. We concentrated on this evangelical obsession in Christman, *Behold*, 36–42; *Gospel*, 122–26, 199–209.

29. We allude to Kierkegaard's early book *Fear and Trembling*.

30. Whether intended or not, we detect an analogous pattern here in which the woman's two responses parallel a broader gospel pattern in which, 1) The redemption of all humankind through the incarnate person and atoning work of Christ is *already* accomplished for all and subsequently "touched" by some in an anonymous "first response" to what light and governance of God they have been given, and 2) Christ "seeks," through the missionary enterprise of his followers, the "second response" of his "sheep" who are *already* "his." (See 2 Cor 5:19; John 1:4; 10:3–5, 16.)

THE "DAUGHTER" WHO TOUCHED THE HEM OF JESUS' GARMENT 57

So, she told him "the whole truth." This illustrates that "confession" before God and men in all its biblical nuance is necessary to the full restoration the gospel brings. But we must emphasize that the societal, or in Mark's terms, familial "fellowship," is integral to what salvation means in the full "kingdom" sense of the NT. Therefore, although she had been "immediately" healed at her touch of the fringe of Jesus, *after* Jesus apprehended and "investigated" her, he says *"Daughter, your faith has made you well; go in peace and be healed of your disease."* It seems that her healing was not truly complete until *after* the personal encounter with Jesus that would draw her into a realized social integration from what would otherwise remain an individualistic anonymity. Nevertheless, her coming integration depended upon her prior (and individual) response to Jesus which in essence began her *new life* as a new self in a new relation to God, herself, and others. Can one gain that form of new life anonymously? It is noteworthy that though first introduced anonymously as "a woman," through the apprehension and investigation of Jesus she became "daughter." She then became a person in relation to family, *to Israel*, as was the dear "little daughter" of Jairus, rather than merely anonymous. An anonymous family member is an oxymoron in God's new family which can be beheld as family from the outside and the inside.

Finally, Christ's "investigation" drew her "faith" out to be his public witness (5:34). This immediately cut her asunder from her old absolute and servile way in the world and placed her in a new relative relation to that world. In a sense Jesus baptized her, albeit without the outward ritual. Christ's gospel draws all from anonymity unto "the obedience of faith for the sake of his name among the nations" (Rom 1:5). For the followers of Jesus are the visible witnesses of his gospel and thereby testify to the invisible God.

> Through this woman whom they could see, the witnesses were enabled to behold the divinity that cannot be seen.[31]

Thus, and with all the new significance accompanying her as "daughter," she would become a visible witness of Christ. This may have been an important underlying message to Mark's hearers, ancient and modern, who can so easily prefer to receive Christ's power but remain relationally anonymous. That desire seems closely related to Kierkegaard's critique of the "religious" desire to be an "admirer" rather than a witness or disciple:

> It is well known that Christ continually used the expression "follower." He never asked for admirers, worshippers, or adherents.

---

31. Ephrem the Syrian, as cited in Oden & Hill, *Mark*, 74.

No, he calls disciples. It is not adherents of a teaching but followers of a life that Christ is looking for. Christ understood that being a "disciple" was in innermost and deepest harmony with what he said about himself. Christ claimed to be the way and the truth and the life (Jn. 14:6). For this reason, he could never be satisfied with adherents who accepted his teaching—especially with those who in their lives ignored it or let things take their usual course. His whole life on earth, from beginning to end, was destined solely to have followers and make admirers impossible.[32]

JESUS BRINGS PEACE TO THOSE WHO VENTURE THE LEAP OF FAITH

The "go in peace" with which Jesus blessed *his* restored "daughter" notarizes the change from past sorrows to present and future joys. But she may well become a persecuted follower of Christ and will certainly suffer subsequent earthly afflictions and trials. Her "salvation" would poignantly speak to Mark's hearers and would-be disciples in the trying conditions in which they must exist and hopefully be Christ-followers within. Anonymity might prevent that, but that would also prevent the fulness of joy and restoration only experienced in the new family of Jesus.

To briefly present the challenging but promising reality of Christ's peace to her, we will list the titles of a series of Kierkegaard's discourses gathered under the heading "Joyful Notes in the Strife of Suffering." He prefaced the discourses with the Scripture epigram: '*I will incline mine ear to the parable, and propound my dark sayings upon the harp*' (Psalm 49.4).[33] The parabolic and paradoxical nature of peace (shalom) is evident in each title and accentuated by the realistic imagery of "dark sayings upon the harp."

The titles were:

I. The Joy of it—that we suffer only once, but triumph eternally

II. The Joy of it—that affliction does not bereave of hope, but recruits hope

III. The Joy of it—that the poorer thou dost become, the richer thou canst make others

IV. The Joy of it—that the weaker thou dost become, the stronger does God become in thee

32. Kierkegaard, PSW, 83. (PC, 237–38.)
33. Kierkegaard, CD, 97.

V. The Joy of it—that what thou dost lose temporally thou dost gain eternally

VI. The Joy of it—that when I 'gain all' I lose nothing at all

VII. The Joy of it—that Misfortune is Good Fortune[34]

Considering the transformative message conveyed in these discourses, we conclude by repeating Jesus' few words in Mark's account, his "red letters." They demonstrate the movement from "anonymous encounter" to entering the kingdom.[35]

> *"Who touched my garments? . . . Who touched me? . . . Daughter, your faith has made you well, go in peace, and be healed of your disease."*

---

34. Kierkegaard, CD, 99.

35. A tantalizing undercurrent in this "reading" is in relation to the idea of Karl Rahner's category of "anonymous Christians." In a sense our reading of Kierkegaard's category of "the single individual" through whom the human race must go, supported by the gospel as we have considered it above, certainly presupposes being in *some* manner of dialogue with Rahner's "anonymous Christian." His view, which we admittedly have not fully studied, may not be the wholly correct answer but is asking necessary questions of the relation to God of true "God-fearers" *outside* of Christianity. Our reading (and personal belief) mitigates against the sense in which these "anonymous" are "Christian," just as Mark's unnamed woman was not *while remaining* "anonymous." Of course, our main intent in this note is merely to say that our reading in this chapter regarding "anonymity" was self-consciously written with this question in the background, and therefore any and all implications therein ought to be "drawn out" just as Jesus drew out the anonymous "woman" to become a "daughter" in intimate relation to God through Christ. Our previous work in Christman, *Gospel*, 266–336, also considered those "anonymously" touching the hem of the garment of the Divine, but, strictly speaking, in no real sense thereby becoming "Christians."

4

The Un-miracle Story in Jesus' Hometown

Reflective Envy as the Social Ethos of the Age of Reflection

Mark 6:1–6 (NIV)

Jesus left there and went to his hometown, accompanied by his disciples. 2 When the Sabbath came, he began to teach in the synagogue, and many who heard him were amazed.

"Where did this man get these things?" they asked. "What's this wisdom that has been given him? What are these remarkable miracles he is performing? 3 Isn't this the carpenter? Isn't this Mary's son and the brother of James, Joseph, Judas and Simon? Aren't his sisters here with us?" And they took offense at him.

4 Jesus said to them, "A prophet is not without honor except in his own town, among his relatives and in his own home." 5 He could not do any miracles there, except lay his hands on a few sick people and heal them. 6 He was amazed at their lack of faith. Then Jesus went around teaching from village to village.

And just as *enthusiasm* is the unifying principle in a passionate age, so *envy* becomes the *negatively unifying principle* in a passionless and very reflective age.[1] —S. Kierkegaard

And eventually human speech will become just like the public: pure abstraction—there will no longer be someone who speaks, but an objective reflection will gradually deposit a kind of atmosphere, an abstract noise that will render human speech superfluous, just as machines make workers superfluous.[2] —S. Kierkegaard

There is nothing, of course, which human envy assails the way it assails the extraordinary. And yet no one becomes a true extraordinary except through the mistreatment of men. Consequently, envy will mistreat a person in order to prevent him from becoming extraordinary, and no one becomes the extraordinary except through human mistreatment—consequently envy produces the extraordinary.[3] —Soren Kierkegaard

Here Mark presents a striking contrast to the miracle stories and general public amazement we have seen so far, not that discordant elements of questioning, unbelief, and rejection have not also been seen. But rather than witnessing a continuation of rapid-fire miracles we instead see what Lamar Williamson called "an un-miracle story."[4] Of course, the ironic "wholesale" rejection of Jesus the Messiah by "national" Israel was what led to his crucifixion, and the "smaller" rejection by his hometown foreshadows that development. It is also ironic that though Jesus has just drawn the unnamed woman of 5:25–34 *out of anonymity*, he is immediately plunged further into it himself.[5]

---

1. Kierkegaard, TA, 81.
2. Kierkegaard, TA, 104. (Seemingly a chilling 1846 prediction of *our* post-speech technological age.)
3. Kierkegaard, JP 1, 794.
4. Williamson, *Mark*, 114.
5. On the incognito theme see Christman, *Behold*, 94–96.

ON OFFENSE AT THE LOWLINESS AND LOFTINESS OF JESUS

Offense at Jesus by his hometown has already been hinted at by Mark in the trouble he previously experienced with his own family (Mark 3:20–21; 31–35). But what is the cause of this offense? Kierkegaard provides a basic analysis of a two-fold cause:

> Offense in the strictest sense . . . therefore relates to the God-man and has two forms. It is either in relation to the loftiness that one is offended, that an individual human being claims to be God . . . or the offense is in relation to the lowliness, that the one who is God is this lowly human being.[6]

In other words, people were offended at two aspects of Christ's person, namely his loftiness and his lowliness.[7] Stephen Backhouse nicely summarizes this saying,

> The lofty offense is that this man before you is *God*. The lowly is that God *is this man*.[8]

Both aspects are seen in this text in Mark, with his loftiness shown in his "miracles" and his lowliness shown in being "the carpenter . . . Mary's son and the brother of James, Joseph, Judas and Simon" (6:2–3). And so *"they took offense at him."* Lamar Williamson explains what transpired in the beginning of this account.

> The astonishment of Jesus' home-town audience represents a potentially positive response . . . *When they reflect on who he is, however, in categories familiar to them* (the carpenter, son of Mary, brother to the neighbors named), their astonishment turns to rejection. They take offense at him. Literally, "they stumbled or "were scandalized"; more picturesquely, "they fell foul of him" (NEB) or "found him too much for them" (NAB); more plainly, "they rejected him" (TEV).[9]

The observation, "when they reflect on who he is," is telling, and reveals how human *reflection* led to envy, how envy led to the rejection of God's Christ, and how these relate to what has transpired in the times of Jesus, the early church, Kierkegaard, and today.

---

6. Kierkegaard, PC, 82.
7. See on Mark 2:18–22 in Christman, *Behold,* 130–31; 196–203.
8. Backhouse, *Kierkegaard - A Single Life,* 254.
9. Williamson, *Mark,* 114, (emphasis mine).

ON PASSIONLESS REFLECTION

That Jesus could respond to his rejecting hometown with a proverb is as telling as was the fact that their "reflection" led them to reject him. In this section we will try to explain why these things are so. A proverb is a generally accepted truism. It is based on observation of the way things are or how things work, in general. To paraphrase, this truism is simply that "an honorable prophet is not honored by the place he came from." The question is, why? What make this to be generally true? We will consider Kierkegaard's view that two "personal" dynamics, reflection and envy, together create a third "social" dynamic, reflective envy which is a negatively unifying sociological principle, or put quite simply, a bad unity. His "formula" by which good things like reflection and passion together "go bad" is as follows:

> And just as *enthusiasm* is the unifying principle in a passionate age, so *envy* becomes the *negatively unifying principle* in a passionless and very reflective age.[10]

Starting with the end of that statement we see that Kierkegaard held his age to be "passionless" *and* "very reflective." So, if reflection is a necessary ingredient of passionate interest, and to Kierkegaard "infinite passionate interest in one's own eternal happiness" was the highest passion, then why was Kierkegaard's "very reflective age" a "passionless" one?[11] The answer is that reflective thought and passion exist together, in both emotion and interest, in a difficult to understand correlation. Robert Roberts presents the correlation:

> The present age is passionless because it is so reflective, and so reflective because it is without passion.[12]

The correlation is perhaps best understood by considering that those in Jesus' hometown used their reflection not merely to properly *deliberate* regarding their response to Jesus, but to "*misuse* deliberation as a strategy for avoiding decisive action."[13] If they had been passionate, their deliberation would be "a necessary *step* towards action."[14] Roberts writes,

> A passion is like a momentum . . . if there is opportunity for acting on a concern, and adequate deliberation has been taken

---

10. Kierkegaard, TA, 81.
11. Roberts, "Passion and Reflection," 89.
12. Roberts, "Passion and Reflection," 92.
13. Roberts, "Passion and Reflection," 92.
14. Roberts, "Passion and Reflection," 93.

> to convince the individual that he should act, then not to act has the tendency to debilitate the concern . . . passions (or at least embryonic ones) *starve*.¹⁵

This rather technical expose of reflection should become a bit more exciting and make more sense as we consider how reflection, when *insufficiently* based in passion, leads to envy which then becomes the "negatively unifying principle" of an age, of a society, of a hometown.¹⁶

ON REFLECTIVE ENVY LEADING TOWARD A SOCIAL ETHOS

The passionless reflection of those in Jesus' hometown led them to envy him. This societal envy thus became their social ethos, something Kierkegaard called a "negative unifying principle." Bruce Malina and Jerome Neyrey provide insight into ancient collectivist cultures that helps us to understand how society-wide envy proliferated in Jesus' hometown because of their reflection on Jesus' person. They write,

> All people in a family (generation) and in a distinctive polis or region (geography) are presumed to have the same experiences and very similar qualities.¹⁷

Before proceeding we need to remember that envy is not only wanting what another has. It is also not wanting another to have what they have. And Jesus, who should have had "the same experiences" and "similar qualities" did not. Thus, Jesus' regional culture reveals the fertile soil in which envy germinated. And the germinated "envy-weed" grows. In the modern age especially, it becomes a societal ethos. Robert Roberts writes,

> Envy is the unhappy recognition of excellence. The envious person, assuming a basic equality between himself and the ethically impassioned hero, recognizes the hero's excellence, but *resents* it because it is not his own. Note that the envious person is still a lover of excellence, though an unhappy one. But envy, being unhappy, is an emotion we tend to avoid . . . "reflection" . . . tends to be called in to rescue the sufferer from envy. For the

---

15. Roberts, "Passion and Reflection," 94–95.
16. A negatively unifying principle could be thought of as "the lie that binds" whereas a positively unifying principle would be "the tie that binds."
17. Malina and Neyrey, *Portraits of Paul*, 157.

> sufferer finds he has plenty of resources for rationalizing away the excellence of the hero.[18]

We can see that those in Jesus' hometown found his "lowliness" to be a handy resource for "rationalizing away" his "excellence." Later in his gospel Mark says of Pilate that "he perceived that it was out of envy that the chief priests had delivered him up," also demonstrating "reflective envy" that became a murderous "social ethos" that infected the crowd (Mark 15:10, ESV).

Of course, there is a sense in which a world lies between the reflective envy of Jesus' day and that of Kierkegaard's and ours. This world of difference is not merely in time, but in the character of the envy. The fact of the matter is that in Jesus' day envy was "real envy." Those caught in envy, though unhappy at Jesus' excellence, at least had the ethical passion that enabled the recognition of greatness. But what was especially arising in Kierkegaard's age of reflection was "characterless envy." Robert Roberts explains,

> Characterless envy is but the shadow of real envy, for what it lacks is precisely the ethical passion for excellence that is the basis of real envy's unhappiness. The passion has been dispelled by "reflection." Characterless envy has deceitfully convinced itself that there really is no such thing as excellence, but, like all self-deceit, it also believes in the denial of what it has deceived itself into believing, and so is threatened, down deep, by the existence of what it perceives to be real excellence. Thus it is convenient for characterlessly envious people to find *objective* ways to discourage excellence. And when we get a society of people who are interested in preventing excellence from rearing its ugly head, it is understandable that there will develop an "objective spirit" subtly opposed to excellence: a poisonous mist that floats out upon the social air the message that impassioned persons are not acceptable, that decisive and extraordinary actions in the ethical sphere will be greeted with the condescension deserved by crusaders and juvenile enthusiasts, or with the scorn appropriate to infantile stupidities, impetuousness, and conclusion jumping—that only deliberation, and not action, will be greeted with approval.[19]

It is difficult to take that all in, not so much because it challenges us intellectually, but because its truth about our society may be repulsive to us. The ethos it describes hits too close to home for us today. The Kierkegaardian

---

18. Roberts, "Passion and Reflection," 95.
19. Roberts, Passion and Reflection," 96.

analysis of Roberts, and the following words of Kierkegaard's from 1846, together present a bone-chilling picture:

> And eventually human speech will become just like the public: pure abstraction—there will no longer be someone who speaks, but an objective reflection will gradually deposit a kind of atmosphere, an abstract noise that will render human speech superfluous, just as machines make workers superfluous. [20]

The "objectivity" that coheres with "characterless envy" and "superfluous speech" demonstrates the broad scope of Kierkegaard's perception of the growth of "the envy-weed" in the modern age. He reveals the "thickness" and "settledness" of "the atmosphere of objective reflection" and over-reflective envy that renders "human speech superfluous."

At this point we will attempt to thread together characteristics of the seemingly ever-expanding "big bang" of societal envy that for this reading began from Jesus' hometown. Hopefully we can thereby discern some application for our time by grounding it in Jesus' first-response to this "atmospheric" disturbance.

ON REFLECTIVE ENVY AND "THE SINGLE INDIVIDUAL"

In a journal entry Kierkegaard wrote, "One solitary man cannot help or save an age; he can only express that it is floundering."[21] It is undoubtedly true that he expresses the answering pathos that any would-be "single individuals" will *feel* when breathing the noxious atmosphere of the pervasive social ethos. We say "would-be" because for Kierkegaard, becoming a self was both gift (or grace) and ongoing *task*. It is likely that Mark proposes the same two "givens" in that the would-be disciples he portrays are generally failing at the most decisive points of both gift and task. Of course, that development is a Marcan theme we will consider in due time. Nevertheless, a task of response to the age is at hand. Kierkegaard "explores" the difficulties of the response to reflective envy as follows:

> Ultimately the tension of reflection establishes itself as a principle, and just as *enthusiasm* is the unifying principle in a passionate age, so *envy* becomes the *negatively unifying principle* in a passionless and very reflective age. This must not promptly be

---

20. Kierkegaard, TA, 104.

21. Kierkegaard, JP 4, 4157. In SK the words "is floundering" are translated "will perish." See Kierkegaard, SK, 165.

interpreted ethically, as an accusation; no, reflection's idea, if it may be called that, is envy, and the envy is therefore two-sided, a selfishness in the individual and then again the selfishness of individuals toward him. Reflection's envy in the individual frustrates an impassioned decision on his part, and if he is on the verge of decision, the reflective opposition of his associates stops him. Reflection's envy holds the will and energy in a kind of captivity. The individual must first of all break out of the prison in which his own reflection holds him, and if he succeeds, he still does not stand in the open but in the vast penitentiary built by the reflection of his associates, and to this he is again related through the reflection-relation in himself, and this can be broken only by religious inwardness, however much he sees through the falseness of the relation. But the fact that reflection is holding the individual and the age in prison, the fact that it is reflection that does it and not tyrants and secret police, not the clergy and the aristocracy—reflection does everything in its power to thwart this discernment and maintains the flattering notion that the possibilities which reflection offers are much more magnificent than a paltry decision.[22]

Kierkegaard's *description* of the difficulties continues for many more pages. In them, reflective envy seems to progressively embolden itself against any would-be single individual. The Pauline-style verbose sentences seem to yield only an anti-Pauline revelation of the well-fortified house of reflection, the strong-man yet to be bound and the house yet to be plundered of its prisoners who would otherwise seek *decision*. As Kierkegaard's expose continues, we see reflective envy reveal the ultimate weapon for its establishment, "leveling."

> Envy in the process of *establishing* itself takes the form of *leveling*, and whereas a passionate age *accelerates, raises up and overthrows, elevates and debases*, a reflective apathetic age does the opposite, it *stifles and impedes, it levels*. Leveling is a quiet, mathematical, abstract enterprise that avoids all agitation.[23]

Many pages later in his expose of the deepening intricacies and extending tentacles of this "Leviathan," Kierkegaard *definitively* reveals the actual response as suffering. He writes,

> These servants of levelling are the servants of the power of evil, for leveling itself is not of God, and every good man will have

22. Kierkegaard, TA, 81–82.
23. Kierkegaard, TA, 84.

times when he would weep over its hopelessness, but God permits it and wants to cooperate with individuals, that is, with each one individually, and draw the highest out of it. The unrecognizables recognize the servants of leveling but dare not use the power or authority against them, for then there would be a regression, because it would be instantly obvious to a third party that the unrecognizable one was an authority, and then the third party would be hindered from attaining the highest. Only through a *suffering* act will the unrecognizable one dare contribute to leveling and by the same suffering act will pass judgment on the instrument. He does not dare defeat leveling outright—he would be dismissed for that, since it would be acting with authority—but in suffering he will defeat it and thereby experience in turn the law of his existence, which is not to rule, to guide, to lead, but in suffering to serve, to help indirectly. Those who have not made the leap will interpret the suffering act of the unrecognizable one as his defeat, and those who have made the leap will have a vague idea that it was his victory. But they will not be certain, because certainty could come only from him, and if he provides one single man with that directly, he is dismissed, for he would be unfaithful to God and would be assuming authority, because he would not in obeying God learn to love men infinitely by constraining himself rather than faithlessly constraining them by dominating them, even if they asked for it.[24]

With these final words of his "literary review" of *Two Ages* proper, Kierkegaard *prescribes* the way of the cross as the ultimate task against levelling, the way of suffering love and witness.[25] And of course, that way has been found and followed by some, perhaps many in the Christian era. It has also been written about extensively elsewhere, by the likes of Dietrich Bonhoeffer and Simone Weil, not to mention Kierkegaard himself in his magisterial *Works of Love,* published the very following year in 1847.[26]

---

24. Kierkegaard, TA, 109. Kierkegaard strikes many very ironic notes here in the complex situation he portrays.

25. Before this *prescription* in TA, Kierkegaard provided a *description* of the foundation for Christian "society," constructed apart from levelling through God as the "middle term" between individuals that are each in relation to God. See Kierkegaard, TA, 62–63; 169–70 n7; WL, 107.

26. Christian suffering became an increasing theme and concern in his later writings since he observed that although it is vitally necessary to discipleship it was sorely lacking in Christendom.

Kierkegaard, following his rather magnificent non-triumphalist ending adds the *off-hand* and *equally non-triumphal comment* that his *Two Ages Review* is only

> banter, for if it is true that every person has to work out his own salvation, forecasting the future is at best tolerable and admissible only as a means of recreation, as an interesting game such as bowling or tilting the barrel.

We conclude that his admittedly puzzling off-hand comment served to *remove* his total argument from any debt to the poisonous atmosphere of "objective reflection." His "review" of the modern age was thus a humble speculation regarding the present and future. But therein he primarily and powerfully witnessed to the way of the cross as the only way of salvation because that way is shaped by patiently suffering *in* the age of reflective envy and *in* practicing enemy-love for envy's practitioners.[27] Kierkegaard's off-hand comment, seemingly humorous and certainly exuding irony, signifies that it is ultimately only the life of the sufferer that teaches. In 1848 Kierkegaard writes,

> The first form of rulers in the world were the "tyrants," the last will be the "martyrs" . . . the martyr is the suffering individual who educates others through his Christian love of mankind, translating the masses into individuals—and there is joy in heaven over every individual whom he thus saves out of the masses.[28]

On this note we must turn to the one who is "the martyr" and "the single individual" par excellence, in whose suffering all true sufferers participate.

ON JESUS, THE "SINGLE INDIVIDUAL" WHO OVERCAME REFLECTIVE ENVY THROUGH SUFFERING LOVE

> There is nothing, of course, which human envy assails the way it assails the extraordinary. And yet no one becomes a true extraordinary except through the mistreatment of men.

---

27. Kierkegaard, TA, 109–110. We admit to universalizing Kierkegaard's regionally contextualized "prophecy." Most prophecy in the Biblical Canon itself is first and foremost, regional. But since the ways of God and man are disclosed in the regional, there is certainly always universal applicability.

28. Kierkegaard, SK, 151.

> Consequently, envy will mistreat a person in order to prevent him from becoming extraordinary, and no one becomes the extraordinary except through human mistreatment—consequently envy produces the extraordinary.[29]

So writes Kierkegaard, and we can be sure that in his Christ-centered thought, Christ would be "the extraordinary" par-excellence and therein also the prototype Christians were to follow in *imitation*.[30] Therefore, what was written in the section above and in that journal entry, we count as the way of imitation for the Christian. Of course, our immediate task is to consider Jesus the extraordinary par excellence in relation to Jesus' response to his hometown's rejection of him.

We first consider what Jesus must have *felt* as he was offensive to, and rejected by, his relatives, neighbors, friends, and acquaintances. In commenting on the proverb Jesus spoke in 6:4, Ben Witherington captures something of what Jesus must have felt in his collectivist culture.

> Mark emphasizes that the lack of acceptance of Jesus involves not only his hometown but even his own family. The saying also stresses that Jesus is operating in an honor and shame culture where one's public honor rating and the "face" one has in one's own home territory is important. Yet paradoxically Jesus must labor in a situation where those very persons who should honor him give him the least "face." This must have cast a considerable cloud over Jesus' ministry in a culture where kinship ties and affirmations by one's kin were considered all-important, and where honoring parents involved accepting their evaluations of one's self and work.[31]

We must also extrapolate what Jesus felt out from his hometown to his homeland, Israel. For the hometown rejection spoke of the coming rejection of the nation, and we can be sure that that non-reception was especially "hurtful" to him who "came to his own" but was rejected (John 1:11).[32]

We next consider Jesus' reflective verbal response, the citation of a proverbial truth regarding prophets, hometowns, and families. It is interesting

---

29. Kierkegaard, JP 1, 794.

30. For instance, Kierkegaard writes, "On each of the later works there is, on the title page: *Poetic*, in order to show that I do not proclaim myself to be an exceptional Christian, or to be what I describe." SK, 165.

31. Witherington, *Mark*, loc 2889–2901.

32. Williamson writes, "In the context of the earliest readers, 'his own people' was extended to include the Jews whose rejection of their own Messiah was so shocking." Williamson, *Mark*, 116.

and instructive that although Jesus was personally hurt, he did not "take it personally." He understood how things work, even when they work wrongly. Therefore, we get no intimation that his demeanor or redemptive disposition was changed toward them. For he did heal a few sick people there (6:5). But the larger note sounded is of Mark's sad and sparse report that, in general, "he could not do any miracles there."

We next note another interior response of Jesus, his *amazement* at their "lack of faith." Mark has highlighted positive amazement many times in his gospel. But here that theme hits an off-key note. This sour note well-fits the "un-miracle" story in Mark's *gospel story* of the "good news" of Christ. Mark's sparse report of the rejection of Jesus by his hometown, with all the pathos that accompanies that sad fact, poignantly presents an underlying ethos for his gospel story. That ethos could be perhaps captured with words like bewilderment and deflation hinting at despair. Mark here and throughout his gospel proves quite Kierkegaardian, or possibly Kierkegaard proved to be quite Marcan. In either case, the authors do not merely tell. Rather, their poetical pathos shows and evokes positive passionate reflection that can overcome the misuse of deliberation that leads to passionless reflection, reflective envy, and societal leveling. Robert Roberts characterizes Kierkegaard's authorial purpose as the promotion of "passion-engendering thought."[33]

At this point in this chapter, we imitate Kierkegaard's lead when at the end of the lengthy "review" called *Two Ages* abruptly said, "I must cut this short."[34] Thus we leave the reader to ponder three devices or "ways that Kierkegaard uses reflection against 'reflection' to foster subjective thinking."[35] Robert Roberts who exposits them in his essay, detected them in Kierkegaard's literary method. It seems that we also detect them in substance in Mark. These devices are: "*intellectual seduction, impassioned psychological analysis, and poetically varied repetition.*"[36] And the purpose of Kierkegaard's literary devices was to promote "passion-engendering thought" so that gospel-hearers could become, like Jesus, "the single individual" who overcomes reflective envy as the social pathos. For that characterless pathos leads to society-destroying *levelling* by effectually *removing* "the single individual." Eliseo Perez-Alvarez provides a brief description of Kierkegaard's method that clarifies his purpose, and we also think, that of Mark.

---

33. Roberts, "Passion and Reflection," 103.
34. Kierkegaard, TA, 109.
35. Roberts, "Passion and Reflection," 104.
36. Roberts, "Passion and Reflection," 103–6.

> Kierkegaard did not seek to isolate the concrete self; rather he wanted to strengthen human beings in order to face the gigantic power of the leveling of the masses, which subsumes the individual.[37]

But with that task at hand, Jesus, "the extraordinary," rejected by his family, hometown, and Israel, left and "went around the villages in a circuit."[38] Jesus is still "going around the villages." And reflective envy still won't receive him.

---

37. Perez-Alvarez, *A Vexing Gadfly*, 25.
38. Farley, *Gospel of Mark*, 88.

5

The Gospel of the Terrible Inversion
The Loftiness of God in the Solidarity of Lowliness

Mark 6:7–13 (NIV)

7 Calling the Twelve to him, he began to send them out two by two and gave them authority over impure spirits.

8 These were his instructions: "Take nothing for the journey except a staff—no bread, no bag, no money in your belts. 9 Wear sandals but not an extra shirt. 10 Whenever you enter a house, stay there until you leave that town. 11 And if any place will not welcome you or listen to you, leave that place and shake the dust off your feet as a testimony against them."

12 They went out and preached that people should repent. 13 They drove out many demons and anointed many sick people with oil and healed them.

Thou plain man! The Christianity of the New Testament is infinitely high; but observe it is not high in such a sense that it has to do with the difference between man and man with respect to intellectual capacity, etc. No, it is for all. Everyone, absolutely everyone . . . Thou plain man! I have not separated my life from thine; thou knowest it, I have lived in the street, am known to all; moreover I have not attained to any importance, do not belong to any class egoism, so if I belong anywhere, I must belong to thee, thou plain man.[1]
—Soren Kierkegaard

1. Kierkegaard, AC, 287. (MLW, 346.)

From on high he will draw all to himself.[2] —Anti-Climacus

Like Jesus their prototype, the witnesses of Jesus exhibit a combination of lowliness and loftiness. A lowliness in mundane human qualities co-existing with a loftiness of divine ability. Such a combination is what makes both aspects puzzling and offensive to the world. But the paradox signifies a divine authenticity because both aspects are necessary for God's perfect kingdom to *redemptively collide* with the world's pseudo-lofty kingdom.

God intends the disciples, representing all Christians, to be "sent into the world" *just as Jesus* had been "sent into the world" (John 17:18). This is not merely the similarity in being sent. It includes similarity in the manner of witness. Jesus did not come "decked out" in royal clothing for honorable presentation and neither do they. In fact, in regard to worldly appearance, the disciples seem to be the ones in need rather than those able to meet the needs of others. The disciples are sent out not as rich benefactors but as themselves impoverished. Their "lowliness" is prescribed by the directions of Jesus: *"take nothing for the journey except a staff—no bread, no bag, no money in your belts. Wear sandals but not an extra shirt. Whenever you enter a house, stay there until you leave that town."* Their lowliness is also dignified by the person of Jesus, the one who became poor to make all rich (2 Cor 8:9).

THE POVERTIES OF THE WORLD AND OF GOD

One reason for the character of this mission was that much of the world lived in near or actual poverty. Since God in Christ entered poverty "in solidarity with the dregs," so also would his disciples.[3] But there is more than one type of poverty in the world, and the physical poverty people are most concerned with ultimately follows the spiritual poverty common to all humanity. It is therefore ironic that the consumerism of those with enough funds to participate in it, leads to increased spiritual poverty while asceticism leads to more abundant life.[4] Therefore, the gospel must be proclaimed

---

2. Kierkegaard, PC, 151.

3. "So it is with Christianity. It is not a doctrine about God's accepting and loving the poor, the dregs, the miserable, the unfortunate—No!, Christianity is this very act, that God in Christ is in solidarity with the dregs." Soren Kierkegaard, as cited in Perez-Alvarez, *A Vexing Gadfly*, 95.

4. "Consumerism is a restless spirit that is never content with any particular material thing. In this sense, consumerism has some affinities with Christian asceticism. The difference is that, in consumerism, detachment continually moves from one product to another, whereas in Christian life, asceticism is a means to a greater attachment to God

and "performed" in the right and holistic way as remedial of all poverties.[5] The "problem" is that humans are generally receptive to God's remedying of the external poverty but not so much concerned with internal spiritual poverty, the polluted fount that overflows the world with inhospitableness and impoverishment.

In the instructions of Jesus to the disciples for their mission, we can see that they were given authority over physical and spiritual poverties. Healings, exorcisms, and preaching repentance cover both types (6:7, 12). But what is easily overlooked is that most of the instructions have to do with "poverty" and hospitality. They were to go as the impoverished in reliance on hospitality. And whether the disciples received hospitality from where they went signified whether those places received the gospel. This strange "divine arrangement" is made even stranger by the fact that many modern-day Christians and missionaries do not see why these are related. The connection is in the fact that "incarnational" mission requires poverty and hospitality on the part of the missionaries and their "mission field." Perhaps "field" was not the best modern "missions" terminology because though the "fields are ripe for harvest" the term does not convey the centrality of poverty and hospitality in God's arrangement (John 4:35).

God is of course, the originator of missions since redemptive history is the record of the mission of God. Central to that mission is the incarnation of God in Christ as the ultimate joining together of poverty and hospitality in relation to God and humanity. Christ, though in the form of God, became impoverished and dependent on the hospitality of those he was sent to (Phil 2:6). Therefore, the followers of Jesus were to go in like manner (Phil 2:5). And as Jesus was not received and given hospitality, as we saw in Mark 6:1–6, it is now the disciples turn to follow. Of course, this may well be *the* apostolic commissioning of Mark's gospel.

HUMANITY'S OFFENSE AT THE LOWLY JESUS

To get back to "the problem" mentioned earlier, humankind in general does not seem to see the wisdom in God's "divine arrangement." In the chapter epigram above, Kierkegaard notes that Christianity is "infinitely high," but that it also aims at human equality and solidarity. He was trying to submit

---

and to other people." Cavanaugh, *Being Consumed*, xi.

5. The "practical" separation in Christian mission is often caused by a theological mistake of dualism which separates humans as soul and body. But Kierkegaard rightly held to the synthesis that "The basic concept of man is spirit, and one should not be confused by the fact that he is also able to walk on two feet." Kierkegaard, EO1, 65.

those aims as his own qualifications for solidarity with his readers. Obviously, he was trying to not be an offense to them since, after all, he was a rich and learned philosophical genius who, without working, lived till the end—albeit an early one—on his inheritance. But he also recognized that human solidarity is extremely difficult to achieve. So, when God becomes flesh, in solidarity with all humankind, are God's "efforts" any more successful?[6] It could easily seem not. Kierkegaard spent much time on this "problem" and examined why it happened. The reasons he gave provide a way to begin to understand the "point of view" of humanity versus the wisdom of God's arrangement to give the world a gospel rooted in solidarity, poverty, and hospitality.

Kierkegaard's Anti-Climacus discusses God's arrangement as a "*terrible inversion of what it seems one ought to have expected.*"[7] He accounts for this inversion by saying,

> Well, this presumably would not have happened if (1) the inviter had conformed to the image the merely human conception of compassion wanted him to have, and if (2) he had had the merely human conception of what human misery is.[8]

It seems that the complaint of humanity is as follows: (1) how can God help us if he does not follow our concept of compassion and exclusively meet bodily temporal needs? and (2) how can God help us if he does not follow our concept of misery and exclusively meet bodily temporal needs? In other words, Jesus' concern for both exterior body and interior soul violated the normal human conceptions of compassion and misery, which are solely concentrated upon the temporal finite existence.

Kierkegaard's Anti-Climacus, concentrating on the "spiritual" aspect of the gospel inflates humanity's complaint to represent a gravely egregious accusation:

> The inviter's conception of the nature of human misery was altogether different from the human conception of it. And to help in this respect was his intention—but he had not taken with him either money or medication or any such things. Thus the inviter's image is so unlike what human compassion would form of him that he really is an occasion for offense. Humanly speaking, it is something downright cruel, something shocking,

---

6. In one sense God *achieved* solidarity with all humanity in Christ. But in another sense God still *seeks* solidarity in which each person hears of and embraces this solidarity.

7. Kierkegaard, PC, 57.

8. Kierkegaard, PC, 57.

> something over which one could become so embittered that one could have the urge to kill the man—to invite the poor and sick and suffering to come—and then to be able to do nothing for them, but instead of that promise them the forgiveness of sins. "Now let us now be human. A human being is no spirit. And when a human being is almost starving to death, then to say to him: I promise you the gracious forgiveness of your sins—this is outrageous. Really, it is laughable, but it is too serious for one to be able to laugh about it."[9]

Merold Westphal further inflates the charges by taking on the solidarity of Jesus with the poor:

> In the long run even the masses turn against him on this ground. Who wants a king whose investiture is symbolized by a manger, a towel, and a cross—who moreover, calls his own to follow in the same narrow way? To say that it requires "a most frightful act of decision for a man to become a Christian" and that "only the consciousness of sin can force one into this dreadful situation" is to do more than simply note the logical leap involved in affirming what cannot be demonstrated, that this man is God. We must recognize that one makes that leap—if it is indeed the leap of true faith and not a poor substitute—not blindly, but in full awareness that the One who is the Way and the Life and the Truth lived the life of a poor, suffering, impotent outcast through his identification with the poor, the suffering, and the impotent people on the fringes of his own society. Is that any way for God to act among us?[10]

In answer to that final question, it is certainly *not* the way that "normal" humans act among us, so perhaps the "problem" of Jesus' *lowliness* is *the* sign that his Kingdom is not of "the normal," i.e., "not of (from) this world," and thus *the* sign of his *loftiness*, his divinity.

To this point in this chapter, we have for the most part only considered the lowly aspects of Jesus as though he did not do the miraculous and lofty works. But we have thought it necessary to give due attention to "God's problem," to then, by way of the lowly disciples following in Jesus' train, rehabilitate God's gospel of poverty and hospitality.

---

9. Kierkegaard, PC, 60–61.
10. Westphal, *Kierkegaard's Critique of Reason*, 25.

HUMANITY'S OFFENSE AT THE LOWLY DISCIPLES

The twelve are, in God's divine arrangement of gospel-witness through poverty and hospitality, necessarily lowly. But they are in fact, in God's arrangement, and *because of* the lowly qualities, also lofty. We did not present arguments to support the loftiness of Jesus because that has generally been a given in Christianized lands, even though in post-Christian times, considered more myth than reality. But to view the disciples, as lofty, especially as portrayed by Mark, needs some supporting argument.

Their loftiness is seen in that Jesus gave them divine "authority" to preach repentance, exorcise demons, and heal the sick. Therefore, they are lofty because they represent Jesus and the Kingdom of God. That is why they must proclaim and "perform" the gospel in the right way, living in solidarity, poverty, and hospitality. And that brings us back to their lowliness, and the dialectic that they, like Jesus, are both lofty and lowly in and for God's divine arrangement which is the gospel for the world. Their loftiness *consists* in lowliness, in the sheer fact of their superlative harmlessness as compared to truly harmful people. They are to be anything but conquerors, invaders, robbers, slaveholders, rapists, or murderers. They are seemingly mere children marching in a crusade without weapons and armed only with the vulnerability of poverty, the bond of human solidarity, and the dynamic of love. Their proclamation and "performance" of the gospel provide a foretaste of the powers of the age to come. And thus, their very being is the call for hospitality as the significant sign of the reception of the gospel.

Another aspect that demonstrates how their lowliness is loftiness is their earthly solidarity with "the plain man" as Kierkegaard called him. Of course, the disciples were culled from the common man. Apart from instances where their concern was for achieving some greatness, they nevertheless were obedient to go forth as lowly followers of the lowly one.[11] But the loftiest aspect of this is simply that gospel-sending creates "kinship" in a solidarity that is existentially founded and fulfilled in the equality of God's non-preferential love that overcomes human sin and separation. "Love thy neighbor," the universal maxim of God's mission, ensures that those who may never receive the gospel nevertheless *encounter* neighbor-love. Kierkegaard's *Works of Love* stands out from his other writings in dealing with Christian love at the societal levels. Kierkegaard thereby shows that

---

11. In this entire chapter we are describing the ideality of the disciples and in them that of the church. But one can easily paint an opposite picture as Mark increasingly does of the original twelve. And this is indeed "God's problem." Our book *The Gospel in the Dock* was an attempt to demonstrate that, all things considered, the gospel of Jesus Christ is nevertheless "good for the church, humanity, and the world."

his emphasis on "the single individual" was not *individualism*. The *familial* disciples were sent to gather God's *whole family* while equipped for the task with the "works of love" just as Jesus was (John 10:15–16).[12]

The final aspect of their loftiness in lowliness, also deriving from following Jesus as their protype, is their essential harmlessness even as agents of judgment. If unwelcomed they simply shake the dust from their feet, as if to say, "we came in peace and leave the same, and leave your dust with you . . . receiving peace was your responsibility." But in the face of such lofty lowliness, the world finds offense at them, just as it did at Jesus, the lofty lowly-one par excellence.

THE GOSPEL IS THE ONLY GOSPEL

Above, we considered "God's problem" of failing to meet human expectations because of Jesus' lowliness. Of course, within his lowliness was true loftiness, signs of his divine way. Mark's gospel of secrets also reveals a "secret loftiness" that is only revealed to those who hear and believe the gospel. The secret loftiness of Jesus and the disciples runs aground because of what Kierkegaard called "the terrible inversion" of what humanity expected or desired. But since the gospel is the only remedy for humankind it cannot be changed to suit the preferences of man.

The first "Christian" heresy, that of the Gnostics, reveals the problem with the gospel as problem. For if salvation—begun in full by Jesus entering humanity in solidarity, impoverishment, and hospitality—is unwelcomed, the truth is, there is no other salvation. Humans are not angels needing return to their heavenly home but humans needing to "be at home" in their earthly home. It seems that the form of despair Kierkegaard viewed as humankind's default despair is indeed, "common to man" (1 Cor 10:13). That despair is the despair of not willing to be oneself (a human) because of despair over the earthly.[13] But salvation cannot be found by becoming something one never was, is, or will be, namely, non-human.

Perhaps the best argument at this point is to reconsider the gospel. And if there is a "problem" with that, it is man's problem, not God's. For God has done all God can do for man's *real* problem. Kierkegaard and Mark seem to consider "the finished work" as the ultimate "apologetic," that cannot be

---

12. For the incarnate Jesus in incarnate solidarity with all humanity was sent in divine solidarity with the "familial" Triune God. This is the gospel-analogy between the gospel-sending of Jesus and of the disciples.

13. Kierkegaard, SD, 49–60.

apologized for. How could it be? So, here's the gospel, as incarnated by Jesus and Jesus-disciples, and as informed by this reading of Mark 6:7–13.

> Hospitality turns out to be an expression of solidarity. Mother Teresa and Dorothy Day did not merely say, "Come in. Live with us." They said, "May I live with you?" more adequately reflecting the incarnation in which God said, "I will live with you." That is transformation that grace works in us as we move from our practice of "come and live with me" to God's practice of "I will live with you." The divine face of hospitality is solidarity.[14]

And there is no salvation apart from human solidarity, poverty, and hospitality.

---

14. Moore, *Limits of Liberal,* 151–52.

6

John the Baptist, King Herod, and *Two Ages*

"The Idea for Which I Can Live and Die"

Mark 6:14–29 (NIV)

14 King Herod heard about this, for Jesus' name had become well known. Some were saying, "John the Baptist has been raised from the dead, and that is why miraculous powers are at work in him."

15 Others said, "He is Elijah."

And still others claimed, "He is a prophet, like one of the prophets of long ago."

16 But when Herod heard this, he said, "John, whom I beheaded, has been raised from the dead!"

17 For Herod himself had given orders to have John arrested, and he had him bound and put in prison. He did this because of Herodias, his brother Philip's wife, whom he had married. 18 For John had been saying to Herod, "It is not lawful for you to have your brother's wife." 19 So Herodias nursed a grudge against John and wanted to kill him. But she was not able to, 20 because Herod feared John and protected him, knowing him to be a righteous and holy man. When Herod heard John, he was greatly puzzled; yet he liked to listen to him.

21 Finally the opportune time came. On his birthday Herod gave a banquet for his high officials and military commanders and the leading men of Galilee.

22 When the daughter of Herodias came in and danced, she pleased Herod and his dinner guests.

The king said to the girl, "Ask me for anything you want, and I'll give it to you." 23 And he promised her with an oath, "Whatever you ask I will give you, up to half my kingdom."

24 She went out and said to her mother, "What shall I ask for?"

"The head of John the Baptist," she answered.

25 At once the girl hurried in to the king with the request: "I want you to give me right now the head of John the Baptist on a platter."

26 The king was greatly distressed, but because of his oaths and his dinner guests, he did not want to refuse her. 27 So he immediately sent an executioner with orders to bring John's head. The man went, beheaded John in the prison, 28 and brought back his head on a platter. He presented it to the girl, and she gave it to her mother. 29 On hearing of this, John's disciples came and took his body and laid it in a tomb.

The thing is to understand myself, to see what God really wishes *me* to do; the thing is to find a truth that is true *for me*, to find *the idea for which I can live and die*.[1] —Soren Kierkegaard, 1835, at age 22

If the essential passion is taken away, the one motivation, and everything becomes meaningless externality, devoid of character, then the spring of ideality stops flowing and life altogether becomes stagnant water—this is crudeness.[2] —Soren Kierkegaard, 1846, at age 33

The destiny of this life is that it be brought to the extremity of life-weariness. The person who when brought to that point can maintain or the person whom God helps so he is able to maintain that it is God who has brought him to that point—such a person, from the Christian point of view, passes the examination of life and is matured for eternity.[3] —Soren Kierkegaard, 1855, at age 42

In this chapter we will see persons truly passionate and dispassionate. This will augment what we saw of that subject in chapter 4. Before doing so we simply point out that many (or perhaps most) today might see the "fanatical"

---

1. Kierkegaard, SK, 44.
2. Kierkegaard, TA, 62.
3. Kierkegaard, JP 6, 6969.

JOHN THE BAPTIST, KING HEROD, AND TWO AGES 83

Baptist as the frivolous one, and Herod as the passionate, due to the modern "rationality" which misunderstands those terms. This chapter hopes to turn those modern notions on their head, by situating true passion and frivolity in the "larger" world as informed by the gospel.

OUR "EXISTENTIAL" WORLD

In the first volume of this series, we noted Mark's "economy of words" in regard to historical space/time references, since his first such reference was John's arrest.[4] Here we find Mark's second "verifiable" space/time reference, again in relation to John's arrest by Herod. By verifiable we simply mean an event that links Mark's narrative to "outside history" wherein there may be found non-Scriptural corroboration of persons, typically, the important political figures of the time.[5] Without such corroboration we are left, apart from Scripture, with the "unrecognizables" of history including most other persons in Mark's gospel. Whatever the reason, Mark does not make a point of such grounding. We only mention this to say that Mark's narrative appears to be somewhat "existential" in this regard. Dan Via's statement seems to note the general "existential" quality of Mark:

> We all live in the midst of the time process, between what Frank Kermode has called "the tick of birth and the tock of death," between creation and apocalypse—the biblical view of world history. The middle of Mark's plot will symbolize for us the middle of time . . . the content of Mark's story . . . the ordering of the world which belongs to its plot corresponds to reality as we experience it . . . Jesus did not simply have a social ethic, but rather his story is a social ethic. It enables us to live coherently amid the conflicts and diversity of our moral existence, making possible our action which is appropriate to the gift.[6]

The "existential" quality of Mark's gospel certainly centers upon "the tock of death" since his first two "historical" markers are about the death of John. At age 22, Kierkegaard's existential search was to find "truth that is true *for me* . . . *the idea for which I can live and die*."[7] The existential challenge asks

---

4. Christman, *Behold*, 38–39.

5. Donald Juel provides a brief account of just such corroboration through Josephus. See Juel, *Mark*, 95.

6. Via, *Mark's Gospel*, 3–4, 10, 14. For the most part we simply seek to apply Via's language inasmuch as it applies in a basic existential sense to the way Mark's story impacts its hearers.

7. Kierkegaard, SK, 44.

whether that *truth* is found in the ascetic wilderness of John, the hedonist palace of Herod, or the new family of God in Jesus? Where is it found "in the middle of time" between the tick of birth and the tock of death? In this chapter we enlist the "crazy" Baptist to help us answer these questions.

MARK'S ACCOUNT OF JOHN AND HEROD

Mark takes considerable interest in details of certain events that other gospel writers do not.[8] The account of the Baptist's death is one such account. One commentator, noting "all the marks of a good story: anecdotal style, vivid and dramatic details, an adulterous king, a scheming woman, a dancing girl, a violent death" asks, "what is such a story doing in the Gospel of Mark?"[9] Lamar Williamson provides an answer by noting that the account draws several important parallels to other parts of Mark, developing themes in Mark's overall story. First, there is a parallel between Herod's treatment of John and Pilate's treatment of Jesus, in which the one "in control" becomes controlled by forces greater than himself. Second, there are parallels between John's preaching and arrest and the same in Jesus and in the disciples.[10]

The question of control, such as when both Herod and John lose it, can be seen as floating transparently over Mark's whole narrative. For the agents of God's kingdom—John, Jesus, and the disciples—doing God's will as only being subject to God, all "fall subject" to other forces leading to their deaths. Mark seems to be calling attention to the question: Who is in ultimate control? Such a concern would perhaps be *the* issue for the hearers of Mark, because of their "subjection" to potentially harmful powers beyond their control. Mark portrays much through "indirect communication" as did Kierkegaard.

Our focus will explore a way that this important and pervasive biblical concern regarding control can be demonstrated. This way of reading the text seems to be invited by Mark as his concern pervades this account, revealing itself in an obvious contrast between the relations of John and Herod to control. The basic thesis is that John's becoming a self through his *passionate ideality* to live and die for *one thing*, namely God, stands in conspicuous contrast to Herod's self-loss through his *passionless frivolity*, because he lived and died for *nothing*, namely for his non-self. The point of

---

8. Of the synoptic gospels Mark provides the fullest account of John's death. (See Matt 14:1–12 and Luke 9:7–9.)

9. Williamson, *Mark,* 122.

10. Williamson, *Mark,* 123. The parallels texts are John the Baptist: 1:4–8 and 1:14; 6:17–29; Jesus: 1:14–15 and 9:31; 10:33; 14–15; The disciples: 6:7–13 and 13:9–13.

this thesis is that Mark transparently subverts the control the "powers that be" exercise, by demonstrating that God's way for humans to achieve true self-hood cannot be prevented by false powers.

JOHN'S TOWERING PRESENCE AND HEROD'S COWERING POSTURE

The first thing to note in this remarkably subversive account, is that Herod first appears as one in abject fear of John. Ironically his fear of John drives and pervades the entire account, so that even in death, he towers over Herod the King. Herod cowers before John, and before all others to a *lesser* extent though it seems with "the crowd" to a *greater* extent. It is amazing that John's death upon Herod's order can be an account of victory. That is gospel truth because it foreshadows Jesus before Pilate, and with "the crowd" actually standing over and behind the "greater" authority! But this was not merely a personal vindication of John, but also the crown of his life achievement that magnified in death what he magnified in life, through what became his motto: "He must increase—I must decrease."

Herod had undoubtedly heard of the clamoring of the crowds after Jesus, and therefore thought that Jesus *was* John, raised from the dead. Thus, John has risen, not as a ghost but as flesh and blood to haunt him with manifestations of *real* and *truthful* power. At least, that was what Herod seems to have thought. In fact, John's power over him (though he was dead) was not merely because of Herod's guilt or paranoia but precisely because the Baptist's person made Herod a non-person before him as we shall see further.[11]

Mark then narrates how Herod *reluctantly* had John killed, again highlighting Herod's fear of John who had *courageously* spoke against his illicit marriage to his brother's wife Herodias. She bore a grudge against John for this, and undoubtedly was behind John's imprisonment, a "half-measure" of Herod's because he feared John's influence enough to *not* want to kill him. But Herodias wanted the full measure. In Mark's account Herod's chief fears are portrayed: John, Herodias, the partygoing "crowd," and the wider "public". Undoubtedly, a real fear of John overshadowed the other servile fears:

11. We can't but think that in this entire account, if it were a comedy, Herod before John could be deliciously portrayed as P. G. Wodehouse's Bertie Wooster was before Aunt Agatha: "She was sitting bolt upright in a chair, staring into space. When I came in she looked at me in that darn critical way that always makes me feel as if I had gelatine where my spine ought to be. Aunt Agatha is one of those strong-minded women ... She has an eye like a man-eating fish, and she has got moral suasion down to a fine point." Wodehouse, *Enter Jeeves*, 1.

"Herod feared John and protected him, knowing him to be a righteous and holy man. When Herod heard John, he was greatly puzzled; yet he liked to listen to him" (6:20). This spoke of a potential fear of God which of course is *the remedy* for wrong fears of men. Obviously, to Mark's point, *King* Herod fearing the one *in his prison* subverts the normal expectations of power and control.

Herodias bided her time waiting for an opportunity to fulfill her murderous grudge against John, and it arrived at a great birthday banquet that Herod threw for himself. Again, the irony comes through as Herod frivolous festivities that he supposed would bolster his power and prestige, stroke his ego, and of course, bring him entertainment, brought instead "great distress"—or "exceeding sorrow" (comparing the NIV & ESV translations). We note in passing that this at least speaks something positive of Herod, the ability to recognize the greatness of John, meaning that he didn't have "characterless envy" of John.

The festive party, as is the case in many such "planned" events, got rather *out of control* as Herod somewhat proverbially "sowed the wind and reaped the whirlwind" (Hos 8:7). The traitor in Herod's midst turned out to be his own flapping tongue—perhaps set more loose than normal through too much wine—as he found it flippantly vowing to Herodias' dancing daughter "*up to half of my kingdom*" in reward for her delightfully wonderful and probably wanton exhibition.[12] Her asking her mother what she should request resulted in the hated Baptist's head on a festive platter. The scene of the ascetic Baptist's head on a hedonist's festive platter drips with irony because that is another graphic statement regarding Mark's subversion of power. Fearing the public scandal of breaking even such an ill-spoken oath before his guests, Herod complied, having lost control. And as mentioned previously, all the while the character of John towered over Herod, though the king had the power. This seems a power struggle, though it may be questionable that Herod had enough strength to even struggle. This was a huge mismatch, and again, foreshadows the coming struggles of the principalities and powers, human and demonic, against Jesus. At this point we will try to consider what made John passionate and Herod frivolous.

JOHN'S PASSIONATE IDEALITY AND HEROD'S PASSIONLESS FRIVOLITY

We turn now to Kierkegaard, to try to better understand the dynamics of John's "victorious" death. We will briefly consider some of Kierkegaard's

---

12. See Farley, *Gospel of Mark*, 94; Garland, *Mark*, 244–45.

concepts regarding personal and social dynamics in relation to God that constitute the basic "physics" underlying the interrelations of John and Herod. These basics include the central importance of an *idea,* the proper *response* to that idea through *passion,* and how *passionate earnestness in relation to the idea* or the lack thereof are manifested in interpersonal relations and societal situations.

The central importance of *the idea* was recognized very early on by Kierkegaard, even before he knew what idea was the one for him.

> The thing is to understand myself, to see what God really wishes *me* to do; the thing is to find a truth that is true *for me,* to find the idea for which I can live and die.[13]

Before knowing what the idea for him was, he knew that he needed a unifying goal in his life which was not simply "God" in general, but specifically "what God really wishes *me* to do." This could be the quest for his God-given call or vocation, perhaps in relation to his writing interests. In this light we can see that John's *idea* was to be "the Baptist," the "forerunner" of the Christ. We also see that even at this early age Kierkegaard was looking for truth in "subjectivity" and not merely in "objective" knowledge of some "formal relation" to God. Thus, when Kierkegaard writes "to find a truth that is true for *me*" we already see the kernel for the momentous *task* in *Concluding Unscientific Postscript* that "truth is subjectivity."[14] So to Kierkegaard, the *idea* for him presupposed a total life response to the idea. Robert Perkins provides a sort of definition:

> "The idea," of course, is and is not all of one kind. It is all of one kind in that its pursuit is . . . a labor. It is of one kind in the sense that the labor to attain the idea is the joyful task that fills a life. All labors for the attainment of the idea are one in the sense that in this effort one's life touches at least the outer fringes of the infinite. The labor for the idea is a passion for the infinite that unifies the multiple aspects of life . . . The idea in its several variations is not all of one kind in the sense that one may vocationally be an excellent painter or plumber and one may psychically concentrate his energies in ethical or in religious development. There are infinite overlays and combinations. Kierkegaard uses the term "stages on life's way" to suggest the rich variety of human life. There are three such stages.[15]

---

13. Kierkegaard, SK, 44.
14. Kierkegaard, CUP1, 189 & c.
15. Perkins, "Envy as Personal Phenomenon," 114.

Of course, Kierkegaard's three "stages on life's way," which are also considered to be "spheres" of life, were the aesthetic, ethical, and the religious. It is also worth noting that the three epigrams for this chapter were from the beginning, middle, and end of a twenty-year period, the chronological stages of Kierkegaard's relatively short-lived adult life. They were chosen to convey Kierkegaard's "labors" for *the idea* for him.

It almost goes without saying that the definition of "the idea" above seems to preclude Herod from having one, based on what the Scriptures and "outside" history know of him. He seems to have lived and died in "frivolity." The definition also further solidifies part of the thesis of this chapter, that John lived contrarily in "ideality." We should further note that Perkins' use of the word "labor" certainly implies "passion," the passionate pursuit of *the idea*. Kierkegaard's thought on the relation of passion to "ideality" provides us with more insight into Herod's frivolity. He writes,

> If essential passion is taken away, the one motivation, and everything becomes meaningless externality, devoid of character, then the spring of ideality stops flowing and life together becomes stagnant water—this is crudeness.[16]

If this applies to Herod, and we think it does, it will mean that he was passionless, lacked "the one motivation" (ideality), lived in "meaningless externality," was "devoid of character," became as "stagnant water," all summarized as "crudeness." Altogether, it seems that "frivolousness" is a sad but fitting summary of Herod. And John, as one with passionate ideality stands in bold contrast to Herod's passionless frivolity, his perverse ideal-less "passions." In perhaps his greatest sermon C. S. Lewis said,

> It would seem that our Lord finds our desires not too strong, but too weak. We are half-hearted creatures, fooling about with drink and sex and ambition when infinite joy is offered us, like an ignorant child who wants to go on making mud pies in the slum because he cannot imagine what is meant by the offer of a holiday at the sea. We are far too easily pleased.[17]

Kierkegaard's less pictorial and more analytical Anti-Climacus said much the same thing:

> It is the same with sin. Most men are characterized by a dialectic of indifference and live a life so far from the good (faith) that

---

16. Kierkegaard, TA, 62.
17. Lewis, *The Weight of Glory*, 3–4.

it is almost too spiritless to be called sin—indeed, almost too spiritless to be called despair.[18]

Certainly, Herod fits the "half-hearted too easily pleased creature" of Lewis, and the "spiritless, devoid of character, stagnant water" man of "flatness and crudeness" of Kierkegaard. And Herodias with her daughter and Herod's party guests fill in Mark's expose of the *passionless* crowd honoring the passionless king.

SEEING JOHN AND HEROD THROUGH KIERKEGAARD'S "DON QUIXOTE"

To reveal John and Herod even further, we will risk an odd reading wherein we will consider several uses of the "Don Quixote" character by Kierkegaard as "fitting" both John and Herod. How this is possible should become evident as we proceed.

In his discussion of Kierkegaard's concept of ideality, Robert Perkins dropped a tantalizing and largely unexplained statement: "*Kierkegaard's own example of the parody of the idea is Don Quixote.*"[19] Perkins also left a sole reference to Kierkegaard's *Postscript*, ostensibly "written" by Johannes Climacus," which reads as follows:

> Don Quixote is the prototype of the subjective lunacy in which the passion of inwardness grasps a particular fixed finite idea. But when inwardness is absent, parroting lunacy sets in.[20]

Of course, *this* Kierkegaardian Don Quixote is of the "Herod" type. But Kierkegaard had a long-term relation with the Knight, covering nearly his entire adult life. Eric Ziolkowski explains why over the course of his authorship, due to his evolving focus and interaction with Christendom, the essentially "comic" character of Quixote was able to also epitomize for Kierkegaard each of the three "stages of life." Ziolkowski writes,

> Indeed, the complexity of Don Quixote's character can be seen to encompass all three existential stages. Insofar as he is preoccupied with the thought of and is in quest of worldly fame and glory, which suggest attachment to the finite, he exists in the aesthetic stage. Insofar as he commits himself wholeheartedly to the chivalric code, which constitutes his ethical absolute, he

---

18. Kierkegaard, SD, 101.
19. Perkins, "Envy as Personal Phenomenon," 116.
20. Kierkegaard, CUP1, 195.

> exists in the ethical stage. Insofar as he maintains, against the arguments of reason and to the extent of becoming ridiculous, his faith in Dulcina and in his illusion that he has been sent by God to restore the Golden Age, he exists in a mode analogous to Kierkegaard's religious stage.²¹

Thus, we can see the Herod type *aesthetic* Quixote in that description in the preoccupation with fame and glory and attachment to the finite. Herod was the aesthete through and through. By contrast, the *religious* Quixote who maintains faith against popular reason in his great restorative mission from God speaks of John the Baptist.

Ziolkowski presents several additional Kierkegaardian descriptive phrases of the aesthetic Quixote that also seem to speak of Herod:

> Don Quixote's quest for fame ("world-historical significance") and his notion that he has been victimized by enchantment ("a jinx")... the archetype of those "stupid" individuals who, in Climacus' words, "forget themselves over their great importance in history,"... the knight's "passion" with "romance," "poetry," and "beautiful *Schwarmerei*,"... along with "subjective madness" or "aberrant inwardness."²²

To further apply one of those analogical phrases, we point out that Herod thought himself "victimized by enchantment," through the "jinx" of John the Baptist, resurrected from the dead. *This* Kierkegaardian Don Quixote is certainly analogous to Herod and helps to further characterize the frivolous King as an aesthete.

But we are also interested in the Don Quixote who became more prominent in Kierkegaard's later thought and is analogous to John the Baptist. Ziolkowski notes that,

> a striking shift occurs after *Postscript;* the allusions to Don Quixote in subsequent journal entries present him clearly as a figure of the religious stage, comparing him with Christ, Christ's disciples, and any aspiring Christian in the modern secular age.²³

Thus, *this* "Don Quixote, who in our reading is analogous to John in "passionate ideality," became Kierkegaard's "final" Quixote, and according to Ziolkowski led to his journal entry from 1848 and "the first analogy ever drawn between Don Quixote and Christ."²⁴ Kierkegaard's entry said this:

21. Ziolkowski, "Don Quixote," 135.
22. Ziolkowski, "Don Quixote," 136.
23. Ziolkowski, "Don Quixote," 136.
24. Ziolkowski, "Don Quixote." 137

> When secular sensibleness has permeated the whole world as it has now begun to do, then the only remaining conception of what it is to be Christian will be the portrayal of Christ, the disciples, and others as comic figures. They will be counterparts of Don Quixote, a man who had a firm notion that the world is evil, that what the world honors is mediocrity or even worse.²⁵

Another journal entry will further demonstrate the "comic" *Christian* meaning of Don Quixote as analogical to John, knowing of course that the "change" Kierkegaard talks about is regarding the substantial de-Christianization of Christendom. For the age, in the sense of the "sensible" world apart from *Christian* values, will always see the passionate *Christ,* the *Christian,* and John, as comic.

> The comic element arises because the age has changed so enormously that it regards this as comic. That a person actually is earnest about renouncing this life, literally that he *voluntarily* gives up happiness of erotic love offered to him, that he endures all kinds of earthly privation, although the opposite is offered to him, that he exposes himself to all the anguish of spiritual trial [*Anfaegtelse*], for spiritual trial comes only to the voluntary—and then that he, suffering all this, submits to being mistreated for it, hated, persecuted, scorned (the unavoidable consequence of essential Christianity in this world)—to our entire age such a life will appear to be comic. It is a Don Quixote life.²⁶

We will next draw out the implications of John the Baptist, Kierkegaard (who said "I am fighting like a Don Quixote"), true Christians, and Christ, as *Quixotic,* with a return to Mark's text and a discourse of Kierkegaard on John.²⁷

KIERKEGAARD'S "HE MUST INCREASE; I MUST DECREASE"

In 1844 Soren Kierkegaard published *Three Upbuilding Discourses* including "He Must Increase; I Must Decrease" on John the Baptist.²⁸ In the sermon Kierkegaard shows that John's entire ministry consisted in publicly

---

25. Ziolkowski, "Don Quixote," 137. (Kierkegaard, JP 1, 317.)
26. Kierkegaard, JP 2, 1762.
27. Kierkegaard's words as cited by Ziolkowski, "Don Quixote," 130, 139.
28. Kierkegaard, EUD, 275–89. We will cite the references to the sermon in the text above in this section.

decreasing in relation to Christ, for that was his calling. But Kierkegaard also shows that all know something of the reality of *decrease*. The death of John is not explicitly mentioned, but we know that it "crowned" his decrease, and as has been seen, his overcoming of the world for the sake of its Savior. Kierkegaard begins by asking,

> An old saying says that everyone would rather see the rising sun than the setting sun. Why everyone? Do you suppose this includes someone whose sun it is that is setting? But why shouldn't he? The rising sun shines for him just as for all the others—indeed, perhaps shines most brilliantly to his eyes precisely because its luster obscuringly hastens the setting (275).

Kierkegaard thus sets the mood for life's increasing and decreasing, moving the reader to identify the one decreasing with the setting sun. He had subtitled the sermon with a fuller statement from John, *"This joy of mine is full. He must increase; I must decrease,"* and thereby bringing *joy* into the picture of the setting sun (275):

> So it was John the Baptizer who said these words. He lived in the Judean desert, far from the vanity that bickers about the place of honor, far from the fickleness that elevates and drags down, celebrates and crucifies, as far as his clothing was from soft raiment and his nature from the pliancy of a reed. He was not the Messiah, not one of the old prophets, not the prophet; he was the voice of one crying in the wilderness ... This was his task; he himself certainly perceived its significance, but he also knew that its significance was that it would be abolished and forgotten, like the night watchman's cry when it is obvious to all that day has broken. Then rose the sun of him whose morning star aroused the wonder of the wise men; its glory shone, and no one understood better than John that its rising was the setting of his sun ... Who does not know that things like these have happened and do happen in the world—that someone who once ruled over countries and kingdoms has ceased to rule and is obliged to see a more powerful ruler take his place; (277–78).

The contrast between the purpose of John and Herod is clearly seen. Kierkegaard then speaks of more "average" people facing the same sort of challenge.

> That the master whose pupil only yesterday sat at his feet must bow his shoulders today under the other's advancement; ... that the girl who once filled her beloved's thoughts now sits and sees his bold ambition pursuing a higher goal; that the singer whose

> words were on everyone's lips is forgotten today and his songs have been more than replaced; that the orator whose words echoed everywhere must now seek the solitude of the desert if he wants echo ... (279).

Kierkegaard then shows that John's life is a prototype for disciples whose lives are meant to magnify Christ's. This magnification follows embracing the task as John did, *in humble self-denial* and with *genuine joy*. Kierkegaard then draws us into that same calling because we too can introduce the bridegroom with joy, as we decrease, that he might increase.

> If you, my listener, recollect as you indeed do, the Baptizer's powerful preaching unto repentance, his prophetic boldness in judging the high and the low, the holy wrath with which he laid the ax to the foot of the tree—then you are bound to be deeply moved when you consider the sad gentleness, the joyous fervency, with which he speaks of his relation to the coming one. That under a camel-hair shirt there can also beat a heart so rich in feeling not only for truth and justice to which his life was indeed dedicated! That he has been able to preserve this feeling out there in the desert! That the soft breeze of self-denying joy can be sensed in the thunder of judgment! His statement points out exactly what it was supposed to point out, but the expression is so celebrative, so festively beautiful, that one is almost tempted to picture the Baptizer's stern figure dressed in festive garments as if he were on his way to a banquet ... (285).

Thus, Kierkegaard shows that the *stern*, austere Baptist partook of *festivity*—*because* he was the self-less friend of the bridegroom—looking to the wedding banquet wherein his decrease would paradoxically lead to his increase as Christ would increase.[29] Herod's life partook of *misery*, looking to his self-glorifying birthday festivities for more "increase" but ironically leading to his decrease. In the Kierkegaardian terms of "becoming oneself through the power that establishes it," John became his self, and passionately so. Herod, passionless in all the ways that matter, lost his self. Mark thus portrays the gospel as the subversion of power, whereby the "powers that be" come to naught, and the things that are not, come to be (1 Cor 2:6).

In this chapter, Soren Kierkegaard has helped clarify the "law" of Mark's gospel, that "passionate" decrease is increase. That Kierkegaard lived this is demonstrated by a journal entry very near the end of his own decrease, his sunset that looked to the sunrise of eternity:

---

29. We note in passing that John's lowliness is revealed by Mark as "secret" loftiness.

> The destiny of this life is that it be brought to the extremity of life-weariness. The person who when brought to that point can maintain or the person whom God helps so he is able to maintain that it is God who has brought him to that point—such a person, from the Christian point of view, passes the examination of life and is matured for eternity.[30]

KIERKEGAARD'S TWO AGES

The decrease/increase motif of John the Baptist, in relation to the eschatological gospel of death and life, provides a doorway into the biblical eschatology of Kierkegaard that framed his lengthy "book review" called *Two Ages: The Age of Revolution and the Present Age, A Literary Review*. The reading in this chapter has been concerned with Kierkegaard's *stages of life* although there were a few mentions of *ages of life*, or more accurately *ages of humanity*. Kierkegaard's concepts in this regard are broadly historical yet informed by the gospel's "critical" eschatology of human life (in its stages). His gospel critique saw two historical *ages* of humanity following paganism. Thus, in *Two Ages* Kierkegaard wrote of

> the revolutionary age . . . that . . . goes astray and the present age . . . essentially a sensible, reflecting age, devoid of passion, flaring up in superficial, short-lived enthusiasm and prudentially relaxing in indolence.[31]

A third age remained strangely unnamed and largely undiscussed by Kierkegaard but seems to be *the age of the future*, or more precisely *the age of Christ* and *the age of the Spirit*.[32]

Our reading at his point will therefore briefly consider that John and Herod, through their respective Kierkegaardian "stages," can exemplify Kierkegaard's first two ages of humanity. In other words, each of them does not merely characterize two "individual" stages (or spheres) of human life, but also two "historical" ages of humanity.

So, what was Kierkegaard's concept of the first age in his *Two Ages*? Pat Cutting describes the *age of revolution* as an age

---

30. Kierkegaard, JP 6, 6969. (Entry of September 25, 1855, at age 42.)

31. Kierkegaard, TA, 68–69; 108–9.

32. Robert Perkins says, "The last age is the future . . . in which envy and the resultant reduction of man to the numerical is overcome." Perkins, "Envy as Personal Phenomenon," 127.

> in which outstanding individuals determine the values and norms for others ... distinct individuals with passionate loyalties, which gave them a degree of inwardness and depth. However, the majority of the people subordinated their values and choices to others—to outstanding orators, to superior officers, to leaders of the revolution, and others.[33]

Based on our discussions above, John's character demonstrates, over against "characterless" Herod, how he exemplified the earlier and relatively higher age of humanity as against the *age of reflection* which was being born in Kierkegaard's day. Kierkegaard thus lived at the intersection of these two ages. It is important to note that Kierkegaard's term *age of revolution* probably does not signify what most hearing the term today would think of, namely, violent totalitarian revolutions. It is better considered as the age of "true heroes, reformers, or leaders (TA, 88–89)."[34]

Herod "foreshadows" the subsequent and relatively lower age of humanity, devolved from the revolutionary age. He exemplifies the *age of reflection* in which it is not heroes, but "the public," that looms largest. Cutting explains that during

> the present age, it is the abstract crowd, namely, the public, rather than the outstanding individual, that leaps in and takes the responsibilities and choices of the members of the society. In Heideggerian terms, this is the level of the "they – self," and like Heidegger's "they," Kierkegaard's "public" is an abstraction. There are no distinct individuals to enter into an essential relationship. Rather, the public is "made up of unsubstantial individuals who are never united or never can be united in the simultaneity of any situation or organization."[35]

In a sense, the public is a chimera, an "accident" of the aesthetic emotive occasion. Thus, the "unsubstantial" Herod and his partying peers were driven by the aesthetic (erotic) dance of Herodius to, in an important sense, "accidentally" behead John—the sole substantial person in that terrifying account of "fate" caused by the mix of human folly and evil in the court of a King. Nevertheless, Herod's wife was diabolically "substantial" enough to orchestrate the outcome of the occasion. Thus, one of many lessons here, the chimeric crowd provides the would-be totalitarian their longed-for day. In *Two Ages* Kierkegaard does not seem to mention the spineless "King" Herod, who lost control in his relative characterlessness. But Kierkegaard

---

33. Cutting, "The Levels of Interpersonal," 75–76.
34. Plekon, "*Towards Apocalypse*," 44.
35. Cutting, "The Levels of Interpersonal," 78.

does mention King Agrippa in a way that can apply to Herod, and thus demonstrates that both Kings struggled at the intersection of pathos and chronos that signified an "age-change" for humankind. Kierkegaard writes,

> To be like that King Agrippa, not far from believing or acting, is the most enervating state imaginable if one remains in it very long . . . Thus an age that is very reflective cannot for that reason be summarily accused of being powerless, for it perhaps has great power, but it goes to waste in the fruitlessness of reflection.[36]

Thus, Cutting aptly summarizes Kierkegaard's "present age" saying,

> The present age, as an age of reflection, is an age devoid of vitality. It has "no hero, no lover, no thinker, no knight of faith, no great humanitarian, no person in despair" (TA, 75) who has had the primitive experience that gives validity to the reflections and utterances of an age . . . The individuals from the first of the two ages, the age of revolution, are viewed as having many of the characteristics of the ethical stage . . . and the people of the present age, the second of the two ages, are seen as having many of the characteristics of the aesthetic stage."[37]

Cutting notes an ironic development in the relation between Kierkegaard's concept of two human stages of existence, the lower aesthetic and higher ethical *stages*, and the concept of the two *ages*, the earlier and "primitive" *ethical* "age of revolution" and the later *aesthetic* "age of reflection." This irony is simply due to a manifesting reversal of human progress so that the moderns of Kierkegaard's day had fallen below the character of "primitivity" which to Kierkegaard meant a more fully human way of human "vitality." Thus, Kierkegaard presents a critique of the Enlightenment project of progress wherein humankind instead *fell*. C. S. Lewis would call this fall *The Abolition of Man*, roughly a hundred years later.[38]

---

36. Kierkegaard, TA, 66.
37. Cutting, "The Levels of Interpersonal," 79.
38. See Christman, "Lewis and Kierkegaard," 123–36.

KIERKEGAARD'S TWO AGES AIMED "TOWARD APOCALYPSE"

It should be obvious that Herod, and the *age of reflection* he exemplifies, were not situated to inherit the coming kingdom of Christ. Of the present age Paul Tyson writes,

> The Present Age is not culturally sustainable in terms of the religious vision it needs in order to give its civilization values and meanings worthy of the human soul . . . We are now like Atlantis just before the rising of the sea; we have extraordinary magical powers, wondrously manipulative knowledge, we are structurally embedded in exploitative immorality regarding the human and natural resources that make our life-form possible, and our centers of power are ingrained in hubristic folly and a tragic spiritual poverty, which means we will not draw back from the brink of destruction.[39]

But were the Baptist and the ethical *age of revolution* he exemplifies better situated to receive Christ's kingdom age? Kierkegaard's discourse on John provides much that helps answer this question.

> Even if no one else comprehended the chasmic abyss between the coming one and the Baptizer, he comprehended it, and yet he gave full expression to it and to his joy that this was precisely the way it was. For him this joy was full, that he was seen in all his lowliness beside the glory of the coming one . . . An old saying says that everyone would rather see the rising sun than the setting sun. Why everyone? Do you suppose this includes someone whose sun it is that is setting? Yes, for he, too, ardently desires to rejoice just as the bridegroom's friend does when he stands and hears the bridegroom's voice.[40]

For what John rejoiced at was the coming of Kierkegaard's "third age," the age of Christ. For Kierkegaard's "given," necessary for the "revival" of Christianity he sought, was that the gospel harvest stood ready in "the category through which the race must go" as is made clear by his allusion to Luke 14:17 toward the end of *Two Ages*.

> It will no longer be as it once was, that individuals could look to the nearest eminence for orientation when things got hazy before their eyes. That time is now past. They either must be lost in

---

39. Tyson, *Kierkegaard's Theological Sociology*, 59.
40. Kierkegaard, EUD, 286, 289.

the dizziness of abstract infinity or be saved infinitely in the essentiality of the religious life . . . because all the individuals who are rescued gain the specific gravity of the religious life, gain its essentiality at first hand from God. Then it will be said: "Look, everything is ready; look, the cruelty of abstraction exposes the vanity of the finite in itself; look, the abyss of the infinite is opening up; look, the sharp scythe of levelling permits all, every single one, to leap over the blade—look, God is waiting! Leap, then, into the embrace of God."[41]

The societal levelling of persons into the "cruel" abstraction of "the crowd" or "the public" is pictured as the anti-gospel harvesting of a low-swinging blade. But those prepared by God's baptizers of any era may "leap" that low and levelling blade unto God's gospel-harvest embrace. Kierkegaard's eschatology, since eschatology is a social revolution of sorts, may appear to be somewhat lacking or possibly even non-existent.[42] But while perhaps hinting at eschatological possibilities beyond, Kierkegaard's view in *Two Ages* for the most part may rest in the idea conveyed in a journal entry:

One solitary man cannot help or save an age; he can only express that it is floundering.[43]

Thus, Kierkegaard "merely" provides another image of the individual's leap of faith—in addition to that more commonly known leap over Lessing's "big ugly ditch" of history—namely the leap over the levelling scythe of the *age*

---

41. Kierkegaard, TA, 108.

42. John Hoberman writes "It is notable that Kierkegaard, on the other hand, does not use *Two Ages* to propound an eschatology of his own, if only because he does not have a conception of history that would permit him to do so. 'When Heidegger asks: what is Being?' Karsten Harris points out, 'he seeks to recover the Greek beginning of our historical existence, to recall us to a new beginning, not to have us simply repeat it, but to transform it into a new beginning.' Kierkegaard has no corresponding historical reality to which he could recall mankind; as a Christian polemicist, his function is to recall the Incarnation." Hoberman, "Kierkegaard's *Two Ages*," 236–37. It is also worth noting at this point Kierkegaard's statement that there is no "new beginning" of the irretrievably passed *age of revolution*: "It will no longer be as it once was, that individuals could look to the nearest eminence for orientation when things got somewhat hazy before their eyes. That time is now past. They must either be lost in the dizziness of abstract infinity or be saved infinitely in the essentiality of the religious life." Kierkegaard, TA, 108.

43. Kierkegaard, as cited in Plekon, "*Towards Apocalypse*," 19. In *Two Ages* he writes, "It is very doubtful then, that the age will be saved by the idea of sociality, of association. On the contrary, this idea is the skepticism necessary for the proper development of individuality, inasmuch as every individual either is lost or, disciplined by the abstraction, finds himself religiously." Kierkegaard, TA, 106.

*of reflection.*⁴⁴ Even so, the "mere" view of Kierkegaard in *Two Ages* is quite *revolutionary.* Michael Plekon provides a lens through which we may see the "singular" *revolution* Kierkegaard envisioned.

> Looking back over the pages of *Two Ages,* the "single individual" and the "instant" are woven throughout as the dominant themes in the diagnosis of the age and its corrective. Individuality is threatened by the age's hyper-reflectivity, by its envy, by the leveling public, by chatter. Most importantly, ethical and religious individuality, the relationship with God, is made extremely difficult when the crucial human quality, passion, is stilled. Yet this tumultuous point in time, this leveling and passionless present age is, according to Kierkegaard, God's decisive moment. God uses this *Kairos* of chaos as his instrument, along with the individual, to effect authentic ethical and religious transformation, just as God used his only Son to make atonement, to win back fallen creation. There is profound theological insight here implied, subtly stated beneath the upper layer of the text of *Two Ages.* It is Kierkegaard's recognition of an actual incarnational encounter, a meeting of God and humankind . . . The convergence of human and sacred history in the apocalyptic vision is signaled by the emergence of the "unrecognizable" ones, God's "secret agents," sent to indirectly help the age, to serve in suffering (TA, 109) . . . a biblical view of the authentic prophets and reformers as suffering, powerless witnesses or martyrs.⁴⁵

We can certainly say that Kierkegaard's *Two Ages* most certainly leaned towards apocalypse. As this reading proceeds, and in future volumes, we hope to further consider Kierkegaard's "singular" eschatological views especially in relation to the "development" of aspects of the *age of revolution* and any *revolutionary eschatology.* For such development may be related to Mark's own eschatological ages that have already been "read" here albeit anthropomorphized in the "revolutionary" John who "prophesied" of the *age of the Spirit.*⁴⁶ In a sort of gospel-solidarity with John, Kierkegaard leaned

---

44. The following chapter will be concerned with the leap over *historical* distance, in contrast to the *sociological* leap just discussed. Both leaps are, at bottom, problems of *rationality,* as Robert Perkins demonstrates with references to Kierkegaard: "The leap called for is not according to prudence and it is against the understanding (TA, 111). Again, we face the incommensurable of the religious and the ugly ditch over which Lessing could not leap (CUP1, 86–97)." Perkins, "Envy as Personal Phenomenon," 127.

45. Plekon, *"Towards Apocalypse,"* 48–49.

46. Hoberman notes that Kierkegaard's present age "is thus a portrait of a man, an exercise in philosophical anthropology that is protected onto the stage of history." Hoberman, "Kierkegaard's *Two Ages,*" 235. This conceptual technique of Kierkegaard is

"towards apocalypse" and may well have been "the first revolutionary theologian of the modern period."[47]

JOHN AND HEROD IN MARK'S GOSPEL

We will conclude this chapter with a brief mention of John and Herod as illustrative of two of the four soils in the Parable of the Seed in 4:1–20. John exhibits the good soil as may be "read" from the fruit of his testimony to Herod in the account we have considered above, and by Jesus' testimony that he was the "Elijah" to come before the coming of the Son of Man (9:11–13). Matthew and Luke also show John as ultimately exemplifying the good soil but as tested by the rocky ground with its "tribulation or persecution on account of the word" of 4:16–17 (see Matt 11:2–6; Luke 7:18–23). Herod's character illustrates the thorny soil of "the deceitfulness of riches and the desires for other things," with the other things certainly including esteem and power (4:19). Viewing the character of both John and Herod through the parable of the seed helps demonstrate how each of them "fills in" Mark's gospel as set forth in what is for him a "master parable" of the gospel, as is his other long parable, the Parable of the Tenants in 12:1–12.[48]

---

what provided the analogical reading of Kierkegaard's *Two Ages* through the lenses of John and Herod.

47. Plekon, "*Towards Apocalypse*," 52.
48. See Christman, *Behold my Mother*, 57–62.

7

Jesus, "Son of Man" on the Mountain and Theophany on the Sea

Historical and "Philosophical" Fragments

Mark 6:30–56 (NIV)

30 The apostles gathered around Jesus and reported to him all they had done and taught. 31 Then, because so many people were coming and going that they did not even have a chance to eat, he said to them, "Come with me by yourselves to a quiet place and get some rest."

32 So they went away by themselves in a boat to a solitary place. 33 But many who saw them leaving recognized them and ran on foot from all the towns and got there ahead of them. 34 When Jesus landed and saw a large crowd, he had compassion on them, because they were like sheep without a shepherd. So he began teaching them many things.

35 By this time it was late in the day, so his disciples came to him. "This is a remote place," they said, "and it's already very late. 36 Send the people away so that they can go to the surrounding countryside and villages and buy themselves something to eat."

37 But he answered, "You give them something to eat."

They said to him, "That would take more than half a year's wages! Are we to go and spend that much on bread and give it to them to eat?"

38 "How many loaves do you have?" he asked. "Go and see."

When they found out, they said, "Five—and two fish."

39 Then Jesus directed them to have all the people sit down in groups on the green grass. 40 So they sat down in groups of hundreds and fifties. 41 Taking the five loaves and the two fish and looking up to heaven, he gave thanks and broke the loaves. Then he gave them to his disciples to distribute to the people. He also divided the two fish among them all. 42 They all ate and were satisfied, 43 and the disciples picked up twelve basketfuls of broken pieces of bread and fish. 44 The number of the men who had eaten was five thousand.

45 Immediately Jesus made his disciples get into the boat and go on ahead of him to Bethsaida, while he dismissed the crowd. 46 After leaving them, he went up on a mountainside to pray.

47 Later that night, the boat was in the middle of the lake, and he was alone on land. 48 He saw the disciples straining at the oars, because the wind was against them. Shortly before dawn he went out to them, walking on the lake. He was about to pass by them, 49 but when they saw him walking on the lake, they thought he was a ghost. They cried out, 50 because they all saw him and were terrified.

Immediately he spoke to them and said, "Take courage! It is I. Don't be afraid." 51 Then he climbed into the boat with them, and the wind died down. They were completely amazed, 52 for they had not understood about the loaves; their hearts were hardened.

53 When they had crossed over, they landed at Gennesaret and anchored there. 54 As soon as they got out of the boat, people recognized Jesus. 55 They ran throughout that whole region and carried the sick on mats to wherever they heard he was. 56 And wherever he went—into villages, towns or countryside—they placed the sick in the marketplaces. They begged him to let them touch even the edge of his cloak, and all who touched it were healed.

Merchant ships are but extension bridges; armed ones but floating forts; even pirates and privateers, though following the seas as highwaymen the road, they but plunder other ships, other fragments of the land like themselves, without seeking to draw their living from the bottomless deep itself.[1]—Ishmael

1. Moby-Dick, chap. 14; as cited in Lorentzen, *Sober Cannibals*, 74.

I must continually see to it that I hold fast the objective uncertainty, see to it that in the objective uncertainty I am "out on 70,000 fathoms of water" and still have faith.[2]—Johannes Climacus

Even if the contemporary generation had not left anything behind except the words, "We have believed that in such and such a year the god appeared in the humble form of a servant, lived and taught among us, and then died"—that is more than enough.[3]—Johannes Climacus

Mark's account of John's death ended with his disciples taking his body and placing it in a tomb, undoubtedly crowning John's foreshadowing of the passion of Jesus. This is followed by a brief note of the disciples' return from their mission with news of all they had done and taught. Mark records no reply to their news. Instead, Jesus invites them to a deserted place for rest, perhaps his "well done!" to their faithfulness. But they were seen departing so that many ran ahead and spoiled their much needed "retreat."

Jesus' attempt for their solitude became another occasion for ministry, since the great crowd was like sheep without a shepherd. Jesus again compassionately taught them, and did so until the day grew late, leaving the "crowd" in need of food. The disciples wanted Jesus to send the people away to fend for themselves, but Jesus wanted the disciples to provide for them. But the available provisions were vastly inadequate considering the number of people. Nevertheless, Jesus remained undeterred that they would serve them. After raising the meager *means* to heaven for blessing he divided them to the *end* of a miraculous feeding of the five-thousand and twelve baskets of leftover "fragments." The leftover fragments were *more provision* than the original means which is the first hint for our reading: all human means are mere fragments, but with God's blessing fragments reap the needed provision, even the eternal.

Still seeking solitude for the undoubtedly weary band, Jesus "immediately" sent the disciples by boat to the other side while he went up the mountain to pray. As they were on the sea, and he on the land, the wind threateningly rose against them. He came to them, "*walking on the sea*" but intended to "*pass them by.*" At the sight of a human form *on the water* they thought him a terrifying ghost. After identifying himself and boarding the boat the wind ceased, much to their astonishment. Mark adds a puzzling note about their "*amazement*" which on the face of it seems disconnected

---

2. Kierkegaard, CUP1, 204.
3. Kierkegaard, PF, 104.

to the situation, *"for they had not understood about the loaves; their hearts were hardened."* The story ends with their arrival to the other side with crowds again swarming and miracles again flowing, even from the fringe of his garment. A second hint for our reading: Jesus, walking on the sea, is transcendent to it.

A Marcan motif of fragments of a whole, begun with the fragment of Jesus' garment in 5:25–34, speaks to God's *full* provisions for life through *faith* in heaven's blessing of otherwise *insufficient* historical elements. Faith receives riches from the transcendent Christ that unfaith does not.

"THE FOLLOWER AT SECOND HAND"

Except for the original disciples in the "sacred history" of Jesus' earthly life, all subsequent disciples of Christ are what Kierkegaard called "followers at second hand."[4] This means that their lives are not literally contemporaneous with Jesus earthly life, and that they follow Jesus on the historical basis of "secondhand information." That situation is the *historical* "problem" on account of which Mark and Kierkegaard have a "faith-concern." Their "solution" is *faith,* rather than *proof.* History, or historical distance to be precise, "digs" Lessing's ugly ditch that *requires* what Kierkegaard called "the leap of faith" as the only way "across" the distance.[5] The faith-solution is ultimately birthed in a meeting "attended" by three things: Christ in theophanic appearance; the proclamation of the good news; and the would-be disciple.

As we proceed, our main goal is to reveal something of the mechanics and dynamics of this meeting, this human/divine encounter. Mark presents it here through the spatiotemporal situation of 6:45–52. We consider that an analogical master-illustration and will further support it through consideration of the *faith-thesis* set forth in Kierkegaard's *Philosophical Fragments.* We must remember that Mark's faith-concern for "the follower at second hand" is presumably the reason he wrote his gospel. And we will enlist Kierkegaard's help to see how Mark does this, requiring us to extrapolate:

---

4. On the "sacred history" see Christman, *Behold,* 55–62.

5. Rae writes, "Lessing argues that if all historical truths are uncertain then they cannot prove anything. That is, if our premises are not indisputable our argument cannot have the status of a proof. His position is articulated in the famous proposition that 'accidental truths of history can never become the proof of necessary truths of reason.' There exists a broad ugly ditch between the two types of truth such that 'it is impossible to get across however often and however earnestly I have tried to make the leap.'" Rae, *Kierkegaard and Theology,* 72.

- *From* Mark's seemingly odd yet purposeful and historical temporo-spatial features including: the disciples' sudden sea-jaunt, the crowd running the long-way-around to find Jesus, nourishment produced by "the eternal" *in* historic space-time, the faith-testimony of "leftover" *historical* fragments, the climax of a planned *theophany* of Jesus *meant to startle* his disciples who were *purposefully* set at spatiotemporal distance from him . . .

- *to* the philosophical musings of Kierkegaard's Johannes Climacus regarding the advantage (or not) of modern would-be disciples, the follower at second hand 1843 years removed from "the jolt" of the appearance of "the god" in human *history*, the capacity of humans to be taught by the eternal . . .

- *in order to* recognize the supposed *faith-problem* of space-time distance from the historical Jesus and understand the *faith-solution* as posited by Mark and Kierkegaard.

Therefore, we first revisit several features of the scene, noting some additional features and giving them significant coloration:

- Through a fragment of history, Jesus and his disciples were historically known to have provided for the needs of "humanity" as "sheep without a shepherd."

- The bounteous historical provision resulted in left-over historical fragments.

- In the course of time Jesus "ascended to the heavenly mountain" (Heaven) becoming separated from the crowd and from the disciples.

- Meanwhile, the "left behind" disciples were *sent* in their "earthly" boat out on the unpredictable sea.

- The contrary winds on the sea hindered the disciples crossing—but Jesus "saw" across the distance—and helps them by coming to them and *passing them by* in his theophanic presence of transcendence, power, grace, and glory.[6]

- The disciples were not able to correctly discern the person of Jesus in his theophany such that their "misinterpretation" of him terrified them.

- Ultimately, the words Jesus spoke to them revealed his person and also calmed the calamity of their situation.

6. On Jesus "passing them by" as a theophany see: Williamson, *Mark,* 130–31; Garland, *Mark,* 263–64.

- The disciples were "utterly astounded" at all this yet they didn't understand about the loaves (fragments) because their hearts were "hardened."

Without at this point further elaborating on the added details above, we summarize that Mark's account of this episode was written for the sake of a later generation and therefore contains elements that make the entire episode analogous to their lives that are "at second hand" from the time of Jesus. If this is one of at least several main purposes of Mark's multivalent gospel, it simply means that his hearers were intended to "understand" from this account the original disciples' spatial *distance* from Jesus as analogous to the spatial distance between their *present* life and Jesus *present* heavenly enthronement. In other words, the *theophanic presence* of Christ, appearing when and where Mark's hearers are "sent," however that theophany is manifest, provides for all earthly boat-bound would-be disciples, whether living in contemporaneity with Christ, a generation later, or *1843 years later,* or now.

That the *theophany of Christ* is somehow linked to "fragments" and "hardened hearts" speaks to the fragmentary nature of the revelation God provides for would-be disciples of every time. The mystery of v.52 seems to be the literary device Mark "plants" at the end of the sea account to evoke the curiosity of his hearers and provoke them to look more deeply into the account for what he intends to communicate. Kierkegaard's *Philosophical Fragments* seems to offer much to fill in the reason Mark mysteriously links fragments of food to hardened hearts.

"JOHANNES CLIMACUS IS IN THE BOAT"

To bring Kierkegaard's *Philosophical Fragments* into this reading we once again place "Johannes Climacus" in the boat with the disciples in "the situation for coming to faith."[7] For Kierkegaard's Johannes and Mark were both concerned to "hold fast the objective uncertainty, see to it that . . . the objective uncertainty . . . out on 70,000 fathoms of water" is portrayed as the "native" place for fallen human existence and therefore for Jesus' disciples and all would-be disciples of all ages.[8] But unlike the disciples who were apt to forget the miraculous loaves and leftover fragments due to their hardened

---

7. See Christman, *Behold,* 204–9.

8. Kierkegaard, CUP1, 204. See Genesis 3:8–10, 22–24 as showing the native place and state of *fallen* humanity but also showing that Eden was the original place and state for *created* humanity. Humanity now lives precariously "out on 70,000 fathoms" rather than in Eden.

hearts, Johannes has his "fragments" with him in the boat out over 70,000 fathoms.⁹

The "philosophical fragments" that Johannes brings into the boat address the *faith-problem* that is our concern in this chapter:

> Can a historical point of departure be given for an eternal consciousness; how can such a point of departure be of more than historical interest; can an eternal happiness be built on historical knowledge?¹⁰

The basic "spatiotemporal" faith-concerns mentioned earlier can be seen in Johannes' question. He poses the "problem" of the relation of historical human location to the reception of eternal truth with "eternal happiness" hanging in the balance. Steven Emmanuel summarizes:

> The first part of this question asks whether it is possible for an individual who is located in history to become conscious of something eternal. The second part asks whether the historical event of learning about the eternal can have more than mere historical interest for the individual. The third part asks whether it is possible for such an individual to base his salvation on what he has learned about a historical event. These questions are aimed at elucidating the relationship between eternal truth and the contingent historical context in which that truth is allegedly communicated to human beings.¹¹

For our purposes we present the following statement and questions based on that summary:

- Underlying all the questions is the problem Johannes called "the jolt," namely that Jesus *the God-man* is always a paradox and thus an offense to the rationality of human beings (PF 93–99).
- What is the capacity of human beings to recognize God, be taught by God as our teacher, and become new selves through God?
- Did those who lived in historical contemporaneity with Jesus have an advantage in coming to faith over those Johannes calls "the follower at second hand" (PF 58, 91)?

---

9. See Mark 6:37–44; 52; 8:1–10; 14–21.

10. Kierkegaard, PF, 1. We will cite further references in the immediate text in the remainder of this chapter.

11. Emmanuel, *Kierkegaard & The Concept*, 61.

- How does Mark's "situation" depicting spatiotemporal separation of all would-be disciples sent "out on the earthly sea" from Jesus who had "ascended to the heavenly mountain" help answer these questions?

At this point we reiterate our thesis: The *spatiotemporal situation* of the disciples at sea while Jesus was on the Mountain is analogical to the *spatiotemporal situation* between believers and Jesus in Mark's time and in all times before the complete consummation. We therefore assume that Mark's depiction helps answer the *faith-problem* of Johannes Climacus (and Lessing).

A NOTE ON JESUS AS THE "JOLT"[12]

That Jesus is the jolt to man helps answer the question of human capacity and the question of advantage or disadvantage of "the follower at second hand." The jolt was "provided" to the disciples "as followers at first hand" *after* they realized the theophany was Jesus and not a ghost. And that Jesus "provides" the jolt to "the follower at second hand" almost goes without saying since the Creed that Jesus is the God-man presents no less offense to human rationality than Jesus' person did.

That Jesus always appears as jolt makes the question of advantage or disadvantage a moot point and shows that humans have in one sense, *only* the capacity to be jolted by Christ. But in another sense, this shows both incapacity and capacity because the jolt, either invokes faith or provokes offense. And though the capacity for offense is natural, the capacity for faith is freely given in the gospel. Johannes speaks of the giving of capacity as occurring in "the moment when *the god* gives the condition for faith" (PF, 64). And the moment is the situation we will continue to consider.

We noted earlier that apart from the words of Jesus the theophany merely terrifies (and offends). Of course, the words of Jesus, who speaks *as* the God-man, always presents the possibility of offense. That is why Kierkegaard's "Anti-Climacus" presents the discourse "Blessed Is He Who Is Not Offended at Me."[13] Hence, in his theophanic appearance and human words, Jesus as the jolt provokes terror, risks the possibility of offense, and

---

12. In *Philosophical Fragments* Kierkegaard uses the language of "the jolt" to human rationality of the paradoxical person of Jesus, the God-man who exhibited both loftiness and lowliness (PF, 89–110). In *Practice in Christianity*, he uses the language of "the halt" in relation to the divine invitation that quickly can become a halt to even so much as an RSVP (PC, 23–68). Both books are concerned with "the follower at second hand" and the scriptural category of the person of Jesus as an "offense." The majority of *Practice* deals with the subject of offense at Jesus.

13. Kierkegaard, PC, 71–121.

provides the condition of faith. For he thereby truly reveals his person, calms life's earthly storms, comforts disciples, and invokes faith. When faith results, the eternal has been recognized, taught, and the human creature saved. In short, this is the divine pedagogy of the fragments of God. But we must now consider these fragments.

HISTORICAL AND "PHILOSOPHICAL" FRAGMENTS

Mark's gospel relates the *historical fragments* gathered up from the life of Jesus. They are only fragments of the miraculous feedings that signify his entire life, gathered up as the "leftover" provisions for disciples on their earthly journey. John's gospel speaks similarly of the fragmentary nature of what was written of Jesus' life in comparison to the books whose fulness thereof would overflow the world itself (John 21:25).

Kierkegaard's Johannes Climacus' humorously relates the *philosophical fragments* of a "human all-too-human" pedagogy to undoubtedly demonstrate many things, several of which are these:

- Climacus reveals that the "philosophical fragments" of "human, (all-too-human) education" are all too often covertly religious.[14]

- Therefore, the "philosophical fragments" of human pedagogy plagiarize the very words of the divine pedagogy. Climacus satirically "coins" terminology for his human pedagogy that was previously minted in the Scriptures, namely, "sin, savior, deliverer, reconciler, judge, fullness of time, new person, conversion, repentance, and rebirth" and then admits "I falsely attribute to myself something that belongs to no human being" while also passing the buck to humankind in general by admitting "I mendaciously want to attribute the invention to you."[15]

- The backhanded way that Climacus presents the "crumby meal" (the "philosophical fragments" of human pedagogy) ironically serves "the main course" of the divine pedagogy. For our purpose here we take this to mean that the admittedly fragmentary "historical fragments" gathered by humans such as Mark result in the main course of Jesus miraculous feeding of disciples of any and every time.[16]

14. Dalton, *How to Misunderstand*, 110.

15. Kierkegaard, PF, 15–19, 21–22.

16. Stuart Dalton demonstrates that *Philosophical Fragments* presents theories of two pedagogies: 1) a "human (all-too-human) education" which is humorously exposed as perennially becoming *religiously* "pious" and "miraculous" with "a misplaced passion for paradoxes" and 2) a "divine education" that rightly changes everything "when God

- The divine pedagogy is provided in the gospel. This Kierkegaardian reading attempts to demonstrate it through the "master illustration" of earthly boat-bound would-be disciples in the situation that is out on 70,000 fathoms of objective uncertainty, met by the theophanic presence and words of Jesus who is ascended to the heavenly mount.

In the times since Jesus' resurrection and ascension he is "seen" in the "fragmentary" theophanic appearances recorded in the gospels: in this account of his passing by on the sea; in the "transfiguration" in Mark 9:1–8; in the paradoxical theophany of the cross; and as the One seated at God's right hand and coming with the clouds of heaven in Mark 13:24–26 and 14:62. The reason for the ambiguity and uncertainty of human perception will be discussed further as we proceed. We also add that the entire Bible can be seen as containing many theophanic descriptions of God and Jesus. It is especially the case that entire books such as *The Gospels, Acts,* and *Revelation* are in effect theophanic descriptions of Jesus, the God-man. That theophany is presented through word (and imagination) does not mean that the possibility of offense through the jolt is alleviated. Regarding imagination, William Lynch writes,

> In all simplicity we first imagine faith and then let faith imagine.
> *Faith is a form of imagining and experiencing the world.*[17]

We simply add that faith that correctly perceives the theophanies of Christ, imagines a wholly new world. (With the strong caveat that the human imagination is what Michael Ward calls the very organ of meaning, that "organ" being what C. S. Lewis called "the seeing eye.")[18]

AMBASSADORS, OF AND AS HISTORICAL FRAGMENTS

Since the time of the ascension, would be-disciples *normatively* encounter Jesus in tandem with his theophanic appearances found in the whole of Scripture and thus also through some instrumentality of prior disciples.[19]

---

gets involved." Dalton calls the first theory the "crumby leftovers" to the "main course," the second theory. Dalton, *How to Misunderstand*, 109–10, 122–23.

17. Lynch, *Images of Faith*, 5.
18. Ward, "Imagine There's No Heaven?", 150.
19. Since all Scriptures are ultimately "concerning" Christ (Luke 24:25–27, 44–47). This does not preclude that fact that Christ also "normatively" appears "on the sea" (in the world) in other theophanies that *may or may not* be providentially accompanied by "word" as we will see below in the discussion of Mark 14:62. This "may or may not"

This "development," in line with the task of Johannes Climacus to make things more difficult, will ultimately "pay off" more than making things easy does.[20] Thus we will begin with one scholar's answer to Johannes' *faith-problem* about this encounter. Steven Emmanuel writes,

> The answer . . . is that one cannot base an eternal happiness on historical evidence . . . there is really only one way to acquire faith: through a personal encounter with Jesus Christ.[21]

We must be careful to note that Emmanuel seems to be setting "historical evidence" at odds with "a personal encounter with Jesus Christ." Climacus' own answer comes in a particularly difficult section of the *Fragments*, wherein he basically states that the contemporary follower of Christ essentially witnesses of "the God" for the "follower at second hand" so that in essence, there are no followers at second hand. He says,

> Just as the historical becomes the occasion for the contemporary to become a follower—by receiving the condition, please note, from the god himself . . . so the report of the contemporaries becomes the occasion for everyone coming later to become a follower—by receiving the condition, please note, from the god himself.[22]

It may be that Climacus, the plagiarist of the Scriptures, is riffing on the basic sense of Paul who writes,

> All this is from God, who through Christ reconciled us to himself and gave us the ministry of reconciliation; that is, in Christ God was reconciling the world to himself, not counting their trespasses against them, and entrusting to us the message of reconciliation. Therefore, we are ambassadors for Christ, *God making his appeal through us*. We implore you on behalf of Christ, be reconciled to God.[23]

---

ultimately seems to *require* a mystery regarding the universal gospel of Christ for all and the outworking of God's providence (1 Tim 4:10; John 3:16–17).

20. Kierkegaard, CUP1, 186–87.

21. Emmanuel, *Kierkegaard and the Concept*, 64, 65.

22. Kierkegaard, PF, 100. Ultimately, how God provides "the condition" entails the totality of the person and work of the incarnate Christ culminating in the sending of the Holy Spirit and the transformation of the "follower." We will essentially use *the Holy Spirit* as "shorthand" for God's provision of "the condition" as we continue.

23. 2 Cor 5:18–20, ESV, emphasis mine.

Considering these statements of Climacus and Paul we can more fully answer the *faith-problem* by noting the following realities that transcend and alleviate the spatiotemporal problem of distance.

- Contemporaneity with the person of Jesus is provided by what Steven Emmanuel calls "personal encounter with Jesus."
- Contemporaneity with the theophanic presence and word-revelation of Jesus is provided by the theophanic presence and word-revelation of Jesus in the Scriptures and *through* his ambassadors.
- Contemporaneity with the jolt of Jesus is provided *through* his word as relayed by his ambassadors and as reduplicated in the lowly lives of his ambassadors.
- Contemporaneity with Jesus that invokes faith is provided *through* his ambassadors who invoke faith.
- Therefore, contemporaneity with Jesus is "mediated" by "the god himself" as seen in these points.
- A final point, more faithfully following Emmanuel's meaning where we started, is that contemporaneity is at the same time "immediate" (not mediated) through the Holy Spirit ("the god himself") who provides encounter with Jesus the God-man.

It seems that what provides a basis for the leap across the big ugly ditch of historical evidence is the presence of Jesus through his Spirit and in his ambassadors and their hearers. For the Spirit provides the "communication" that mere historical testimony cannot fulfill by being *the Spirit in the communication*. Does this provide certainty or remain absurd? It all boils down to the hearer's canon of reason. For,

> "historical evidence . . . *any of the normal canons of historical reasoning*" cannot provide a "base" for one's eternal happiness, "because the true basis "*even contradicts some broadly held canons of historical reasoning.*"[24]

That humans become bearers of "historical fragments," and are themselves "personal fragments" of the divine Person may offend the canon of human reason and pedagogy. But are the fragments of the human, all-too-human pedagogy something that humans can truly "take heart" in (Mark 6:50)? Is it better to be enamored by the self-deification of the human pedagogy that *begins and ends with fragments* or be "utterly astounded" by the divine pedagogy that begins with fragments but reaps an *eternal* happiness? In our

---

24. Roberts, *Faith, Reason, and History*, 10.

first chapter epigram above, Melville's Ishmael critiques the human-all-too-human enterprise of merchant ships as fortified "extension bridges" from the land, and pirates or privateers as plundering "other fragments of the land like themselves," both of which therefore do not seek to "draw their living from the bottomless deep."[25] But Mark, and Kierkegaard after him, lead us *through* fragments to draw our very life from the bottomless deep of the theophanic God-man who walks "over 70,000 fathoms."

DISTANCE, FRAGMENTS, AND CHRIST'S CONTINUAL THEOPHANY

It is interesting to consider the closing words of Mark's account in relation to the foregoing discussions. We will further press and extrapolate our thesis based on Mark's conclusion to this account. Mark reports that

> When they had crossed over, they landed at Gennesaret and anchored there. As soon as they got out of the boat, people recognized Jesus. They ran throughout that whole region and carried the sick on mats to wherever they heard he was. And wherever he went—into villages, towns or countryside—they placed the sick in the marketplaces. They begged him to let them touch even the edge of his cloak, and all who touched it were healed (6:52–56 NIV).

Pressing our reading, Mark's report of crossing over, landing, anchoring, and deboarding the vessel, may be taken to signify a return to normal history apart from the previous spatiotemporal-bending account. In this sense, the account of the disciples precariously journeying across the earthly sea of time while Jesus is ascended to the heavenly mount is a sort of transfiguration account revealing the greater reality that encompasses the "normal" one (Mark 9:2–7). Jesus is again recognized in mundane history and carries on with his usual healings of those brought to where he was and of those where he went. But Mark also shows that the touching the hem of Jesus' garment for healing in 5:30 was not a one-off occasion but became more commonplace. And this also implies some measure of distance from Jesus and posits "fragments" of his person as a medium of saving contact.

If we consider an account of Mark near the end of his gospel, we can see that distance is no barrier to Christ's mission. But we may also see that historical fragments are necessary for rightly recognizing the person of Jesus

---

25. Extrapolating from the chapter epigram above.

in what we will call his continual theophanic appearing. We will separate and italicize the prediction of the coming of Christ in theophanic presence.

- And the high priest stood up in the midst and asked Jesus, "Have you no answer to make? What is it that these men testify against you?" But he remained silent and made no answer. Again the high priest asked him, "Are you the Christ, the Son of the Blessed?"
- And Jesus said, "*I am, and you will see the Son of Man seated at the right hand of Power, and coming with the clouds of heaven.*"
- And the high priest tore his garments and said, "What further witnesses do we need? You have heard his blasphemy. What is your decision?" And they all condemned him as deserving death (14:60–64, ESV).

"The Son of Man seated at the right hand of power and coming on the clouds of heaven" is the classic language of theophany from Daniel 7:13. In the gospel of Matthew, with the words "from now on you will see," this coming is emphasized as continual rather than one-time or occasional (Matt 26:64). Thus, Matthew and Mark, reveal that the then-coming theophany of Christ would be constantly appearing in all coming history.[26] That the high priest would see this signifies that Jesus' transcendent theophanic appearance was accessible to human perception. But this perception, as is everything in the gospel, is dependent upon eyes that see and perceive and ears that hear and understand (Mark 4:12). Regarding the *particular historic form* of theophany the high priest and the council would see in history, we can surmise the following. They will see Mark 13 category events. Unless they receive beforehand historical fragments of the word of Christ, i.e., gospel testimony that prepares them to "hear," "Take heart; it is I . . . Do not be afraid," they will only see a terrifying apparition of death which haunts their lives as it haunted the disciples (Mark 6:48–50; cf Heb 2:15). Christ's theophanic presence in his theophanic storm of judgment can only terrify them.

These accounts in Mark as historical fragments of the gospel "beg," as did the fragment of Jesus' earthly garment, to be touched by those of all ages. In other words, the theophanic account of the disciples at sea, and the then-coming theophanic account of the high priest and council, are historical fragments begging to be touched by all those the gospel reaches. These are not merely historical accounts. In accord with our entire reading in this chapter, they are fragments meant to be conduits by which the theophanic presence of Christ passes by us, so that his gospel that provides his presence

---

26. See Talbert, *Matthew*, 296–97.

may come to us.²⁷ We may initially or perpetually respond in terror and offense. We may even respond in faith which, though "astounded," exists within hearts that though "healed" remain "hardened" and still see men, as trees walking (Mark 6:51–52; 8:23–24).

In all this reading we see that distance, fragments, and theophany, are not barriers. They are invitations that provoke us to our core and aim to evoke passionate faith in that very place. As noted above, Melville's Ishmael seems to have intuited that we must draw our life from life's bottomless deep. And Christ's gospel reveals that the bottomless deep only yields its life through the bottomless depths of the theophanic God-man who walks over its 70,000 fathoms. An eternal consciousness and happiness *can* be built from *our* historical point of departure out over the 70,000 fathoms where Jesus comes to us, to pass by us in theophany. And the past historical point of departure, the report from history, does not need to be more sufficient than what seems an extravagant exaggeration by Johannes:²⁸

> Even if the contemporary generation had not left anything behind except the words, "We have believed that in such and such a year the god appeared in the humble form of a servant, lived and taught among us, and then died"—that is more than enough.²⁹

All things considered, Johannes' statement seems more a *slight exaggeration*. For to faith, that point of departure is more God's *revelation* than *historical certainty*.³⁰ But neither the revelation, nor the sacred history, arise from the human, all-too-human heart of man (1 Cor 2:9; Hab 1:5; Acts 13:41; Mark 4:11).

---

27. Our reading of Mark 14:62 implies that Christ's perpetual theophanic appearances are potentially universal. We believe that their historic forms cannot be delineated for they can range from very particular to quite universal historical occasions. Thus, description would be like delineating the historic manifestations of Acts 14:17, which is perhaps an apt analogy to the perpetual nature of the theophanic reality. Christ's theophanic appearance may accompany but perhaps most often precedes the verbal gospel witness of Christ which serves to exegete its gospel to us.

28. For this view see Roberts, *Faith, Reason, and History*, 138–39.

29. Kierkegaard, PF, 104. Kierkegaard's allusion to Philippians 2:6–10 could possibly be a "shorthand" account of the gospel "cited" by Johannes Climacus to lend support to his downplaying of the historical report.

30. See Emmanuel, *Kierkegaard & the Concept*, 66, 71–72.

8

"Corban" and The "Christian" Bourgeoise Settlement

God's Eternal "Like for Like"

Mark 7:1–23

God is actually himself this pure like for like, the pure rendition of how you yourself are . . . God's relation to a human being is at every moment to infinitize what is in that human being at every moment.[1]—S. Kierkegaard

Never is that evil, mediocrity, more dangerous than when it is dressed up as "geniality."[2]—Soren Kierkegaard

A TURNING POINT IN MARK: CRITIQUE OF "CHRISTIAN" BOURGEOISE SETTLEMENTS

This section of Mark is an important turning point in his gospel. It is an integral part of what Lawrence Farley calls "withdrawal beyond Galilee."[3] His designation nicely encapsulates that the withdrawal is in one sense from nonreceptivity in Galilee and in another sense to receptivity beyond it. The movement at this key point centers upon the religious leaders of Israel, the

---

1. Kierkegaard, WOL, 384.
2. Kierkegaard, JP 1, 225.
3. Farley, *Gospel of Mark*, 6.

"CORBAN" AND THE "CHRISTIAN" BOURGEOISE SETTLEMENT 117

law of Moses, their interpretation and practice thereof, and the society their "law practice" creates. We will therefore posit that the central issue at this turning point, theologically speaking, concerns the gospel—that enables fulfilling God's commanded love of God and neighbor—in saving and critical relation to *any* society's views of love of God and neighbor, *however* those are conceived by that society.

This central issue will allow us to apply the collision of Jesus with his Jewish society to human societies that have since collided with Jesus, namely the "mega-societies" of Modern Christendom and Post-Christendom. In all three collisions, we hope to show that Jesus collided with different forms of a "Christian bourgeoise settlement."[4] And with the help of Kierkegaard, from whom that term is derived, we hope to also demonstrate through Jesus' encounter with these Pharisees and scribes that each "settlement" falls terribly short of loving the neighbor and God. In other words, these societies' "love" of neighbor and of God only manifest human, all-too-human pale facsimiles thereof.

Our identification of these three societies as "Christian" bourgeoise settlements (noting the scare quotes) enables us to consider Jesus' critique of the Jewish settlement, narrated in Mark 7:1–23, as applicable to nineteenth century Christendom and twenty-first century Post-Christendom. We now proceed to the reading and will divide Mark 7:1–23 into three sections, each of which reveals points of critique by Jesus that signify divine judgment.

Mark 7:1–5 (ESV)

Now when the Pharisees gathered to him, with some of the scribes who had come from Jerusalem, 2 they saw that some of his disciples ate with hands that were defiled, that is, unwashed. 3 (For the Pharisees and all the Jews do not eat unless they wash their hands properly, holding to the tradition of the elders, 4 and when they come from the marketplace, they do not eat unless they wash. And there are many other traditions that they observe, such as the washing of cups and pots and copper vessels and dining couches.)

5 And the Pharisees and the scribes asked him, "Why do your disciples not walk according to the tradition of the elders, but eat with defiled hands?"

---

4. We borrow the Kierkegaardian term from Perkins, *Works of Love*, 2–3. We obviously posit an anachronistic *Jewish* "Christian bourgeoise settlement." The designation simply signifies that the Jewish settlement fell under the judgment of *Christ's gospel* of God, the law, and their faulty following of both. So, in a sense, Mark shows the Jewish settlement as fallen from Christ and therefore become a "Christian bourgeoise settlement."

MARK'S HISTORICAL TURNING POINT IN THE GOSPEL MISSION

In 7:1 and 7:14 Mark narrates two situations that together convey a historical turning point in his gospel: the Pharisees "gathered to him" and Jesus "called the people to him again." Given the context of the "withdrawal beyond Galilee" mentioned above, these situations signify Jesus' transition from the mission to Israel to the mission to the Gentiles. It functions much as does the summary preview for John's gospel:

> He came to his own, and his own people did not receive him;
> But to all who did receive him, who believed in his name, he gave the right to become children of God (John 1:11–12, ESV).

The Pharisees and scribes "gathering to him" can ironically signify the mission of gathering to Jesus God intended for the covenant children of Israel. Jesus "calling the people" to him and correcting the Pharisees' law-views in effect distances them from their restrictive views and previews the way the gospel will be proclaimed in the mission to the Gentiles. Of course, the mission to Israel had always been God's means to that end (Gen 12:2–3). And Mark increasingly depicts Gentiles coming to Jesus to signify the "withdrawal beyond" that Luke's two-part gospel makes explicit in Acts 10–13.[5]

Thus, it seems Mark here depicts a definitive turning point for Israel where there is judgment instead of "gathering to" (see Matt 23:37–38). Mark gradually depicts this by using OT "road-signs" that picture Israel's increasingly wayward steps. First, we see God's invitation of Israel in 1:2–3. Second, we see Israel's perception of that invitation in 4:12. Third, we see Israel's rejection of God's invitation in 7:6–7. We must now consider the way of Israel that led to Jesus' "points" of divine critique and judgement. In the process we increasingly try to demonstrate how the Jewish settlement's "fall" mirrors the fall of the previously mentioned societies and mirrors our present society *as* a "Christian" bourgeoise settlement."[6]

THE ETERNAL "LIKE FOR LIKE"

The first point of judgment is revealed through Mark's narration in verses 2–5. The Jewish leaders observe the disciples and judge them according

---

5. Especially noting the turning point of Acts 13:46–47, but also noting that Luke on the whole portrays more definitively than does Mark, a reception by a "remnant" of Israel (just as Paul also does in Romans 9–11).

6. Remembering Kierkegaard's dictum that God's word is to be our mirror, as set forth in Christman, *Behold*, 1–10.

to their standards. But their main criterion was not God's law but their faulty conception of God and the law. Thus, their criterion of judgment was themselves.

The judgment God metes upon them was to "echo" their false conceptions back on them *as though* they were wholly divine conceptions. Kierkegaard calls this divinely governed reciprocity the "echo of like for like" and sees it as the mechanism whereby God *immediately* judges all humans.[7] This is, so to speak, John Lennon's "instant karma." We thus see a *deep turning point* revealed in Mark whereby the concerns with Israel are expanded to universal concerns with humanity, including the expansions of God's law for Israel to God's law for humanity. Of course, that's the given of the gospel from the beginning. Martin Andic explains Kierkegaard's "*Christian like for like, eternity's like for like*" as

> an idea of *justice* that marks what is fully Christian by contrast with what is Jewish . . . It has indeed given up the temporal and Jewish like for like, by which you are to take an eye for an eye; but has replaced this with an eternal one, whereby God judges or blesses you as you judge or bless others . . . For now your every relation to others is finally and essentially a relation to God, who looks on you in your conscience leniently or rigorously, exactly as you look on others: in a way God looks on you with your own rigor, or with a rigor that is leniency if you acknowledge and obey God by practicing God's equal, unconditional love.[8]

Andic's explanation of Kierkegaard's view of divine judgment is easily applied to the Jewish leaders in Mark 7:1–23 as they judged the disciples just as they were accustomed to judging everyone. It is also easily applicable to humans who universally judge others, thus also marking this turning point in Mark.

At this point we must present Kierkegaard's view in his own words, noting that he presents this definitive principle of *universal judgment* at the very conclusion of his massive "Christian deliberations in the form of discourses" (WOL, 1). This, again, signifies that his "religious" *Works of Love* is a "philosophical tract" for all humanity, albeit a "thoroughly theocentric book."[9] Kierkegaard's delineation of God's "eternal like for like" is as follows:

> The Jewish, the worldly, the bustling like for like is: as others do unto you, by all means take care that you do likewise unto them.

---

7. Kierkegaard, WOL, 384–85. We will cite references to *Works of Love* in the remainder of this chapter in the main text above.

8. Andic, "Love's Redoubling," 9.

9. Perkins, *Works of Love*, 1, 3.

> But the Christian like for like is: God will do unto you exactly as you do unto others . . . In the Christian sense, *to love people is to love God, and to love God is to love people*—what you do unto people, you do unto God, and therefore *what you do unto people, God does unto you* . . . God *is* actually himself this pure like for like, the pure rendition of how you yourself are. If there is anger in you, then God is anger in you; if there is leniency and mercifulness in you, then God is mercifulness in you. . . . God's relation to a human being is at every moment to infinitize what is in that human being at every moment (WOL, 383–384).

Before moving to the next section of Mark we merely point out that Kierkegaard finds God's "like for like" in texts like Mark 4:24, "with the measure you use it will be measured to you." In *Works of Love*, he cites Matthew 6:14, 7:3, and 8:13, in his explication of the principle (WOL, 378–383). Of course, one could also add Matthew 7:1–2 as the classic text about judging others and which also uses the "measure" language of Mark 4. We also point out that Kierkegaard's description of the Jewish way as "the worldly, the bustling" was probably an intentional *coloring* of the Jewish "law settlement" that was *suitable* for his critique of the "Christian" bourgeoise settlement. His mirroring supports our own regarding this "Jewish" account in Mark as critically interpretive of the societies we are considering here as "Christian" bourgeoise settlements.

Therefore, we point out that Kierkegaard's conception of the divine "like for like" radicalizes the gospel so that it is "deeply subversive" to any human "settlements" whether they claim to be sacred or secular, or some mix.[10] For Kierkegaard's radical claim is that "Christianity . . . makes every one of your relationships to other people into a God-relationship . . . you will surely receive like for like in both the one and the other sense" (WOL, 376). In other words, we humans may compartmentalize our relations to others as related to the secular or the sacred. But God's "like for like" makes these all of one as "a God-relationship" and thereby makes them the mechanism for *immediate* judgment, or, as we said earlier, "instant karma."

Mark 7:6–13 (ESV)

6 And he said to them, "Well did Isaiah prophesy of you hypocrites, as it is written,

"'This people honors me with their lips,

---

10. Stephen Backhouse calls *Works of Love* "a deeply subversive book" and we hope to introduce it as that as we continue. See Backhouse, *A Single Life*, 152.

> but their heart is far from me;
>
> 7 in vain do they worship me,
>
> teaching as doctrines the commandments of men.'
>
> 8 You leave the commandment of God and hold to the tradition of men."
>
> 9 And he said to them, "You have a fine way of rejecting the commandment of God in order to establish your tradition!
>
> 10 For Moses said, 'Honor your father and your mother'; and, 'Whoever reviles father or mother must surely die.' 11 But you say, 'If a man tells his father or his mother, "Whatever you would have gained from me is Corban"' (that is, given to God)— 12 then you no longer permit him to do anything for his father or mother, 13 thus making void the word of God by your tradition that you have handed down. And many such things you do."

THE PRACTICE OF "CORBAN"

This section of Mark's narration reveals a practice which epitomized the ways the Jewish settlement had replaced God's commands with those of man. We will discuss three things in relation to God's law and its replacement by man to further demonstrate the gospel critique of human, all-too-human "Christian" bourgeoise settlements provided in Mark.

First, God has indeed commanded love, so that love is both definable and not an oxymoron as we moderns and post-moderns tend to think.[11] Regarding this supposed oxymoron we seek to turn the tables of language exchange in the modern temple and pose the following: Inasmuch as the now-current slogan "love is love" is a non-definition that is "innocuously" given content by whatever preferences the human settlement that coined it decides, it only avoids being an oxymoron by being nonsensical. It appears to be an ideological propagandizing tool useful for buttressing the "Christian" bourgeoise settlement. Kierkegaard writes

> "One should love one's neighbor as himself," say the bourgeoise, and by this they mean the well-brought up children and now useful members of the state—those who have great susceptibility to every transient emotional flu.[12]

---

11. Perkins, *Works of Love*, 1.
12. Kierkegaard, JP 1, 221.

As we all know, there are many literal and "emotional" flus going around today, and they militate "moral" forms of "love is love" based more on the "Christian" bourgeoise settlement's *ideas* of love than on love as commanded by God. This "teaching as doctrines the commandments of men" (7:7) is what makes them bourgeoise, because "the powers that be" cultivate the power of "the crowd" to militate these "loves" *as* human law.

On this point, for the sake of transparency, we add that our use of "love is love" is not to pose a specific critique of current ideas of human "loves" or laws. We are merely trying to demonstrate the replacement of the divine love-commands with human ones by a "Christian bourgeoise settlement."

Second, the human shortcoming regarding loving neighbor and God is not due to their being commanded, but simply due to the commands not being obeyed because their content is intentionally and selfishly (a)voided (7:13). As for the Jewish settlement's failure to obey God's commandments to love God and man, Jesus' emphasis on the internal evils of man in 7:14–23, and the material "payoff" the "Corban" *provisions* only provided its creators, Mark shows that sin was at the bottom. In other words, the religious bourgeoise settlement designed its new doctrines of "love" of neighbor and God for self-serving sinful reasons. They fulfill by "dignified" charade the second chapter epigram above: "Never is that evil, mediocrity, more dangerous than when it is dressed up as 'geniality.'" This falsely founded respect gains the servile obedience of the "proletariat" masses who therefore bow to a mediocre spiritless bourgeoise "priesthood" which evades the self-sacrificial duties that are necessary to true priests.

The heartlessness (7:6) of such practices becomes more evident by considering *the material gain* that "Corban" delivered to those other than its practitioners. For "Corban" voided God's major commandment to honor one's parents, which did not mean mere verbal or genteel respect but providing for their life-needs in a day when that meant survival (Ex 20:12). And if the Jewish settlement at that time "wrote off" taking care of one's own parents, we can be sure that the poor of that society fared no better.

Third, the Jewish settlement's pseudo-religious way of "loving God and neighbor" through "Corban" signifies more than that one historical occasion when we consider that all quasi-religious bourgeoise settlements require "Corbans" of their own. The perennial necessity of Corban-like practices for bourgeoise existence leads to new traditions that employ propagandizing slogans to promote "geniality," i.e., *clout*, to the masses. And the "benefits" such hollow ideological slogans provide are as vaporous as the ideologues who create them. For they are not creative (*dabhar*) *speech-acts* of spirited humans that beneficially *love* the neighbor according to God's love already defined in God's love-commands (God's creative speech-acts).

"CORBAN" AND THE "CHRISTIAN" BOURGEOISE SETTLEMENT 123

In other words, calling some "transient emotional flu" of the bourgeoise settlement "love," does not make it God's love of neighbor which as we saw earlier, *is* "a God-relationship." But, whether by design or default, to *not* fulfill God's commanded love the "Christian" bourgeoise settlements need a "Corban." In the next verses in Mark Jesus reveals the dark materials from which all "Corbans" are created and then practiced to the defilement of their host settlements.

Mark 7:14–23 (ESV)

14 And he called the people to him again and said to them, "Hear me, all of you, and understand: 15 There is nothing outside a person that by going into him can defile him, but the things that come out of a person are what defile him." 17 And when he had entered the house and left the people, his disciples asked him about the parable. 18 And he said to them, "Then are you also without understanding? Do you not see that whatever goes into a person from outside cannot defile him, 19 since it enters not his heart but his stomach, and is expelled?" (Thus he declared all foods clean.) 20 And he said, "What comes out of a person is what defiles him. 21 For from within, out of the heart of man, come evil thoughts, sexual immorality, theft, murder, adultery, 22 coveting, wickedness, deceit, sensuality, envy, slander, pride, foolishness. 23 All these evil things come from within, and they defile a person."

THE "VOID" OF MERELY HUMAN MORALITY AND RELIGION

Here Jesus pulls away the veil to reveal the interior that all shows of exteriority hide in the charade of mere human morality that "voids" God's commands. Apart from quoting Isaiah regarding the far-off "heart" of those claiming to "honor" God, and naming their "hypocrisy," Jesus had not yet addressed what lies at the root of these religious leaders and their evil practices. Now Jesus unearths the "heart" of all "Christian bourgeoise settlements" and "calls the people to him" to reject the hollow exterior morality that Kierkegaard held to be the "badge" of the crowd and the "bane" of the single individual that would live differently, leading him to write in his journal "beware of people."[13]

In our day virtue signaling seems the sign of the cross for the crowd accompanied by a false puritanical and scapegoating demonization of the

---

13. Kierkegaard, WOL, 418; JP 4, 4596.

single individual. We speak thus because this section of Jesus' critique signifies Mark's previously mentioned turning from a merely Jewish milieu to the universal human milieu, and the evil interiority that lies beneath all merely humanly derived social exteriority masked as God's "love thy neighbor." And therefore, Jesus reveals "the skeletons in the closet" of "Christian" bourgeoise settlements as defined earlier.

At this point we need to remember Kierkegaard's radical claim that "Christianity . . . makes every one of your relationships to other people into a God-relationship" (WOL, 376). Of course, this claim is radical because Jesus and his gospel were radical. But this statement, based on the divine "like for like," means that Jesus saw no essential divide between religion (how humans worship God) and social morality (how humans treat others). Kierkegaard merely realized that the gospel removes the false divide between the sacred and the secular that so defines modern life. Jesus reveals that internal and external reality both exist and are integrally related to one another. The internal spiritual reality of a person causes the external social reality as it is manifested therein. The book of James portrays this graphically when it speaks of "fights among you" as being caused by "wars within you," which inner wars are symptoms of "coveting" (Jas 4:1–2).

In Mark 7:14–23 Jesus narrates this "Genesis" of evil in more detail and we should note that the "evil thoughts" that "defile a person" flow out in a flood of *social sins*: "sexual immorality, theft, murder, adultery, coveting, wickedness, deceit, sensuality, envy, slander, pride, foolishness." None of these sins, though arising from the cesspool within, remains within.

Therefore, the sacred/secular divide cannot so divide human acts. It is also why human acts toward neighbor are, in God's *eternal* "like for like," *infinitized* to be acts toward God. Therefore, no person or society can divide human activity into sacred and secular compartments, even in the United States with its "wall of separation." For all "Christian" bourgeoise settlements this side of Christendom are such because they derive their democratic ideals of equality and liberty from latent Christian morality. But, like the Pharisaical bourgeoise settlement, they inevitably collide with and *crucify* the person(s) by whom God exposes the moral nakedness of their mediocre "geniality." Following a litany of the crowd singing the high praises of "Christian" bourgeoise Babylon, John's *Revelation* calls this "dangerous" evidence found in her "the blood of prophets and of saints and of all who have been slain on earth" (Rev 18:11–24).[14] We won't overly belabor this point other than to delineate the immorality of:

---

14. See Gorman, *Reading Revelation Responsibly*, 147. We are alluding in these last several sentences to Kierkegaard's words in our second chapter epigram.

- Modern "morality" with its quasi-divine "Corbans" that eviscerate the true neighbor-love owed the lowly by voiding its being defined by God.
- Modern democracy's dehumanization of "its citizens" by promoting its sacred/secular divide through the very existence of human beings.
- "Christian bourgeoise settlements that always crucify those sent to reveal its charade and intend to turn it to true love of neighbor and love of God.

In sum, "all these evil things come from within, and they defile a person," and unfortunately, they also *defile a society* because God "makes every one of your relationships to other people into a God-relationship . . . you will surely receive like for like in both the one and the other sense"—the internal and external senses (WOL, 376–77). We need to remember:

> Never is that evil, mediocrity, more dangerous than when it is dressed up as "geniality."[15]

God has decreed a two-fold judgment, that the merely human morality and religion of individuals and societies reaps the defilement of merely human morality and religion to both individuals and societies. It does so by making God's *defined* love of neighbor and God null and void. The merely human, sowing under the condition of sin, reaps like for like. The evil mediocrity of the "Christian" bourgeoise settlement is extremely dangerous because it is dressed up in a "geniality" of new "divine" traditions that dupe the crowd through a "transient emotional flu." And as Bob Dylan noted in a song from his 1983 album "Infidels," someone with less than divine aspirations caught stealing a little will be thrown in jail, but someone with "divine" aspirations stealing a lot will be made king.[16] Man as would-be king becomes the "Christian" bourgeoise settlement of "love" for neighbor and God, but, of course, without fear of God. Kierkegaard narrates this evil mediocrity quite satirically:

> The bourgeois' love of God commences when the vegetative life is in full swing, when the hands are comfortably folded over the stomach, when the head is reclining on a soft easy chair, and when a drowsy glance is raised toward the ceiling, toward higher things.[17]

---

15. Kierkegaard, JP 3, 225.
16. See Bob Dylan, "Sweetheart Like You."
17. Kierkegaard, JP 1, 220.

Of course, what is easily overlooked in all this sham is the reason the pseudo-Christian bourgeoise settlement makes such sense and works so easily: "We are all Christians."[18] The comment of Robert Perkins shows why the "truth" of the "Christian" bourgeoise settlement is self-evident to its crowd:

> Now, of course, if we are all Christians in heart and mind, whatever we think of the love commandment is the truth of the matter. Since we are all Christians, our common life is a social expression of the Christian ethic.[19]

Some may doubt that this works so well in places like "post-Christian" America. But two things: First, the term "Christian" is also determined through the social consensus of the bourgeoise which as we have shown divinizes its quasi-religious "traditions" no matter how it self-identifies. Second, the "Christian-atheists" and especially "Christian-humanists" know otherwise, since they know, like the Christian Chesterton knew that "The modern world is full of the old Christian virtues gone mad."[20]

"LIKE FOR LIKE" AND THE GOSPEL

We will conclude the reading of this chapter by trying to tie up a few loose ends that some readers may be wondering about.

We will begin by countering what many in our pluralistic pantheistic age might falsely conclude from Kierkegaard's radical claim that "Christianity . . . makes every one of your relationships to other people into a God-relationship" (WOL, 376). We won't spend much time here other than to cite the disclaimer of Martin Andic, who writes

> Kierkegaard is not committed . . . to any "immanence" or anthropomorphism or subjectivism that reduces divine love to human love, or divine reality to its appearance to us.[21]

---

18. Kierkegaard, MLW, 117–18.

19. Perkins, *Works of Love*, 3.

20. Chesterton, *Heretics/Orthodoxy*, 192. Tom Holland makes the best case for the *historical basis* for Christian atheism. See Holland, *Revolutionary*, xi–xx. Theologian Jens Zimmerman presents the best case we know of for Christian Humanism. See Zimmermann, *Incarnational Humanism*, 52–162.

21. Andic, "Love's Redoubling," 12. Andic writes that Kierkegaard's claim differentiated between God and the human in this "like for like" and shows that Kierkegaard believed that "God redoubles us and we reduplicate. *We* are redoubled by allowing God to make us nothing and to create us anew. But *the Divine* redoubles itself, in boundlessly communicating itself or what it itself is, and so for ever and continuously acquires what it gives; our highest perfection is to become nothing but an instrument of divine redoubling" (37–38).

"CORBAN" AND THE "CHRISTIAN" BOURGEOISE SETTLEMENT 127

Another question may arise concerning the "mechanics" by which the "like for like" works. When Kierkegaard says, "If there is anger in you, then God is anger in you," how does God make that happen. Is not God's purpose to always "make it happen" that we know God in truth?

The first answer is to affirm that God's purpose is always to be known in truth, but for that to happen God must first "deconstruct" our idols of "God." The purpose of Jesus narrated in Mark 7:1–23 was to deconstruct the false "God" of the Pharisees and scribes along with their practices in service to that God. Of course, this task was subservient to the reception of the true God through the gospel of Jesus. That the "construction" of *reception* follows "deconstruction" simply means that humans all too often go the long way around to salvation, if at all, as may be implied in the case of the Pharisees and scribes in Matthew 23:39.

A second answer is to try to present the mechanics by which the "like for like" is subservient to God's truth which always judges, but not for condemnation but for redemption. The mechanics by which "if there is anger in you, then God is anger in you," or conversely "if there is forgiveness in you, then God is forgiveness in you," are based in basic principles of human formation. Broadly speaking, this means that God's governance is both preliminary to and subservient of human redemption. In Jesus diagnosis of human evil in Mark, he says

> What comes out of a person is what defiles him. For from within, out of the heart of man, come evil thoughts . . . all these things come from within, and they defile a person.

This shows that the *second* "like" of God's "like for like" signifies the autonomous person's inner desire which, when expressed, forms the person's habit or character. These evil desires thus form the person in defilement. Philosopher James K. A. Smith characterizes the process through which good or evil comes by the descriptive words "we are what we love," due to the fact that we humans are "desiring, imaginative animals."[22] The *desire* of the heart finds consummation of the desire's *love* through first *imagining* the desire as satisfied in a "target or object."[23] This rather technical description is made more graphic and world-centered when Smith says "what we love is a specific vision of the good life, an implicit picture of what we think human flourishing looks like."[24] Smith carries this further, bringing this vision from the internal imagination-world to the more concrete world where our *desire*

---

22. Smith, *Desiring the Kingdom*, 37.
23. Smith, *Desiring the Kingdom*, 48.
24. Smith, *Desiring the Kingdom*, 52.

hopes to find satisfaction, namely in a world that is a domain, or a kingdom. He writes,

> To be human, we could say, is to desire the kingdom—*some* kingdom . . . it's not a question of *whether* you long for some version of the kingdom but of *which* version you long for. This is true for any human being; it is a structural feature of human creatureliness . . . The heart is like a multifunctional desire device that is part engine and part homing beacon. Operating under the hood of our consciousness, so to speak—our default autopilot—the longings of the heart both *point us* in the direction of a kingdom and *propel* us toward it.[25]

Through the "mechanics" of the human heart Smith provides we should be able to see how our hearts drive us, as Jesus said. We should also note that Smith is describing the basic or *neutral* structural make-up of every human being. The structural make-up set in place by God does not itself pre-determine an evil outcome.

This mechanics helps us see that a person with an evil character, like Mark's Pharisee, who continues to cultivate their evil thoughts and desires, sees the world as the arena where their desires may be fulfilled. Thus, the world becomes *viewed* through the person's own evil construct. It sees through those eyes, judges everyone else with those eyes, and thus reaps what it sows through God's governing "like for like." If it lives in anger, it reaps anger in a world governed by an angry God. If it lives in forgiveness, it reaps forgiveness in a world governed by a forgiving God. Of course, between those two examples transformation has occurred. Kierkegaard cites God's "like for like" in relation to the gospel's centurion (Matt 8:13) to demonstrate how it "plays out" for good *because of the gospel*, but only for those whose character and "like," is like his.

> Therefore, if you listen carefully, in what most definitely must be called Gospel you yourself will hear also the rigorousness, For example, what Jesus says to the centurion from Capernaum, "Be it done for you as you have believed." Indeed, no more joyful tidings can be imagined, no more lenient, more merciful words! And yet, what is said there? There it is said, Be it done for you as you believe." Or what would Christ have thought if, instead of coming to him believing, the centurion had come to him secretly in order to find out if he had faith! "Be it done for you as you believe"—that is, it is eternally certain that it will be done for you as you believe. Christianity guarantees you that,

---

25. Smith, *You Are What You Love*, 11–12.

> but whether you, precisely *you,* have faith certainly does not belong to Christianity's doctrine and proclamation, so that it should declare to you that you have faith. Then when the fearful concerns arise that you perhaps do not have faith, Christianity, unchanged, repeats, "Be it done for you as you believe." How rigorous! From the story of the centurion you find out that he had faith; this actually does not pertain to you at all. Then you find out something essentially Christian, that it was done for him as he believed—but you, after all, are not the centurion (WOL, 377–78).

Kierkegaard shows two reasons why the unbelief of the Pharisees and scribes returned to them rigorousness. Because their "God" was not lenient but rigorous, and because they therefore showed no leniency or love to others. They received rigorousness for rigorousness, "like for like." Their rigorous "God" created them in his image, which was not the "nurturant" God imaged before them and before all the people in Jesus.[26] And the Jewish bourgeoise settlement and coming "Christian" bourgeoise settlements, by replacing God's commanded love with pale facsimiles thereof, also create other "Gods" and false "loves' in their images.

Kierkegaard rightly held to a more intimate love, "a spontaneity *after* law" based in the "gentleness" of "invitation and permission" of the exhortation, "Beloved, let us love one another" (WOL 375).[27] But that spontaneity was not for the beginning of Kierkegaard's *Works of Love,* precisely because it was not (and is not) for the "drowsy glance . . . raised toward the ceiling, toward higher things" of the mediocre "Christian" bourgeoise settlement.

> If there is anger in you, then God is anger in you; if there is leniency and mercifulness in you, then God is mercifulness in you. *It is infinite loving that he will have anything to do with you at all and that no one, no one, so lovingly discovers the slightest love in you as God does. God's relation to a human being is at every moment to infinitize what is in a human being at every moment* (WOL, 384, with the crucial line we previously omitted inserted).

---

26. See Sanders, *Embracing Prodigals,* 40–48.
27. See Ferreira, *Loves Grateful Striving,* 241–42; Kierkegaard, WOL, 375–76.

9

The Syrophoenician Woman and Fragments from the Children's Table

The Parable of the Offensive Invitation

Mark 7:24–30 ESV

24 And from there he arose and went away to the region of Tyre and Sidon. And he entered a house and did not want anyone to know, yet he could not be hidden. 25 But immediately a woman whose little daughter had an unclean spirit heard of him and came and fell down at his feet. 26 Now the woman was a Gentile, a Syrophoenician by birth. And she begged him to cast the demon out of her daughter. 27 And he said to her, "Let the children be fed first, for it is not right to take the children's bread and throw it to the dogs." 28 But she answered him, "Yes, Lord; yet even the dogs under the table eat the children's crumbs." 29 And he said to her, "For this statement you may go your way; the demon has left your daughter." 30 And she went home and found the child lying in bed and the demon gone.

If I have ventured wrongly, well, then life helps me by punishing me. But if I have not ventured at all, who helps me then?[1] —Anti-Climacus

---

1. Kierkegaard, SD, 34.

The Canaanitish woman lives more happily without a name, than Herodias with one.²—Sir Thomas Browne

Humor is always a concealed pair.³ But humor is also the joy which has overcome the world.⁴—Soren Kierkegaard

Before moving into Mark's next scene, we will gather several loose historical "fragments" begging to be touched for the power of Christ that flows from them across the centuries to the sick and unclean (7:56). For Jesus has just shown the true uncleanness flowing from the unclean hearts of men whose "like for like" sees only uncleanness—rather than their *neighbor*—standing before them. Through their religious "Corban" they "worship" the invisible God while blind to those God has set before them to love and serve.⁵ So Mark shows a bourgeoise woman the Jewish bourgeoise settlement would not even see who insists on being seen by Jesus who will "play the good Pharisee."⁶ She is as unnamed and passionate for healing as was the one we only know as "daughter" who also only sought a fragment from Jesus to provide the whole of what God provides (5:25–34). And therefore, God's "like for like" provided the love for her "uncleanness" that she provided for her own "unclean" daughter. She thus "immediately" provides in Mark the first "reduplication" of the "like for like" of *love* that in Jesus *stood* before the Pharisees and scribes, and the people, in the previous account.⁷ Given the richness of her account, she is, along with the Gerasene demoniac, Mark's "Cornelius" of Luke's "turning point" to the Gentile harvest in Acts. Though unclean and unnamed she "lives more happily" than does the frivolous Herodias, daughter of the bourgeoise, whose lewd dance was more than merely acceptable to the merely human, all-too-human morality of her

---

2. As cited in Trueblood, *The Humor of Christ*, 116.

3. As cited in Trueblood, *The Humor of Christ*, 33.

4. Kierkegaard, JP 2, 1717.

5. "The matter is quite simple. A person should begin with loving the unseen, God, because then he himself will learn what it is to love. But that he actually loves the unseen will be known by his loving the brother he sees; the more he loves the unseen, the more will he love the people he sees. It is not the reverse, that the more he rejects those he sees; the more he loves the unseen, since in that case God is changed into an unreal something, a delusion." Kierkegaard, WOL, 160. From Kierkegaard's "deliberation" on "Our Duty to Love Those We See," based on 1 John 4:20.

6. We have good reason to believe she was of the bourgeoise, as will be seen below.

7. Martin Andic explains the reduplication of love: "whereby love does to the lover what the lover does for others . . . existing in it, one will exist in it for other people, or communicate it so that they may exist in it too." Andic, "Love's Redoubling," 15, 19–20. Kierkegaard writes, "the one who loves is or becomes what he does." (WOL, 281.)

mediocre bourgeoise society. The Canaanitish woman's truly passionate love that risked so much, as we will see, serves to model for all time the love that cannot be lived by or through the bourgeoise "love of God" that "commences when the vegetative life is in full swing, when the hands are comfortably folded over the stomach, when the head is reclining on a soft easy chair, and when a drowsy glance is raised toward the ceiling, toward higher things."[8] Also, and more importantly, any bourgeoise settlement's "love of God" can no more contain God's love, even when "reduplicated" in and through us, than can any human-made temple contain God (1 Kgs 8:27, Acts 17:24).

Thus, in Mark's next scene, he abruptly (or maybe not considering these things) shows the kingdom's expansion through the daring faith of a Gentile woman, a "single individual," coming out from the "natural" prejudices of her own bourgeoise crowd which would restrict her from doing so.[9] Helmut Thielicke writes,

> For to come she has to overcome the prejudices of her people against the figure of the Nazarene. She has to cross the frontier of another land. She has to enter a country which in nationality and outlook is divided by an abyss from all that is accepted around her. Finally, her coming involves a risk. She knows of Him only by hearsay. Perhaps the reports are deceptive. She has to accept the possibility not merely that her actions will be disappointingly futile but that it will leave her open to censure.[10]

Mark thus interjects great moments of drama through this high-stakes situation for one individual woman which has ramifications for many nations.[11] He presents a serious dialogue at turns dangerous, humorous, and witty, between two equally passionate and colorful individuals. And God's kingdom power is again released as the consequence of the vital interaction.

---

8. Kierkegaard, JP 1, 220.

9. In regard to women in particular becoming separate from the crowds in Mark's gospel, Rhoads, Dewey and Michie write "Many of the minor characters are women. They are in the crowds. They are among Jesus' new family of mothers and sisters and brothers. As part of the crowd, they receive the invitation to renounce themselves and follow Jesus . . . Many show courage in flouting social expectations and religious customs . . . Jesus lifts up women as examples for the disciples to follow, such as the woman who anoints him and the poor widow." Rhoads et. al., Mark *as Story,* 133.

10. Thielicke, *The Silence of God,* 11–12.

11. "We must remember that the Marcan story was written primarily for Gentile Christians, who had much in common with this woman" Turlington, *Mark,* 327. This statement may be qualified by noting that her social status may not have been in common with many or most Gentile Christians (as we will see).

Therefore, we will consider four main aspects of this scene: a bold venture for an answer to a pressing need; a parabolic and humorous response that was both repelling and inviting; the highest passion of faith which overcame the "offense;" and the "crumbs" of new life that fall from the table of the mirthful "surplus savior."

A dry yet bold humor seems to pervade this account. It is perhaps hinted at from the very beginning, since the immediate but comically ongoing "intention" of Jesus and the disciples has been to find some rest. Since the time the disciples returned from their "two by two" mission in 6:31 we have seen several dramatic scenes of "near escapes" from the incessant activity across land and sea only at every point be drawn back into the fray. It perhaps portrays a "comedy of errors" in which the mishaps invariably give way to the miraculous works of God. The comedic atmosphere seems pervasive, so that just as Jesus "*could not be hidden*" (7:24), perhaps neither can the childlike humor of Jesus which Mark may have known of and intentionally portrayed in his gospel. The humor of Kierkegaard has often been noted and there is some evidence he thought that Jesus had a well-developed sense of humor.[12] At any rate, as we proceed, we will note the humor of both Jesus and of Kierkegaard in this chapter's reading of the divine humor that "has overcome the world."[13]

THE BOLD VENTURE OF A GENTILE WOMAN

One of the epigrams at the head of this chapter has to do with what Soren Kierkegaard called "venturing," an activity requiring "earnestness." In a sense, the statement simply fills in the adage, "nothing ventured—nothing gained":

> If I have ventured wrongly, well, then life helps me by punishing me. But if I have not ventured at all, who helps me then?[14]

The woman in this story certainly ventured and did so earnestly. If she ventured "wrongly . . . life would punish her." Life is helpfully corrective but can only be so when given the opportunity. In her case, life might have corrected her by showing her to the door others thought she should not have entered. But her venture, for the sake of her demon-possessed daughter, was worth her risk. She would have probably appreciated Pascal's wager, or

---

12. Kierkegaard notes humor in various statements of Jesus, much the same as does Elton Trueblood. See Kierkegaard, JP 2, 1682; 1686.
13. Kierkegaard, JP 2, 1717.
14. Kierkegaard, SD, 34.

Kierkegaard's leap, and have taken them up on their faith ventures. W. H. Auden wrote,

> Pascal's "wager" and Kierkegaard's "leap" are neither of them quite adequate descriptions, for the one suggests prudent calculation and the other perverse arbitrariness. Both, however, have some value: the first calls men's attention to the fact that in all other spheres of life they are constantly acting on faith and quite willingly, so that they have no right to expect religion to be an exception; the second reminds them that they cannot live without faith in something, and that when the faith which they have breaks down, when the ground crumbles under their feet, they have to leap even into uncertainty if they are to avoid certain destruction.[15]

She seemed to be one who simply recognized how life works and was willing to risk its correction for what she hoped to gain. She had heard how Jesus routinely dismissed the demons. With a demon-possessed daughter, her response was a foregone conclusion. If anything, her earnestness sought to steal the fire of God's attention in the face of the likely "life-correction" her female and Gentile approach to a Jewish Rabbi portended.

There may be another aspect of her personal status which speaks to a quality of her person which was exhibited by her willingness to fall before Jesus in her lowliness of need. David Garland explains that she may have been of the upper crust in her society and how her exchange with Jesus might further reveal that she was rather "remarkable." He writes,

> The city of Tyre was well stocked with produce from the hinterland of Galilee (see Acts 12:20), while those who grew the food frequently went hungry. Economically, Tyre took bread away from Galilee. Galileans perceived Tyre politically as posing a permanent threat with expansionist policies since there were no natural boundaries to mark off the two regions. The hostility between Tyrians and Jews is reflected in Josephus's statement that the people from Tyre are "our bitterest enemies" (*Aq. Ap.* 1 § 70). At the outbreak of the Jewish revolt against Rome, he reports that Tyrians killed and imprisoned many Jews (*J.W.* 2.18.5 § 478). This woman is, therefore, not just a Gentile but a member of a resented class of privileged foes. She has a lot of Gentile chutzpa to ask a Galilean Jewish healer for help. It would be analogous to a rich Brahmin pulling up in a fancy limousine to a shelter run by Mother Teresa and insisting that

---

15. Auden, LTK, 17–18.

she leave her untouchable charges to pray over her sick child. Would we be surprised if she were treated less than kindly? If this woman does come from the domineering high society, her acceptance of such a term as little dog for herself and for her daughter would be "all the more remarkable."[16]

If she was from the higher strata "bourgeoise" of Tyrian society, this would reveal even more of her earnestness and the possibility of "life-corrections" in the form of insult or derision had she been rebuffed by Jesus. In any case, she certainly evidenced a venturesome boldness that probably surpassed that of others seen to this point in Mark's gospel. Yet we also see a humility in the fact that she came before Jesus kneeling as a beggar. This seems to reveal a humility before God. In his ironic portrayal of "The Anxieties of the Heathen"—aimed at contemporaneous "Copenhagen Pagans" (Christians)—Kierkegaard says the following about "the anxiety of highness":

> The heathen in the high place is without God in the world . . . the heathen is ignorant of what true highness is. He knows no other highness than this earthly sort—and to know truly what highness is, is impossible, since he is in himself untruth, vapor, vain imagination, from which no cognition of truth can issue, except that this is what it is . . . Thus it is the heathen of high estate lives in highness. That there are many beneath him he knows full well; but what he does not know is beneath him, that nevertheless is beneath him—the abyss. One can become or be a Christian only as, or in the character of, a lowly man.[17]

Given what we have seen (and will come to see) of this woman, it is likely that she was humble regarding the temptation of "the anxiety of highness." Her humility could have been caused by prior societal humiliation due to her daughter's possession. That may have deepened her resolve to go to the Galilean Jesus. The past histories of people appearing in the gospel accounts are not revealed except in the barest details or intimations. But it must be supposed that their histories were important preparation for the gospel so that this account is part of what Jesus called the work in "the fields" that were already "white for harvest" (John 4:35). That divine "agriculture" is here seen in the harvest stage in an unnamed Gentile woman's bold venture answered by a very interesting "invitation."

---

16. Garland, *Mark*, 293.

17. Kierkegaard, CD, 59, 60, 56. The term "Copenhagen Pagans" is from Possen, "On Kierkegaard's Copenhagen Pagans," 35–59.

THE PARABLE OF THE OFFENSIVE INVITATION

The short exchange between the woman and Jesus becomes centered upon his verbal and essentially parabolic response to her petition. She comes begging Jesus for the sake of her daughter and his "answer" is to tell her *a story about a master of a household, children, their bread, and house dogs*. The story is perhaps more obviously "invitational" than some other parables because his obvious inference is that she and her daughter are *in* the parable, albeit as "the dogs."[18] Her needful determination was obviously accompanied by an intuitive mind that quickly grasped several "talking points" in this odd and seemingly odious invitation: She and her daughter were *in the scene*, albeit as the dogs; They were *in the master's house*, although apparently of less "immediate" concern to the master; There *was bread*, although the children must be fed *first;* This "first" implied a wondrous *second,* the opportunity implicitly "hidden" in what on the face of it appeared an insulting and offensive brush-off. We note the following regarding this seemingly harsh story with a wondrously serendipitous result.

The first thing to note is how easily Jesus was able to subvert the accepted narrative of the relation of the Gentiles to God. It *seemed* that Jesus simply narrated a typical story that did not hide the "given" Jewish estimation of the Gentiles as dogs. His story *seemingly* "put them in their place." But a few "innocuous" elements in his creative telling of the Jewish status quo, seized upon by the venturous Gentile woman, subverted what might otherwise have been the outcome of such a "put off."

The second thing is to note why Jesus gave her this subversive invitation. There were at least several reasons but the most important is that Jesus' subversion of the story was essentially a reversion, so to speak, to the Abrahamic covenant wherein "Israel" was chosen to be the means of blessing for all nations, not the means of their exclusion (Genesis 18:18, 22:18, 26:4). That Jesus affirmed the priority of the order of means and end, also recognized by Paul in Romans 1:16; 2:9–10, only confirms that his "riddle" to her was based in the redemptive aim of the Abrahamic Covenant. Of not less importance is that Jesus here draws the "universal" focus of the Abrahamic covenant from the nations in abstract to the nations in concrete. He brings it to the very specificity of this Gentile woman he saw before him begging for the "salvation" of her offspring. Thus, Jesus *saw* her, in distinction to the Pharisees and scribes, his own disciples, or anyone else unable to see

---

18. This common usage of "dogs" to refer to Gentiles is shown in a comment in the Babylonian Talmud: "As the sacred food was intended for men, but not for the dogs, the Torah was intended to be given to the Chosen People, but not to the Gentiles." As cited in Juel, *Mark,* 108.

persons *as persons*. Jesus wonderfully exhibits the "works of love" centered upon "the person we see" and the God of love who *commands* us to love *non-preferentially* as God does. John Baggett writes,

> The eyes of Jesus did not view . . . the despised in terms of the popular stereotypes and distinctions of superiority and inferiority of the day; the eyes of Jesus always saw *others*, regardless of their shortcomings, as human beings, fellow children of Adam, and loved of God.[19]

Moreover, this Syrophoenician woman, by "entering" the story as a "dog" that can eat the crumbs falling *now,* "begs the question" that the time of the Gentile harvest had already arrived.

The third thing of note is the reason Jesus used the parabolic method to subvert the usual narrative that had ungodly and dehumanizing results. We noted in the discussions of the parables in Mark 4 that they were examples of what Kierkegaard called "indirect communication," devised to communicate the gospel at a deeper potentially transforming level if/when people accept the invitation to place themselves *in* the parabolic scene. James Edwards says:

> The woman is the first person in Mark to hear and understand a parable of Jesus . . . That she answers Jesus from "within" the parable, that is, in the terms by which Jesus addressed her, indicates that she is the first person in the Gospel to *hear* the word of God to her.[20]

The fourth thing of note is the humorous aspect of the parable, which is easily overlooked. We will dedicate the next section to this.

THE HUMOR OF THE OFFENSIVE INVITATION

The humor in this parable and in others Jesus told, and his general sense of humor, most often consisted in *irony*.[21] Irony, and humor in general, are present in statements or scenes when two aspects within it present *a surprise*. In the case of this parable, the surprise is that it *eventually*—through the *witty* contribution of the woman—portrays Israelites and Gentiles both

---

19. Baggett, *Seeing Through the Eyes,* 136–37, emphasis mine. Terry Cross sees Jesus' action toward others as essential for the next century, saying "It is this making-room-for-the-other that must become the very essence of the life of the church in the twenty-first century." Cross, *People of God's Presence,* 51.

20. Cited in Keller, *Kings Cross,* 89.

21. See Trueblood, *The Humor of Christ,* 55.

eating of the same bread, in God's house, and doing so as nearly as possible at the same space-time moment, given the historical outworking of what is called "the scandal of particularity."[22] How humor "works" in this regard in relation to Christ's humor is noted by Trueblood who says,

> What we require, for Christ's kind of humor, are two ingredients, *surprise* and *inevitability*. There is a connecting which we do not expect, but which nevertheless, seems absolutely valid when once it is presented. "First of all," said Robert Frost, "the coupling that moves you, that stirs you, is an association of two things you don't expect to see associated." Frost was repeating, in essence, the insight of Soren Kierkegaard . . . "Humor is always a concealed pair."[23]

The way irony works in an ironic statement is that it appears to say one thing while in fact denying it's "truth." Thus, the statement itself is not the truth of the answer, but the way *to* the truth which is *the surprise*. Applying this to Jesus' statement to the Gentile woman, the apparently true answer to her request was the "no" of "*it is not right to take the children's bread and throw it to the dogs.*" But as we saw above, this ironic statement is not the truth, but "the way" *to* the truth which was a permissive "yes" and thus agreeable to her*: "Yes, Lord; yet even the dogs under the table eat the children's crumbs."*

Trueblood calls this ironic back-and-forth discussion "a humorous dialogue" because of the surprising outcome, a reversal of the expectations.[24] Many commentators have questioned the presence of humor in this account, but Trueblood seems to be correct that her response certainly contained humor by reversing the outcome of the whole story, and that Jesus'

> "immediate and friendly response to the woman's wit" was a "clue to the whole encounter"—because "if Christ could respond so readily to the banter of another, there is reason to suppose that there was an element of banter in *His* own earlier and apparently insulting comments."[25]

In sum, the potentially offensive statement of Jesus was a parabolic and ironic riddle that, for that reason, became the means of providing her an invitation to the bread of life. She perceived and willingly placed herself in

---

22. In his many books Lesslie Newbigin treated important aspects of this "problem" in a valuable way. (For an introduction see Weston, *Lesslie Newbigin*, 48–53, 102–3; and Christman, *Gospel*, 95–99.)

23. Trueblood, *The Humor of Christ*, 50.

24. Trueblood's chapter on this encounter is called "*A Humorous Dialogue.*" See Trueblood, *The Humor of Christ*, 116–25.

25. Trueblood, *The Humor of Christ*, 122–23.

Jesus' parabolic mirror, exhibiting the earnestness God calls forth, in answer to the gospel thus declared.

> When you read God's Word, in everything you read, continually say to yourself: It is I to whom it is speaking, it is I about whom it is speaking—this is earnestness, precisely this is earnestness.[26]

THE HIGHEST PASSION OVERCOMES OFFENSE

The possibility of offense at Jesus statement must not be overlooked. The ironic outcome could not have transpired had she simply taken offense.[27] The potential offensiveness of Jesus' "answer" was indeed a "means" of grace but could only be so if she perceived and responded to it as such. For her to respond "correctly" necessitated an inner transformation, and that was indeed the reason Jesus presented her such a means. Baggett clarifies Jesus' intentions, saying,

> In the dialogue we see Jesus challenging the woman, who responds in a way that Jesus approves. Jesus' challenge, which to us may seem to be uncharacteristically depreciating, is not intended to degrade but to evoke consciousness.[28]

From this perspective, Jesus' answer to her exhibits God's own earnestness that calls forth the earnest response of faith. Kierkegaard's statement regarding God's incarnation applies to all his redemptive purposes:

> When God lets himself be born and become man . . . when God does this, then this fact is the earnestness of existence. And in turn, the earnestness in this earnestness is this: that everyone *shall* have an opinion about it.[29]

---

26. Kierkegaard, FSE/JFY 36. See Christman, *Behold*, 1–10.

27. This overall narrative whereby she achieved "ironic faith" exemplifies the growth from "childish (Dionysian) faith in the expected" to "mature (ironic) faith-imagination that grows in/through the unexpected" so masterfully narrated and expounded upon in Lynch, *Images of Faith*, 10, 35–45, 111–32.

28. Baggett, *Seeing Through the Eyes*, 135. Helmut Thielicke, following Matthew's version of this story notes that Jesus' first response was silence, "he answered not a word" (Matt 15:23). Matthew's account may add another layer to the possibility of offense due to the silence of God she had to overcome. In Mark's account one could posit God's silence in the fact that her desperation may indicate that God had been silent regarding her daughter's need before she even came to Jesus. See Thielicke, *The Silence of God*, 10.

29. Kierkegaard, SD, 130.

God calls forth our earnestness and passion through means such as the riddle Jesus "answered" the woman with which could have offended her. God's aim is to call forth and cultivate the passion of faith in us, as he did with her by "communicating capability" through the means of a potentially faith-offending yet faith-inciting revelatory parable.[30] Kierkegaard writes,

> Faith is the highest passion in a person. There perhaps are many in every generation who do not come to faith, but no one goes further.[31]

FRAGMENTS FROM THE BANQUET OF THE MIRTHFUL SAVIOR

What is most surprising in the daring faith of the Gentile woman is that she "got it." She "got" what the disciples had repeatedly *not* gotten about Jesus and faith. Her "perception" develops an easily overlooked theme in Mark's gospel which is evident in the following texts that lead up to her dialogue with Jesus.[32] We have placed emphasis on the two aspects of the theme.

- 4:13 And he said to them, *"Do you not understand this parable? How then will you understand all the parables?*
- 5:28–30 For she said, **"If I touch even his garments, I will be made well."** And immediately the flow of blood dried up, and she felt in her body that she was healed of her disease. And Jesus, perceiving in himself that power had gone out from him, immediately turned about in the crowd and said, **"Who touched my garments?"**
- 6:41–44 And taking the five loaves and the two fish, he looked up to heaven and said a blessing and broke the loaves and gave them to the disciples to set before the people. And he divided the two fish among them all. And they all ate and were satisfied. **And they took up twelve baskets full of broken pieces and of the fish.** And those who ate the loaves were five thousand men.
- 6:47–52 And when evening came, the boat was out on the sea, and he was alone on the land. And he saw that they were making headway painfully, for the wind was against them. And about the fourth watch of the night he came to them, walking on the sea. He meant to pass

---

30. See Tietjen, *Kierkegaard, Communication, and Virtue*, 49–57.
31. Kierkegaard, FT, 122.
32. The texts in this list are from the ESV.

- by them, but when they saw him walking on the sea they thought it was a ghost, and cried out, for they all saw him and were terrified. But immediately he spoke to them and said, "Take heart; it is I. Do not be afraid." And he got into the boat with them, and the wind ceased. And they were utterly astounded, **for they did not understand about the loaves,** *but their hearts were hardened.*
- 6:56 And wherever he came, in villages, cities, or countryside, they laid the sick in the marketplaces and implored him **that they might touch even the fringe of his garment.** And as many as touched it were made well.
- 7:17 And when he had entered the house and left the people, his disciples asked him about the parable. *And he said to them, "Then are you also without understanding?*
- 7:27–28 And he said to her, "Let the children be fed first, for it is not right to take the children's bread and throw it to the dogs." But she answered him, "Yes, Lord; **yet even the dogs under the table eat the children's crumbs."**

The common two-fold thread is the disciples' lack of understanding of the power of Jesus that comes through "fragmentary" means. To help illustrate the twofold theme we have italicized the explicit words that show the disciples lack of understanding and bolded the explicit words that show the fragmentary means of healing. In a very real sense, the disciples have been living in a parable of the power of God they do not understand. But the woman in 7:24–30 placed herself in the parabolic picture of life Jesus presented to her and thereby understood.

The connection of fragmentary means of healing and understanding was already made explicit in Mark 6:52, when Jesus linked their hardened misunderstanding to the *leftover fragments* of the loaves. But this Gentile woman, upon encountering Jesus for the first time, *understands* and *has faith* that mere crumbs are sufficient for her. In this way she is similar to the woman who had faith that only needed a touch of the hem of Jesus' garment. But the difference between the women is that the Gentile woman had to first understand the "life-parable" that the disciples did not. James Edwards points out the contrast between the Gentile woman and the disciples:

> She appeared to understand the purpose of Israel's Messiah better than Israel does. Her pluck and persistence are a testimony to her trust in the sufficiency and surplus of Jesus: his provision for the disciples and Israel will be abundant enough to provide for one such as herself... What an irony! Jesus seeks desperately

> to teach his chosen disciples—yet they are dull and uncomprehending . . . after one sentence she understands his mission and receives unambiguous commendation . . . How is it possible? The answer is that the woman is the first person in Mark to hear and understand a parable of Jesus . . . That she answers from "within" the parable, that is, in the terms by which Jesus addressed her, indicates that she is the first person in the Gospel to *hear* the word of Jesus to her.[33]

Edwards' comments summarize the theme we have been following as emphasized in the pertinent passages. It is in this account that we see the theme made most explicit, namely that the gospel works faith through fragmentary and parabolic means. This is perhaps *the faith apologetic* for Mark's gospel that has therefore been seemingly penned for the follower at second hand. Before moving on, we should call attention to the fact that in 8:1–21 Mark brings this theme to a head regarding the disciples, we could even say, to a "boiling point."

To conclude this chapter, we will further consider the significance of the Syrophoenician woman as Mark's "Cornelius" at this "turning point" of his gospel.

JESUS' SUBVERSION OF "EXCLUSIVITY"

Simply put, Jesus subverted religious exclusivity through redefinition. He essentially redefined the characters in the longstanding narrative of the coming of God's kingdom. He redefined "us" and "them." This account encapsulates the redefinition of God's family which has already been seen earlier in Mark's gospel, in which the emphasis was for the most part given to who was or was not "doing the will of God" (Mark 3:35). At this point Jesus parabolically "playing the good Pharisee" provides a pointed *illustration* of the ungodly heart which he had just *exposited* in his challenge to the Pharisees regarding *Corban* (Mark 7:20–23).

The way that Jesus redefined the people of God in this account in Mark was by redefining "the dogs." An interesting and somewhat humorous illustration of this redefinition is provided in a discussion by Drusilla Scott

---

33. Cited in Keller, *King's Cross,* 89. See also in Garland, *Mark,* 288–89, who says: "The woman's response reveals that she comprehends more about the bread that Jesus offers than even his disciples do. They have witnessed the feeding of the five thousand (6:31–44, 52) and will witness the feeding of four thousand (8:1–10) but still do not understand the bread that Jesus offers (8:14–21)."

of scientist/philosopher Michael Polanyi's concept of "tacit knowing." She writes,

> Here is a story about dog identification from Leila Berg's book – 'Look at kids'.
>
> "At the time I ran a nursery group we had an Old English sheepdog. The first time I let him into the garden, the children were amazed. 'What is that?' 'It's a bear!' 'It's a pussy.' 'It's a bunny.' 'It's a lion – (at this last, everyone ran away into a small flurry and came back half a minute later) 'What is it?'
>
> "It's a dog," I said. All hell broke loose. Tom hurled himself at me as if he were fighting for his life. 'It's not a dog! It's not a dog!' He screamed, feet and fists pulverizing me.
>
> "In the middle of saving myself and comforting him, I wondered how any two-year-old comes to learn that alsatians, pekinese, collies, Great Danes, chihuahuas, are all dogs?[34]

This story can illustrate Jesus' redefinition of "dogs" in several ways.

First, Jesus is the only "scientific" classifier of what breeds of "dogs" are *offensively invited* to the house and if coming let in to partake of the children's crumbs. Other would-be classifiers might be provoked to a fearful frenzy at this admittance process as their old categories for qualification are shattered.[35]

Second, the "scientific" method of Jesus is much the same as that of Kierkegaard's anonymous preacher of the "Ultimatum" appearing at the end of *Either/Or*. His *offensive invitation* given to all is the ultimatum: "THE EDIFICATION IMPLIED IN THE THOUGHT THAT AS AGAINST GOD WE ARE ALWAYS IN THE WRONG."[36] Applying this to Jesus' own redefinition of "sons" in the parable of Luke 15, we can wax Kierkegaardian and say that the "younger brother" (aesthetic pleasure-seeking Gentiles) and the "older brother" (ethicist moralizing Jews) are both "in the wrong." This means that both "sons" (Jewish and Gentile) are "dogs." This is how Paul summarizes the gospel: "God has consigned all to disobedience, that he may

---

34. Scott, *Everyman Revived*, 53–54.

35. In rather Kierkegaardian fashion, what Timothy Keller writes of the parable of the two sons in Luke 15 applies well to Jesus' subversion of the Jewish norms in the original situation here and potentially in relation to every retelling thereof, such as Mark's: "No, the original listeners were not melted into tears by this story but rather they were thunderstruck, offended, and infuriated. Jesus's purpose is not to warm our hearts but to shatter our categories." Keller, *Prodigal God*, 10.

36. Kierkegaard, EO2, 343. This was an early understanding of Kierkegaard regarding the human/divine relation as evidenced by the nearly exact journal entry from 1840–41. See Kierkegaard, JP 5, 5486.

have mercy on all" (Rom 11:32, ESV). Timothy Keller provides a veritable Kierkegaardian and Pauline commentary in his exposition of the parable of the two sons:

> This means that Jesus's message, which is "the gospel," is a completely different spirituality. The gospel of Jesus is not religion or irreligion, morality or immorality, moralism or relativism, conservatism or liberalism. Nor is it something halfway along a spectrum between two poles—it is something else altogether. The gospel is distinct from the other two approaches: In its view, everyone is wrong, everyone is loved, and everyone is called to recognize this and change.[37]

Third, although the gospel views all as "dogs," this does not mean that the reconstituted family of dogs is just a homogeneous group. Rather, just as in the story above the fact is that "alsatians, pekinese, collies, Great Danes, chihuahuas, are all dogs." Likewise, God's *one* family or "kingdom" consists in people "from every tribe and language and people and nation" (Rev 5:9, ESV).

The sheer positivity of the gospel, which is captured by Kierkegaard's "edifying" *Ultimatum*, must not be obscured by any over-sensitivity to its "offensive invitation." Its positivity is exhibited by considering that Jesus' subversion of religious exclusivity included at least four components that "all things work together for good, for those who are called according to his purpose" (Rom 8:28). First, Jesus exposed and subverted the "religious" othering of the Gentile "dogs, the reducing the Other to the meaning I give him or her," and as though they are essentially different than God's "children" seated at the table in his parable.[38] Second, Jesus viewed the Gentile woman and her daughter as real *others* in the sense that each person is unique and made in the image of God, the ultimate *other*.[39] Third, Jesus was the ultimate *other* who became (and had to become) the incarnate and atoning God-man in order to confer true *otherhood* for all humans and humanity itself.[40] Fourth, Jesus is the *other* who *in love* receives all *others* as God's children, as

---

37. Keller, *Prodigal God*, 44–45.

38. The quoted phrase is Westphal's narration of the thought of Emmanuel Levinas. Westphal, *Levinas and Kierkegaard*, 39.

39. Westphal writes, ". . . Kierkegaard's God is unambiguously personal, an interlocutor . . . who is other than the human precisely by being the 'first other,' the 'other par excellence,' or the 'absolute other.'" Westphal, *Levinas and Kierkegaard*, 71.

40. We are consciously emphasizing the view of T. F. Torrance wherein the incarnation and atonement of the God-man are inseparable parts of redemption. See Torrance, *Incarnation*, 194–96.

should we also as those *in* God's love.[41] For all these reasons and more, as Sir Thomas Browne said, "the Canaanitish woman lives more happily without a name, than Herodias with one." For her bold venture became an integral part of the story of the ages, the gathering of the world's grain that is white for harvest.

---

41. M. Jamie Ferreira writes, "Note that Kierkegaard imagines God as not saying "if you want to *show* that you love me," but saying "if you want to *love me*"—service to others is not the sign of love for God, it *is* the love." Ferreira, "Levinas and Kierkegaard," 50.

10

Sighing to Heaven, Spitting and Restoring on Earth

The Gospel of Groaning, Hearing and Speaking

Mark 7:31–37

31 Then he returned from the region of Tyre and went through Sidon to the Sea of Galilee, in the region of the Decapolis. 32 And they brought to him a man who was deaf and had a speech impediment, and they begged him to lay his hand on him. 33 And taking him aside from the crowd privately, he put his fingers into his ears, and after spitting touched his tongue. 34 And looking up to heaven, he sighed and said to him, "Ephphatha," that is, "Be opened." 35 And his ears were opened, his tongue was released, and he spoke plainly. 36 And Jesus charged them to tell no one. But the more he charged them, the more zealously they proclaimed it. 37 And they were astonished beyond measure, saying, "He has done all things well. He even makes the deaf hear and the mute speak."

Jan. 29 But have you never been so indescribably distressed, that the power of sorrow over your whole being was almost like the power of nature: then you experienced what it means to be dumb, experience the feeling of being unable, even though your life were at stake, to express the agony that rocked deep within you, and selfish of itself made you dumb—in order that you might not rid yourself of it. For that is how infinite sorrow is egotistical; it makes a man dumb in order to keep him in its power.[1] —*Soren Kierkegaard*

One could imagine the above excerpt from the journal of Soren Kierkegaard as also being the "unspoken thoughts" of the deaf and speech-impaired man in Mark 7, before Jesus healed him. That his impediment prevented him pleading on his own behalf could simply be a statement of fact, but perhaps Mark has chosen this incident to demonstrate individual hopelessness that cannot even *wish* internally, let alone outwardly express it. He seems almost in the despair that is "egotistical" by keeping him "in its power." Perhaps that is why he appears to have presented—even epitomized—a slightly more difficult case for Jesus who usually works miracles instantaneously. We are obviously to some extent pressing our Kierkegaardian reading here but cannot say that Mark could not have sought to demonstrate hopelessness regarding truly following Jesus such as will be increasingly seen in his gospel, for instance in the account of the "rich young ruler" in 10:22–26, and even in all the disciples. Whatever the real reason, in this "unusual" instance, the healing seems to require extra time—taking him aside privately, placing his fingers in the man's deaf ears, mysteriously spitting and then presumably touching his inarticulate tongue with some spittle, and finally, deeply sighing and then saying, "be opened." Only then were his ears opened and his tongue loosed so that plain words could flow forth.

Imagining a correlation of thought between this man in Mark and that exhibited in Kierkegaard's journal excerpt helps to demonstrate that the process of becoming healed by God is a work that begins in *one moment in the fulness of time* but stretches into all *moments*.[2] A Marcan theme of faith in *process*, which has all along been present by implication in many of those coming to faith, is coming closer to the surface. Mark is beginning to overtly draw together several factors: 1) the stubborn inability of the disciples to understand and have full faith, 2) the truth that a mere fragment from the surplus power of Jesus is fully sufficient for us, 3) the fact that full healing and understanding, faith and conversion, is a process, 4) the outworking of this process is confusing and difficult.

Mark's concern of a faith-process has always been implied in a relation between physical deliverances and the inner processes of faith since he has continually shown the necessity of (someone's) faith (even if only that of Jesus) for there to be deliverance. But now Mark seems to be more

---

1. Dru, *Soul of Kierkegaard*, 136.
2. See Christman, *Behold*, 36–42.

conspicuously shifting to a more direct treatment of that necessity by calling attention to the parallel between the *miraculous deliverances* and the *mundane* human needs. That parallel is directly related to the person's "mundane" need of *conscious* God-relation. In other words, healing the blind signifies giving spiritual *sight;* healing deafness signifies giving spiritual *hearing;* healing muteness signifies giving spiritual *speech;* and so on. And all such things have to do with gaining spiritual *understanding* and/or *faith* for living *today* in relation to God. One commentator notes the significance of miracles as such signs in that they

> symbolize the Christian faith—sight, hearing, resurrection— which become full realities only after the death and resurrection of Jesus, these physical cures cannot really be spoken of with understanding at this stage, because they point forward to events and spiritual changes which still lie in the future.[3]

But Mark's post-resurrection writing to an audience privy to this insider's view already directs attention to Jesus' miracles pointing to such future realities, namely our present-day mundane life-realities.[4] The difficulties humans face is in understanding the true significance of miracles as signs pointing to their basic needs as holistic creatures of finitude and infinitude, temporality and eternity, necessity and freedom. In sum, at this point in Mark the dynamics within the process of coming to practical faith and understanding are more conspicuously surfacing. We need faith to live *now* in light of the gospel that provides spiritual sight, hearing, and speech.

BEING HEALED AND BECOMING A CHRISTIAN

Mark's deaf and speech-impaired Gentile man in this account and the Jewish blind man in 8:22–26 frame the disciples' lack of spiritual sight and hearing lamented by Jesus in 8:18. Thus this Gentile man serves to preview the Jewish man so that in a sense both serve as counterpart of the disciples (and all disciples to come) and thus implies that all will likewise require divine *process* to receive full healing.[5] Thus the man signifies discipleship's tension

---

3. Morna Hooker, as cited in Garland, *Mark*, 299.

4. "After reading just one page of Mark the reader has become an initiate, already knowing more than most characters will ever get to know in the story." Iersel, *Reading Mark*, 42.

5. We are following (but also expanding upon) Bas van Iersel when he writes of the significance of Mark's blind man that Jesus healed (also by a process) just after lamenting the spiritual blindness of the disciples in 8:18: "The blind man whom he cures resembles the disciples and is at the same time their counterpart." Van Iersel, *Reading Mark*, 23.

between being Christ's follower (as a state) and becoming Christ's follower (through a process). His *being* healed—though in sum only requiring a very short span of time, nevertheless, was in reality a process of *becoming* healed. Likewise, given that such physical miracles were outward signs of spiritual and *present* workings of God, *being* a Christian is *also* the process of *becoming* a Christian. The process of Jesus doing things to this man's ears and tongue therefore *signifies* ongoing work God does to heal *our* spiritual faculties, or lack thereof, for hearing and speaking. Presumably, such "hearing" would signify an *increasing reception* of the gospel and "speaking" of that gospel reception would signify an *increasing understanding*. In sum, Mark's concern is to exhibit and promote *the process* of hearing the gospel in increasing reception and understanding.

Similarly, Kierkegaard rarely spoke of *being* a Christian, and instead typically spoke of *becoming* a Christian. Most of his descriptions of Christian faith exhibit this quality:

> Christianity is "*existence communication*," the "*communication of capability*;" Believing the objective truths of Christianity is worthless apart from the existential practice summarized by the statement "truth is subjectivity;" Christianity is *following*—not merely *admiring*—Christ our *prototype,* in active *contemporaneity* with him; Christian faith is only authentic when manifested in "*works of love*."[6]

These emphases make some uncomfortable, especially those whose Christian tradition emphasizes the objective doctrines and the "status" of *being a Christian* through assent to objective truth. But that is often to the detriment of *becoming a Christian* by subjectively and increasingly living in a faith-relation to God and for others through Jesus (James 2:14–26). Following James, his favorite book of the Bible, Kierkegaard rightly recognized an imbalance in the Protestant Christian tradition and saw the danger when Christianity is reduced to doctrinal assent.[7] He saw a merely outward objectivity as the essence of "Christendom." For it is not Christianity but *Christ*, the God-man, who *is* the way, the truth, and the life. Kierkegaard wrote,

> It is the other and really decisive side of Christianity which has been abolished in Christendom. Christianity has become a doctrine, but conversion, rebirth, imitation, dying away from

---

6. An ad-hoc summary.

7. Richard Bauckham says that Kierkegaard may have been unique in Church history as regards his favorite book of the Bible. Bauckham, "Kierkegaard and the Book of James," 39.

this world, renunciation, self-denial, etc.—they are as if blown away.[8]

It is those essentials that Kierkegaard speaks of as "blown away" that are the difficulty in the process of *becoming* that requires Christ to put his fingers in our ears, put his spittle on our tongue, and deeply sigh to heaven's power to fully heal. It is those essentials that lie beneath the following journal entries which narrate his deep difficulties in *being* a "converted" Christian, notwithstanding the breakthrough of April 19th.

- *Wednesday, April* 19, 1848. My whole being is changed. My reserve and self-isolation is broken—I must speak. Lord give thy grace . . . Now, with God's help, I shall be myself; I believe that Christ will help me to be victorious over my melancholy, and so I shall become a priest. And yet in that melancholy I loved the world, for I loved my melancholy.
- *April* 24, 1848, Easter Monday. No, no, my self-isolation cannot be broken, at least not now. The thought of breaking it occupies me so much, and at all times, that it only becomes more and more firmly embedded.
- *May* 11 There is something of despair in such resignation . . . then the possibility of faith presents itself to him in this form: whether he will believe by virtue of the absurd that God will help him temporally, (Here lie all the paradoxes.)[9]

The cause of his conflict was the "dying" side of *conversion,* or more accurately, *discipleship*. Thus, we'll next explore the dynamics of this process of *becoming/being* a Christian wherein "God will help him temporally" in this gift/task.[10] (It seems best to construe Christianity as a dialectic tension between becoming and being a Christian *through faith* that requires both essential aspects.)

DYING TO SELF AND LIVING BY THE SPIRIT

"Dying to self" seems the biggest problem for "would-be" and "already" disciples as Mark will make increasingly clear in his gospel. Thus, from our point of view, it seems that God's biggest problem is "making" disciples which therefore becomes God's primary and universal "gospel-purpose"

---

8. Kierkegaard, JP 1, 397.
9. Dru, *Soul of Kierkegaard*, 137–39.
10. We will thus augment the prior reading in our "Epilogue" in Christman, *Behold*, 210–16.

(Matt 28:19). Most serious Christians, whether they use the Pauline terms or not, know that dying to self is the difficult but necessary *negative* side to the dialectically opposite *positive* side of Christian living. For the dialectical complex of *dying and living* are part and parcel of the one gospel, the proverbial two sides of the one coin. Sylvia Walsh calls this gospel dialectic "*Dying to the World and Self-Denial / New Life, Love, and Hope in the Spirit*" in her masterful treatment of the Christian life.[11] This dialectic is the reason that "the cross" of death is the central symbol of Christianity, with the understanding that the "resurrection life" follows it. But the order is important and cannot be bypassed. There is no spiritual "by-pass surgery" that can connect the arteries of God's new life in the Spirit to the diseased ones of a person's old life in sin. Kierkegaard was very concerned that we don't take God's grace in vain by merely "adding" Christ to our fallen human life and thus by-passing the "ordeal" of death-to-self:

> There is not one, not one Christian qualification into which Christianity does not first of all introduce as the middle term: death, dying to [*at afdoe*]—in order to protect the essentially Christian from being taken in vain . . . This life-giving in the Spirit is not a *direct* heightening of the natural life in a person in *immediate* continuation from and connection with it—what blasphemy! how horrible to take Christianity in vain this way!—it is a new life...literally a new life—because, mark this well, death comes in between, **dying to**, and life on the other side of death—yes, that is new life.
>
> Death goes in between; this is what Christianity teaches, you must die to. The life-giving Spirit is the very one who slays you; the first thing the life-giving Spirit says is that you must enter into death . . .
>
> Christianity is not what we human beings, both you and I, are all too eager to make it; it is not a quack doctor. A quack doctor is promptly at your service and immediately applies the remedy and bungles everything. Christianity waits before it applies its remedy.[12]

Following Paul, Kierkegaard held that the Spirit who gives new life does not simply enter the old life. If that were possible, the Spirit would be buried beneath the still-operating complex of sinful human desires. In essence, the human would remain king of his castle, and the Spirit the dutiful servant of his fortified self-centered life. A good illustration of this is Simon the

---

11. Walsh, *Living Christianly*, 79–112.
12. Kierkegaard, FSE/JFY, 75–77, 80. (Emphasis in bold print is ours.)

Magician, seen in Acts 8:9–25. He vainly sought to "purchase" the Holy Spirit from Peter and John to further his magic-career as "the power of God that is called Great" (Acts 8:10, ESV). Simon the magician may illustrate a more blatant desire than "normal" to add the Spirit to one's corrupt desires. But such a desire is nonetheless operative when persons seek to receive the Spirit while hoping to preserve and enhance their old self-seeking lives.

But this raises a question regarding how the Spirit of *life* brings "death." That process sounds like an oxymoron, but it is not, since "death" signifies the denial of the sinful desires of the *old-self*. *A first point* is that the self-denial in view is centered upon all that is taught in the gospels regarding the paradigmatic death of Christ. In Kierkegaardian words, it is "dying to" serving oneself for the sake of serving the gospel of the kingdom.[13] Salvation is being fitted into God's kingdom rather fitting salvation into our kingdom. For that is the oxymoronic contradiction and impossibility, as is the Spirit entering our old life. But this must also be dialectically qualified by *a second point*, the fact that the *passivity* of being fitted *coexists* with the *activity* of fitting ourselves into God's kingdom.

Both aspects, the passive and active, mean that this death to self is no matter of self-striving to imitate Christ under our own steam. We become new creatures through the Spirit. Nonetheless there is striving involved in that relation. Our striving to positively follow Christ in that relation, which by the way is rooted and grounded in God's love, reveals the need of negation, of "dying to," and helps bring it about.[14] The positive *living* of Christian life which consists of seeking first the kingdom, imitating Christ as our prototype, being willing to suffer for the gospel, loving all others as God loves them, necessarily presupposes and therefore includes *living* the negation of "dying to." The "positive" life-aim reveals our *natural* inability to "die to" and "live for" and therefore reveals the need and induces the faith for the empowering Spirit who thereby "kills" our old self that stands in the way of life in the Spirit. God also employs providential circumstances which Kierkegaard called "governance" to help "kill" our self-desires and self-reliance that would feign "achieving self-hood in God." For the two ways, "becoming a self by resting transparently in the power that establishes it" and "invent yourself whole cloth," are mutually exclusive.[15]

---

13. Kierkegaard, FSE/JFY, 80.

14. Thus M. Jamie Ferreira's apt commentary on the Christian life in active love as exhaustively expounded in Kierkegaard's *Works of Love* is called *Love's Grateful Striving*.

15. The first way is the already culturally unpopular (Christian) "formula" for selfhood from Anti-Climacus in Kierkegaard's *The Sickness Unto Death* and the second way seems the chosen "formula" promulgated to the masses in much of the world today. In essence, the second way is a form of "by-passing" the Christianly necessary *death* that

SIGHING TO HEAVEN, SPITTING AND RESTORING ON EARTH 153

In sum, God's gospel love and grace "pressure" us externally and internally, squeezing our new self out from the confines (death) of our old self into the new life of God's kingdom. Of course, this also necessitates a faith that willingly agrees and even desires to be so squeezed into the life beyond our old one.[16] Kierkegaard writes of this process in which Christian severity prevents taking the gospel in vain.

> Therefore Christianity's severity . . . lest it confirm you in nonsense . . . Is it cruel to be, if you please, cruel when it is unconditionally the only thing that can save from ruin and help to pull through? So it is with dying to.[17]

But this "beginning" with Christian severity does not end there, for it is "followed up" by the Spirit:

> Then, my listener, then—then comes the life-giving Spirit. When? When this has happened, when you are dead to . . . The Spirit brings *faith, the faith*—that is, faith in the strictest sense of the word, this gift of the Holy Spirit—only after death has come in between . . . Faith is against understanding; faith is on the other side of death. And when you died to yourself, to the world, then you also died to all immediacy in yourself, also to your understanding. It is when all confidence in yourself or in human support, and also upon God in an immediate way, is extinct, when every probability is extinct, when it is dark as on a dark night—it is indeed death we are describing—then comes the life-giving Spirit and brings faith.[18]

Thus, Kierkegaard shows that *true faith* is not an increase of what we humans may call faith but is only part of the old life. For it is a different type of faith, an ironic faith against the common understanding, born on the other side of death. It is born as a gift through the Spirit who, himself a gift given

---

"comes in between" to manufacture a "direct heightening of the natural life."

16. The reader should detect that faith must already be present for one to willingly respond to God's process. At the risk of seeming to contradict the emphasis on an "order" we have been (and still are) occupied with, we must add that Kierkegaard did not agree with the prevalent "order of salvation" in which individuals first repent in order that God may then give forgiveness and reconciliation. Kierkegaard writes of the true orthodox view: "Heterodoxly one may say that conversion precedes and conditions the forgiveness of sins; orthodoxly one may say: the forgiveness of sins precedes conversion and strengthens men to truly be converted." Cited in Rae, *Kierkegaard and Theology*, 101. Murray Rae's excellent discussion on forgiveness from 98–101 explains this important distinction. See Kierkegaard JP 2, 1208.

17. Kierkegaard, FSE/JFY, 80.

18. Kierkegaard, FSE/JFY, 81–82.

following death (John 16:5–16), brings faith along with him in the beginning of the new becoming that is *Christian* life.

Kierkegaard's "late" writings on the Holy Spirit are minimal in relation to the entirety of his authorship. And even in that minimal treatment we find complexity, tension, and unresolved questions. From the few excerpts we have already looked at, it might seem that he posited a neat, chronological order that would seem to result in the idea of a Christian norm, of *becoming* a Christian through that process. In other words, Christianity *is* about being a Christian *after becoming* one, after all. But Mark's accounts of *various* methods and necessities on the part of Jesus and the *varied* aspects of the human needs and responses would mitigate against a tidy system. Kierkegaard's thought on the working and reception of the Spirit would seem to also resist homogeneity. Thus, one commentator wisely states that we should probably not seek to systematize Kierkegaard's writings on the Holy Spirit:

> Kierkegaard is clear that the Holy Spirit is tremendously important for the late *For Self-Examination* and the unpublished *Judge For Yourself!* The scattered and undeveloped references throughout the rest of his corpus do not easily relate to each other or with the later explicit statements. A systematic articulation of the role of the Holy Spirit is, therefore, very difficult, and perhaps impossible. Perhaps Kierkegaard would not desire one.[19]

And this probably holds true regarding overly relying on systematizations of Mark or the entire Bible, mainly since we humans are doing the systematizing.

We have hopefully somewhat adequately demonstrated Kierkegaard's view of the ongoing realities of the process and tensions of Christian *becoming and being*. As our reading continues, especially in the volumes to follow on Mark 9–16, we hope to demonstrate that Mark saw the same ongoing realities. This process is ultimately due to the problems "disciples" have in overcoming spiritual blindness, deafness, and muteness. And those problems call for humility, patience, grace, and hope. Moreover, the gospel itself demonstrates God's own condescension to human weakness to the extent that the problem's "call" was also a call for God to humbly enter patience, grace, and hope. In Christ God has indeed humbled God's self to the lowest depths (Phil 2:5–8). But as for us, the call is as Kierkegaard describes:

---

19. Martens, "Emergence of the Holy Spirit," 221.

> Imitation must be affirmed to press toward humility. This, quite simply, is how it is done. Everyone must be measured by the prototype, by the ideal . . . Everyone has to measure himself before God by the requirement of ideality, and then before God—but responsibly—flee to grace.[20]

HEARING AND SPEAKING THE GOSPEL

At the beginning of this chapter, we noted that the healing of Mark's deaf and speech-impaired man *signified,* as part of the gospel message, gaining spiritual hearing (or understanding) and spiritual speech (or witnessing) as one transformed by that gospel. We also saw that the problem of truly hearing and understanding the gospel challenges (and ultimately "kills") the old self and necessitates the new self. Spiritual speech is "naturally" one of the first actions of the new self whereby the person simply witnesses to their newness. Mark's healed man did not need to tell others about Jesus to be a witness of what Jesus *did*. In other words, he would witness of Jesus' power even if he spoke "plainly" about the weather. Of course, the good news that God has unleashed such miraculous life-changing power in the world ought to be a worthy subject for *new speech* also.

What we are getting at is that there is *indirect* communication of the gospel that is based in the "mundane" acts of a disciple. But those can be "filled in" regarding their spiritual significance by *direct* communication of how the healing came to be. This is the "method" cited in 1 Peter 3:15 wherein active living in "hope" (indirect communication) leads to the opportunity for direct communication. The problem with much "witnessing" is that the latter is sometimes done apart from the former and in essence contradicts the indirect communication. Of course, the reason for this shortcoming is often because the "dying to" and "living for" has not much taken place. Mark Tietjen discusses this problem with a reference to a journal excerpt of Kierkegaard's:

> Indirect communication through lives rather than words is far more gripping and possibly more effective, and in the case of Christianity, appropriate:
>
> "To teach in actuality that the truth is ridiculed, etc., means to teach it as one ridiculed and scoffed at himself. To teach poverty in actuality means to teach it as one who is himself poor . . . To that extent all instruction ends in a kind of silence; for when

---

20. Kierkegaard, FSE/JFY, 198; JP 2, 1785.

> I existentially express it, it is not necessary for my speaking to be audible (JP 1:286 [#653])."
>
> Actions speak louder than words. Kierkegaard would simply add the following: (1) this is all the more true when the words have become so familiar that they've lost their meaning and (2) indirect communication through actions can more successfully draw actions out of the one who receives the communication.[21]

In his total communication with the Canaanite woman in Mark 7:24–30 Jesus perfectly embodied the gospel. This embodiment is something we will fall short of but nevertheless are meant to *be*. But the lack of perfection in this regard need not necessarily prevent witnessing if one is authentically pointing out that their "highest perfection" is in needing God. Therefore, regarding "speech," whether indirect or direct, the gospel witness of *needing God* can easily and even boldly be communicated, because it stands in great contrast to the secular view of life. Kierkegaard demonstrates why, saying:

> In a human being's relationship to God ... the more he needs God, the more deeply he comprehends that he is in need of God, and then the more he in his need presses forward to God, the more perfect he is. Therefore, the words "to be connected with the grace of God" will not only comfort a person, and then comfort him again every time earthly want and distress make him, so to speak mundanely, needful in comfort, but when he has really become attentive to the words they will call him aside, where he no longer hears the secular mentality's earthly mother tongue, the speech of human beings, the noise of the shopkeepers, but where the words explain themselves to him, confide to him the secret of perfection: that to need God is nothing to be ashamed of but is perfection itself, and that it is the saddest thing of all if a human being goes through life without discovering that he needs God.[22]

One major hindrance to proper *gospel witnessing* can be that the form of words is correct, like those of Jacob to Isaac, but the speaker's dialect reveals a "secular" imposter with an "earthly mother tongue." This happens if the gospel is shared as being a good *addition* to the old life—bypassing the utter imperfection of "normal" human life in its *infinite qualitative difference* from God. Therefore, gospel speakers should indirectly witness to the gospel of love by embodying their utter need thereof and by practicing its "works of love" toward "the other." This is an example where the importance

---

21. Tietjen, *Christian Missionary,* 113–14.
22. Kierkegaard, EUD, 303.

of the dialectic between dying to self and living in the Spirit comes to bear. Paul Martens' explanation of Kierkegaard's view of the Christian's works of love helps to explain this embodiment of the gospel way of *Christ* that the disciples eventually learned:

> Lastly but more importantly, the Spirit gives love. This spirit-given love is embroiled in a polemical relationship with what Kierkegaard calls self-love, and nowhere is this expressed as sharply as in the second chapter of the earlier *Works of Love* (WL, 17–90). In a sense, Christian love has died to selfishness, to the world, to spontaneous warmth and enthusiasm, and especially to romantic love. For Kierkegaard, Christian love must be learned the same way it was learned by the apostles: they were hated, they were mocked, they were spat upon, and they were left alone by the death of their leader. In this way, they died to the world, and in this unloving world the life-giving Spirit brought them love (FSE, 85). Ultimately, then, the apostles did not learn to love through their suffering, but they took the first step: they learned to die to the world and the way it loves. The Spirit then gave them love, Christian love.[23]

Many or most Christians, reading Marten's description of Christian love and how the Spirit taught it to the apostles, will find themselves coming up short. It is so easy to *not* die to self and the world, and so naturally *human* to want God to simply send the *Holy* Spirit to enhance our *undead* dead lives. The Holy One is looking for those he can send but we speak all-too-well *the secular mentality's earthly mother tongue.* How shall *we* speak?

> *And I said: "Woe is me! For I am lost; for I am a man of unclean lips, and I dwell in the midst of a people of unclean lips; for my eyes have seen the King, the Lord of hosts!"* (Isaiah 6:5, ESV)

"HE HAS DONE ALL THINGS WELL"

Thankfully, we can conclude by repeating the words of the astonished crowds that this account ends with: "*He has done all things well. He even makes the deaf hear and the mute speak.*" Dare we put Kierkegaard in even the astonished crowd? Maybe just this once:

---

23. Martens, "Emergence of the Holy Spirit", 21:206–7

> Amazing! He who invites all and wants to help all—his method of treating a patient is just as if intended for each one individually, as if in each patient he had only this one patient.[24]

This singularity of divine purpose once again takes the individual "aside from the crowd." And Jesus' mediating "look and sigh to heaven" opens the ears and loosens the tongues to "plain speaking" which cannot be restrained. And the world of onlookers could not be restrained from "zealously proclaiming," albeit in "astonishment," at all things "done well" by Jesus, the God-man who died for the life of the world (John 6:51).

At the end of this part of Mark's narrative, dramatically punctuated by the individual Syrophoenician woman's tenacious faith against a "stern" Jewish Jesus, and a Gentile crowd begging hearing and plain speech for a helpless man who could not call out for himself, we see previewed the coming harvest of Gentile disciples. The healing of the "deaf-mute" also represents the power available for the Israelite disciples, themselves representative of the twelve tribes of Israel, giving them a note of hope that Jesus can make all deaf and tongue-tied people, including Jewish disciples, hear and speak plainly.

But Mark has us at the edge of our seats, so to speak, wondering what "extra" measures Jesus will need to take for the disciples to hear and speak rightly. We are become like those bringing the "deaf-mute" to Jesus, begging for him, knowing that what is represented in this gospel story has universal implications and hoping that in the end we will be enabled to say, "he has done all things well." If we fully realized God's ever-present "problem" of making disciples of all nations, we would be more hopeful that the discipling process seen in Mark's gospel and Kierkegaard's gospel readings will gain purchase in today's world that as much as ever needs "healed" disciples with gospel hearing and gospel speaking. For the world, whether it knows it or not, is eagerly expecting the day when it can say "he has done all things well" regarding the "deaf-mute" children of God (Rom 8:19). Perhaps we should *try* to summarize what Jesus has done:

- He "took him aside privately"—something only the God-man can *personally* do with every person.
- He "put his fingers in his ears"—an *intimacy* only the God-man can provide for every person.
- He "spit," normally an act of disgust (Mark 10:34, 14:65, 15:19)—and "touched his tongue," to signify hopeful, willful defiance against the

---

24. Kierkegaard, PC, 15.

- "futility" in all creation (Rom 8:20)—a defiance only the God-man could *safely* exercise.

- He looked "up to heaven" and "sighed"—experiencing and voicing the "groaning in childbirth" of the entire creation, including *our* groans, and entering "a symphony of sighs"—something only the God-man could do *redemptively* (Rom 8:22).[25] Mark presents a mini-theology of "sighing" in 7:34 and 8:12 and is the only canonical gospel to mention his sighs.

- He "said to him, 'Ephphatha,' that is, 'Be opened'—to open humanity's ears and release humanity's tongue—something only the God-man could do *effectually*.

Regarding the non-verbal "sigh" of Jesus followed by his healing words, we can easily apply Kierkegaard's words regarding the ever-narrowing path he had to follow to death. He writes,

> This is a sigh—the way is narrow. A sigh! What is a sigh! A sigh signifies that something is locked up inside, something that wants to get out but cannot or must not come out, something that wants to have air. Thus a person sighs and gets something off his chest (in order not to perish) just as he gasps for air in order not to perish . . . "Oh faithless generation, how long must I be with you? How long must I bear with you? This is a sigh . . . Then he says to Judas, "What you are going to do, do quickly." This is a sigh . . . then he is nailed to the cross—then just one more sigh and it is over. One more sigh, the deepest, the most terrifying: My God, my God, why have you forsaken me!"[26]

It should be evident that the total "life-sigh" of Jesus signified the sheer difficulty of his task as the God-man to fulfill the "double movements of grace" for the redemption of the world. Jeff McSwain writes that

> In Christ we discover the movements of grace, a God-humanward and human-Godward double movement, all by the Holy Spirit.[27]

---

25. Moo, *Romans*, 518.

26. Kierkegaard, FSE/JFY, 62–64. Kierkegaard's lengthy segment of these "sighs" of Jesus more explicitly weaves together the element of difficulty regarding the sorrow and terror that *time* presented to Jesus in these episodes. Our selection was meant to portray his movement into the "*groaning*" of the futile sufferings of humankind.

27. McSwain, *Movements of Grace*, xviii.

What Jesus did in his healing actions for Mark's "deaf-mute" was, and demonstrated to us, the double movement of grace. The God-humanward movement is of course simply that "the Word" (the logos) entered history as "the God-man" to encounter and transform this deaf man and all of humanity. The human-Godward movement is that the God-man was able to do all the actions listed in the bullet points above. Jesus not only encountered "humanity" but entered its futility, sufferings, spittings, and groanings to lift and transform the groaning of "all creation." The double movement was God-humanward toward the groaning of humanity and human-Godward in entering that groaning, spitting at its futility, and redeeming it in a sighing (groaning) that opens the deaf ears and loosens the bound tongues.

In passing we also need to mention that Mark also introduces a "theology of spitting" which is positively developed further in 8:22–26, against the usual practice of shaming and scapegoating spitting presented in 10:34, 14:65, and 15:19. Spitting has been the serious business of earth just as "joy is the serious business of heaven." And Jesus was redeeming spitting for that serious business of heaven that his disciples are to be about, on earth.[28]

To summarize and conclude, we will consider Dietrich Bonhoeffer's astounding statement, written while imprisoned by the Nazi's not long before his execution, revealing the practical significance of the double movement of grace for discipleship. For he delineates *the* way of life disciples can participate in because God's divine-humanward and human-Godward movements have already been provided *in Christ*.

> He must live a "worldly" life and so participate in the suffering of God. He *may* live a worldly life as one emancipated from all false religions and obligations. To be a Christian does not mean to be religious in a particular way, to cultivate some particular form of asceticism (as a sinner, a penitent or a saint), but to be a man. It is not some religious act which makes a Christian what he is, but participation in the suffering of God in the life of the world. This is *metanoia*. It is not in the first instance bothering about one's own needs, problems, sins, and fears, but allowing oneself to be caught up in the way of Christ, into the Messianic event, and thus fulfilling Isaiah 53. Therefore, "believe in the Gospel," or in the words of St. John the Baptist, "Behold the lamb of God that taketh away the sin of the world."[29]

---

28. Lewis, *Letters to Malcom*, 93.

29. Bonhoeffer, *Letters and Papers (Prisoner)*, 222–23. See Bonhoeffer, *Letters and Papers*, 480–81.

Some may find this entire extrapolation from the bare report of Mark overdone. But in essence, whatever the possible variety in details, Jesus, the new man, transformed our *hopeless* human, all-too-human spitting on earth and sighing to heaven into hopeful means of prayer (and action) for the restoration of creation. Therefore, just as Paul concluded "Romans 8" with a lengthy benediction, so also, Mark's benediction is in order: May we be "astonished beyond measure, saying, 'He has done all things well. He makes even the deaf hear and the mute speak.'"

11

Beware the Leaven . . . Welcome the Gadfly

"Socratic" Gadflies and the Established Order

Mark 8:1–21

In those days, when again a great crowd had gathered, and they had nothing to eat, he called his disciples to him and said to them, 2 "I have compassion on the crowd, because they have been with me now three days and have nothing to eat. 3 And if I send them away hungry to their homes, they will faint on the way. And some of them have come from far away." 4 And his disciples answered him, "How can one feed these people with bread here in this desolate place?" 5 And he asked them, "How many loaves do you have?" They said, "Seven." 6 And he directed the crowd to sit down on the ground. And he took the seven loaves, and having given thanks, he broke them and gave them to his disciples to set before the people; and they set them before the crowd. 7 And they had a few small fish. And having blessed them, he said that these also should be set before them. 8 And they ate and were satisfied. And they took up the broken pieces left over, seven baskets full. 9 And there were about four thousand people. And he sent them away. 10 And immediately he got into the boat with his disciples and went to the district of Dalmanutha.

11 The Pharisees came and began to argue with him, seeking from him a sign

from heaven to test him. 12 And he sighed deeply in his spirit and said, "Why does this generation seek a sign? Truly, I say to you, no sign will be given to this generation." 13 And he left them, got into the boat again, and went to the other side.

14 Now they had forgotten to bring bread, and they had only one loaf with them in the boat. 15 And he cautioned them, saying, "Watch out; beware of the leaven of the Pharisees and the leaven of Herod." 16 And they began discussing with one another the fact that they had no bread. 17 And Jesus, aware of this, said to them, "Why are you discussing the fact that you have no bread? Do you not yet perceive or understand? Are your hearts hardened? 18 Having eyes do you not see, and having ears do you not hear? And do you not remember? 19 When I broke the five loaves for the five thousand, how many baskets full of broken pieces did you take up?" They said to him, "Twelve." 20 "And the seven for the four thousand, how many baskets full of broken pieces did you take up?" And they said to him, "Seven." 21 And he said to them, "Do you not yet understand?"

Strangely enough, this deification of the established order is the perpetual revolt, the continual mutiny against God . . . And then—then along comes a singular one, a Mr. Impudence, who fancies himself as being higher than the established order . . . it could very well be that he is the "gadfly" the established order needed to keep it from falling asleep or from falling into what is even worse, self-deification. Every human being is to live in fear and trembling, and likewise no established order is to be exempted from fear and trembling . . . And fear and trembling signify that there is a God—something every human being and every established order ought not forget for a moment.[1]—Anti-Climacus

Where in the world could one get rid of a dead man who had carried on a one-man theological revolution during the final years of his life, calling the pastors cannibals, monkeys, nincompoops, and other crazy epithets? What

---

1. Kierkegaard, PC, 88. The reference to the "gadfly" is clarified in footnote #88, p. 384; It references Plato who represents Socrates saying: *"It is literally true, even if it sounds rather comical, that God has specially appointed me to this city, as though it were a large thoroughbred horse which because of its great size is inclined to be lazy and needs the stimulation of some stinging fly. It seems to me that God has attached me to this city to perform the office of such a fly, and all day long I never cease to settle here, there, and everywhere, rousing, persuading, reproving every one of you."*

sense did it make to give such a person a Christian burial in consecrated ground?[2]—Joakim Garff

What did Socrates, Jesus, and Kierkegaard all have in common? They were all "gadflies" to their respective "thoroughbred horses" of Greece, Roman occupied Jerusalem, and Denmark. In Kierkegaard's words they all functioned as stimulants to awaken and prevent the hosts they irritated from the "*perpetual revolt, the continual mutiny against God*" of self-deification. Thus, they were all seen as impudent nuisances, with both Socrates and Jesus eventually being executed and a riot arising at Kierkegaard's funeral. Kierkegaard had relieved the authorities by dying—shortly after delivering a fervent flurry of pesky gadfly stings (the famous/infamous *Attack upon "Christendom"*)—and leaving them with a dilemma regarding the "proper burial" of a recent nuisance to their established order!

All three gadflies were concerned with an evil influence in their respective cultures which Jesus called "leaven." Like common yeast leavens dough, this influence could "leaven" an entire culture, but not for good but for subjugation to its power. We will begin our consideration of this leaven by considering it in relation to the one who identified it as such.

JESUS AND THE LEAVEN OF THE PHARISEES AND OF HEROD

In some Scriptures leaven had a "usual Jewish sense of something evil (see Lev. 2:11; 1 Cor. 5:6–8; Gal. 5:9)."[3] This is probably because the way it worked easily portrayed the "corrupting and the infectious power of evil" since the type of leaven used was "*fraught with health hazards because it could easily become tainted; it would then spread poison when baked with the rest of the dough. It, in turn, would infect the next batch.*"[4] In his encounters with the Pharisees and by his knowledge of Herod, Jesus recognized that they were infected carriers of a dangerously "tainted" leaven.

What their leaven was is never explicitly described, but it's nature can be surmised from the context in which Jesus warned his disciples about it. At this point in Mark a sub-current regarding "bread" comes to the surface. The theme that has been loosely running "beneath" the narrative is noted in the following:

---

2. Garff, *Soren Kierkegaard*, xvii.
3. Williamson, *Mark*, 143.
4. Garland, *Mark*, 310.

- the account of the miraculous multiplication of the meager provisions of bread (and fish) for the feeding of five-thousand which left many baskets of leftovers in 6:30–44.
- the mention of the leftovers later that evening in connection with the disciples ongoing unbelief in 6:52.
- the allusion to the internal corruption of the Pharisees over their views of clean and unclean foods in 7:1–23.
- the faith that saw divine sufficiency in the breadcrumbs that fell from the table of the Israelite children in 7:22–30.

Now Mark narrates another miraculous multiplication of bread and fish which occurred in Gentile territory and probably signified the extension of the "banquet of the Kingdom of God" to the Gentiles.[5] Following this the Pharisees reappear as they "*came and began to argue with him, seeking from him a sign from heaven to test him*" (8:11). In reaction to them, "*he sighed deeply in his spirit and said, "Why does this generation seek a sign? Truly, I say to you, no sign will be given to this generation."*"

Jesus had long known of their hardened hearts, but his deep sigh reveals the same pathos Mark had just shown in him as he healed the deaf and speech-impaired man (7:34). Certainly, this man symbolized the spiritually deaf condition of the Pharisees that was capable of "leavening" his disciples also. The Pharisees' sign-seeking signifies two sides of their "leaven-problem." First, they had obstinately missed the significance of everything they had already seen Jesus do. Second, they missed what he did because his acts fell short of their criterion, their test for Messiahship.

Leaving them, Jesus and the disciples got into the boat again and went to the other side. Apparently, they were discussing having forgotten to bring all the bread, having only "one loaf" (14). That is perhaps an ironic detail, considering that "one (full) loaf" (that they then consider as "no bread" in v16) is what they were ultimately after as we will show in the next section. Jesus cautioned them about this, seeing in their words that they were still without understanding and faith, since everything they had already seen should have been enough to prevent worries for their provision. They had seen two miraculous feedings with bountiful leftovers and yet they were worried about not having enough bread. Jesus detected in them an obstinacy dangerously near that of the Pharisees. And so, he said "*Watch out; beware of the leaven of the Pharisees and the leaven of Herod.*" That he brought Herod into his warning is interesting, because Herod had also heard of Jesus' miraculous works but had not believed. Moreover, those of Herod's

5. See Horne, *Victory According to Mark*, 126–27.

party were *already* in league with the Pharisees to destroy Jesus (3:6). Mark Horne shows that the Pharisees, Herod and the Herodians, were enamored, and the disciples nearly so, with expectations and attending signs of the Messiah according to their worldly likings.[6]

We thus scan the surface of this account. But much remains mysterious. Therefore, we must look more deeply and try to understand what an argument over seeking signs and a "heated" discussion regarding bread, fragments, leaven, hardened hearts, forgetfulness, and lack of understanding is getting at. What is the point of this seemingly confusing collage?

THE ETERNAL CHOICE: FRAGMENTS OF BREAD OR A LEAVENED LOAF?

At this point Mark's themes can easily lose us in the complexity of mixed metaphors. For the theme of bread and fragments has now become entangled with a theme of bread and leaven. Bread, fragments, and leaven are all woven together in 8:1–21 in a climactic warning against "not understanding" that the Pharisees already epitomize (11–12) and the disciples nearly so (15–21). We have already shown in previous chapters that the fragmentary "bread" provided in Jesus' ministry is sufficient to faith and life. Here Mark presents the alternative: the full loaf of bread! Everyone would agree that having a whole loaf of bread is better than having some fragments of a loaf. But Mark here begins to definitively demonstrate that the sufficient fragments are what God provides, and the "whole loaf" humans offer instead is leavened by evil. In essence, Mark here demonstrates the danger of misplaced faith in the established order's promise of a whole loaf of merely human certainty.

We quite naturally seek certainty in "divinized" works of completion, a "full loaf" of bread, a "Christ" on a throne without a cross. That cross-less throne was sure to elate Israel, given the innumerable Roman crosses seen lining their famous roads. (The cross-less throne elates all existing and would-be established orders.) But that idea only evoked the deepest of sighs from the very one who would die thereon (11–12). For his sigh was not for himself, but for the suffering misplaced faith in the cross-less way would bring them. So, Jesus narrated the only sign that would be given, and left the Pharisees— with hardened hearts too enamored with the full loaf—behind (13). Would Jesus have to also sigh deeply at the same misplaced faith of the disciples and their hankering for the full loaf? For the sigh of Jesus was over the fact that the full loaf was leavened with evil. This was the concern

---

6. Horne, *Victory According to Mark*, 128; See Garland, *Mark*, 310–11.

of Jesus as he probed the hearts of the disciples as they left the Pharisees and went in the boat to, hopefully, another side of this "imperception."

For before the Pharisees came and argued with Jesus, the disciples had just witnessed another instance of Jesus' ability to "break" and distribute "insufficient" means of nourishment to "satisfy" the crowd (1–9). Mark 8:1–21 is a summary of the theme that God uses what by any "reasonable" human being would seem insufficient to provide God's sufficiency. The antitheme is "leaven" that provides a full loaf. It is the theme that humans, after becoming a bona-fide established order (of course with "God's" subservience and "stamp of approval") will become the fully sufficient means for meeting all human needs. In short, Mark 8:1–21 reveals the choice between God's sufficient fragments for man and man's insufficient yet self-divinized full loaf for men, along with the question whether the very followers of Jesus will also fall from him and misplace their faith in the tainted leaven. And Jesus' deeply sighing in his spirit signifies the tragic consequences that always (eventually) follow placing faith in the established order rather than in Christ. For God's kingdom's ways are radically otherwise than the leaven-dynamic of the established order's self-conceived, self-constructed full loaf.

Part of the way that God "deconstructs" the leaven-dynamic of the established order is to send "gadflies" against it, as we have already posited above. Therefore, we will next consider how gadflies dethrone the quasi-divine credentials of the established order by showing its "miraculous" ability to bake "a full loaf" of provisions for spirit soul, and body as counterfeit. Gadflies thus show them unworthy of faith, and also as ultimately destructive of humanity.

"GADFLIES" AND THE ESTABLISHED ORDER

Herod and the Pharisees represented the established order of their day, as also did Pilate and Caesar. It is interesting that Jesus lumped Herod and the Pharisees together as overcome with leaven, given that Herod would have represented a treasonous cooperation with Rome but the Pharisees a determined opposition. Of course, we mentioned earlier that the Pharisees and Herodians had already plotted together for the death of Jesus (Mark 3:6). On a technical note, the evil leaven ultimately signifies naked force and owes no ultimate allegiance to "enemy of my enemy" allegiances. (Another reason to "beware.") Playing with such dark undercurrents did not bode well for Israel regarding her own fate in following the leaven of "self-deification, perpetual revolt, and continual mutiny against God."

Socrates, Jesus, and Kierkegaard were individuals against the established orders of their respective times. Since the established order represents a perpetual revolt against God, in the remainder of this chapter we will focus on how Kierkegaard has supplied a veritable "gadfly" training for tactical relation to the established orders in the world. Of course, Kierkegaard and Socrates were both following Jesus as *the* "gadfly" for all human history, but the one did so unknowingly and *prospectively*, in a sense "through a glass darkly" which was something Socrates readily admitted, and the other knowingly and *retrospectively*.[7]

KIERKEGAARD AS A MISSIONARY

Kierkegaard wrote that *"Christendom has abolished Christianity . . . As a result, if something must be done, one must attempt again to introduce Christianity into Christendom."*[8] That being his main task, Kierkegaard was first and foremost a "Christian Missionary to Christians," a description ascribed to him by Mark Tietjen.[9] The term "Christians," in Tietjen's description, is a cultural designation which therefore determined Kierkegaard's missionary task. Some may think it reductionistic to claim that Kierkegaard was primarily a Christian missionary. Tietjen clarifies that Kierkegaard wore many hats and often wore them at the same time: *"philosopher, theologian, biblical interpreter, psychologist, prophet, missionary and poet."*[10] But after discussing each of those roles, Tietjen nevertheless sees each as subservient to his main calling:

> However one reads Kierkegaard, through whatever discipline one wishes to do so, one cannot in good faith ignore his Christian commitments and the degree to which he envisions his authorship as serving God by making use of his particular talents and gifts.[11]

Therefore, noting all these clarifications, due to his varied capabilities and their expressions, one should only conclude that his talents suited his task,

---

7. Socrates admitted that the guidance of his *"Daimonion"* only warned against bad actions but didn't prescribe good actions: "I have had it from childhood; it is a kind of voice, which whenever I hear it, always turns me back from something which I was going to do, but never urges me to act." As cited in Guardini, *Death of Socrates*, 49; cf. 42 n1; 43. Socrates, at the least, prefigured Jesus in significant ways.

8. Kierkegaard, PC, 36.

9. Tietjen, *Kierkegaard, Christian Missionary*, 1.

10. Tietjen, *Kierkegaard, Christian Missionary*, 47.

11. Tietjen, *Kierkegaard, Christian Missionary*, 54.

and his "missionary theology" was as the proverbial mustard seed that brought surprisingly parabolic growth. And it should go without saying that such growth evidences the vitality of the tiny, nearly invisible seed from which it began, the man walking, observing, conversing, thinking, praying, and writing at his desk. The pen is indeed mightier than the sword, and Kierkegaard wielded his well against the established order and probably contributed to his early demise from such strenuous and continuous "battle." Because Kierkegaard was a "missionary" for restoring Christianity to Christendom we should always consider his antagonistic gadfly activity as subservient to that positive end. And that aim applies to all established orders inasmuch as their self-deification renders them due for Christian correction.

KIERKEGAARD AS A PROPHETIC "GADFLY"

Kierkegaard as a gadfly presents at least two challenges to any would-be "Christian" established order (the state). First, at the level of the *authenticity* of its *Christianity*, whether it is faithful to God's kingdom; Second, at the level of the *quality* of its *Christianity*, whether it edifies God's people both individually and collectively. It must be noted that both levels are concerned with faithfulness relative to the manner of carrying out the responsibility of the state as an *order* of God.[12] The first of these challenges might be called the "prophetic" task, and the second the "pastoral." Both were immediate concerns of Kierkegaard, essentially two sides of the coin of God's overall "governance" in relation to the order of the state. Thus, Kierkegaard's gadfly character as prophet and pastor was for the "preservation" of the proper order of *delegated* government lest it overstep God's bounds and deify *itself*. Therefore, Kierkegaard was in a sense an unofficial schoolmaster to subsequent prophets and pastors of the church by setting forth how they may serve as gadfly to the established order.[13]

Regarding prophetic "schooling" for the authenticity of the Christianity of all supposedly "Christian" established orders, we simply wish to point out that Kierkegaard's authorship continues to provide important criteria by which disciples can "beware of the leaven of . . ." (fill in the blank). Merold

---

12. The "theory" of this section is based in Bonhoeffer's view of the relative (rather than absolute) "orders of preservation toward Christ" that God has instituted in human government. See editor's introduction in Bonhoeffer, *Ethics*, 17–23.

13. For a book-length treatment of Kierkegaard as "prophet" see Roberts, *Emerging Prophet*. For a chapter on Kierkegaard as "pastor" see Edwards, *Taking Kierkegaard Back*, 24–40.

Westphal holds Kierkegaard to be "a religious philosopher in a prophetic mold" so that "the mantle of prophecy" did not have to be wholly "fallen to the Babylonians and Assyrians" such as Marx, Nietzsche, and Freud.[14] Westphal sees Kierkegaard as providing what these secular prophets' rebukes cannot, the potential alleviation of the "tragedy" wherein "many outside the faith are misled into drawing conclusions about God that do not follow from the faithlessness of his people."[15] Therefore, as another "master of suspicion"—like Marx, Nietzsche, and Freud but therein not bringing suspicion on the true God but rather upon God's *leavened* followers—Kierkegaard provides the necessary "ideology critique" of any "Christian" would-be established order.

One such order, that receives most of the attention today, is the hybrid that is modernistic "Christian" fundamentalism.[16] It is modernistic due to its over-reliance on rationalistic philosophical foundations. Ironically, the fundamentalists are themselves "masters of suspicion" but only by looking outwardly at those who are the "them" to their "us." In an interview Westphal relates that

> Fundamentalism is a hermeneutics of suspicion about everything except itself, and one way to learn the hermeneutics of suspicion is to practice it on "them," whoever they may be. The trick is to get to a place where you can put aside those things as exercises and turn that skill, if it is a skill, into self-examination, and that's what Kierkegaard was up to. He's a Christian thinker who puts Christendom in question, the very community to which he belongs and of which he's a part. It's a little bit different, therefore, from what Nietzsche does when he puts Christendom on trial. I have often said that there's a terrible danger of pharisaism in the hermeneutics of suspicion, and it becomes that for sure if you only practice it on people that are different from yourself, the "them" that have different beliefs and different practices.[17]

Passing by explicitly relating this to God's "like for like" we will say that the problem of evangelical rationalism is the failure to be suspicious of one's

---

14. Westphal, *Kierkegaard's Critique of Reason*, viii, 20.

15. Westphal, *Kierkegaard's Critique of Reason*, 20.

16. Of course, its nemesis is its "evil twin" that we will call "modernistic 'Christian' liberalism." In a sense each of these "twins" is the *raison d'etre* for the other's existence, revealing that neither has what we would call a "gospel-derived" self-existence. Ironically, because of their similar genetics, our "Westphalian" (Kierkegaardian) critique of the one could just as fittingly be a critique of the other.

17. Putt and Westphal, "Talking to Balaam's Ass," 187.

similarity to the secular established order. That rationalism has been historically evident in Christendom's "system building"—it's *ontotheology,* which continues in much of evangelicalism. Discussing Westphal's own work as a gadfly in this regard, his theological sparring partner John Caputo says,

> Merold has deployed many gifts around a watchword from Johannes Climacus that the world may not be a system for us, but that does not mean it is not a system for God. On that basis he has sketched a generous vision of Christian philosophy that is organized under what he sometimes calls "epistemological humility."[18]

And to bring this all back to the problems of *leaven* that may be an immediate danger to *us,* and *established orders* that we live in, we present the following excerpts:

- Kierkegaard's attack on Christendom is not primarily a theological critique of doctrines; for the most part, he has no problems with historic Christian beliefs. It is, instead, a critique of how the doctrines are understood and used.[19]

- Theologically deployed ontotheology yields to fundamentalism, God becoming at our conceptual and political disposal to legitimate every form of political theocracy.[20]

- The true Christian is not merely someone who assents to God's transcendent revelation, but someone who allows that revelation to have authority over his or her practical life. This means that the true Christian necessarily will come into conflict with "the established order" and will face suffering as a consequence, a suffering that is voluntary in that it could be avoided if the individual were content with a religious "hidden inwardness."[21]

In sum, Kierkegaard's *prophetic* "gadfly" schooling challenges all to the following aspects of Christian *authenticity:* a circumspect response to Jesus' call to "beware" the Pharisaic and Herodic types of "leaven;" an avoidance of oxymoronically using God to gain power; a serving the needs of "seen" others rather than serving an ideology called "God"; a willingness to follow Christ who suffered under the established order but did so for the sake of

---

18. Caputo, "What is Merold Westphal's Critique," 101.
19. Evans, "Merold Westphal," 36.
20. Matustik, "God Who Refuses," 90.
21. Evans, "Merold Westphal, 36.

those living "under" it; a following of Christ alone as Lord, rather than of the deified established order as such.

KIERKEGAARD AS A PASTORAL "GADFLY"

Kierkegaard's pastoral "schooling" challenges the established order through the *gospel upbuilding* wherein individuals become true *selves*. In a sense the difference between the prophetic and pastoral "schoolings" Kierkegaard provides is that between the outward actions and the inward transformed character, though these are but two sides of the same coin of *Christian* discipleship. We will thus consider how this "pastoral schooling" takes place within the outer context, the "universe," so to speak, of the established order.

Most would probably not disagree with the idea, and even the evidence, that Kierkegaard's "age of anxiety and despair" is the "universe", the existential reality within which our present established order exists. We will try to demonstrate how this works. We start by simply saying that, like any established order worth its salt, such as the Roman one, it promises its "Pax Romana." But truth be told, these are mere slogans of "peace, peace when there is no peace" that the OT *Jeremiad* revealed concerning the "Pax Romana" of Jerusalem centuries earlier (Jer 6:14, 8:11). Therefore, the "peace" of established orders propagandizes the herd, the mass men, manipulating and controlling them through the many anxieties its "barrage" of and for *conformity* produces. The conformity barrage "promises" freedom from anxiety but ironically produces anxiety simply because in essence, the *deified* established order cannot provide what it is not, namely, salvation in relation to *the eternal* which, at the least, properly relativizes anxiety such that its *despair* can be overcome.[22] Thus Kierkegaard's Anti-Climacus, albeit as a rather over-intellectual pastoral gadfly, nevertheless writes at the beginning and conclusion of *The Sickness Unto Death*,

> The formula that describes the state of the self when despair is completely rooted out is this: in relating itself to itself and in willing to be itself, the self rests transparently in the power that established it.[23]

---

22. Ultimately, the failure of the human, all-too-human established order is that it presents *itself* as the means for relief from anxiety which in the nature of the case it cannot be since it is in essence using the crooked to "make that which is crooked straight" Eccl 1:13–15).

23. Kierkegaard, SD, 14, 131.

And "the power" signifies Kierkegaard's somewhat Jewish name for God, *the eternal,* and most definitely does not signify "the established order."

Walter Brueggemann's "dominant script of therapeutic, technological, consumer militarism that permeates every dimension of our common life" perhaps best summarizes the "barrage" of the established order.[24] And that script produces anxieties. The script feeds Eugene Peterson's unholy "Replacement Trinity" which he describes as

> a very individualized personal Trinity of my Holy Wants, my Holy Needs, and my Holy Feelings . . . we enter adulthood with the working assumption that whatever we need and want and feel forms the divine control center of our lives."[25]

The dominant script of the established order "promises" to fulfill our unholy trinity and bring us relief from anxiety. But it cannot deliver "the goods." Its promises simply breed more anxiety. The established order deems it that Kierkegaard's gadfly-like "good news" that *"there is no bliss except in despair, hurry up and despair"* will fall on deaf ears. This is because its "Pax Romana" tells us that we have peace. But this requires much *diversion* from our essential despair that it cannot cast out.

Meanwhile, Walter Brueggemann preaches nearby as a street-corner evangelist, *"Do you renounce the dominant script?"*[26] Thus should be evangelism in the "present age of anxiety in the wilderness of despair" following the examples of John the Baptist and Soren Kierkegaard.[27] For Jesus can still cast out the demons of the age of anxiety, if we are willing to recognize that we are possessed.

Our consideration of the "pastoral schooling" Kierkegaard provides in response to the established order has to this point mostly focused on the socio/psychological "barrage" of *diversion* from the real and personal challenge, namely "Christianly" *psychological* character formation. Of course, that real challenge is part and parcel of Kierkegaard's entire mission of presenting the "difficult" radical cure of the person-forming gospel against the

---

24. Brueggemann, *Mandate to Difference,* 192.
25. Peterson, *Eat This Book,* 32.
26. Brueggemann, *Mandate to Difference,* 200.
27. See our Christman, *Behold,* 11–16. David Kangas rightly characterizes Kierkegaard's public gadfly activity: "His polemic against 'speculative thought,' prosecuted in the pseudonymous writings, grew to all-consuming proportions: he unleashed a scathing critique against 'the present age,' the media, the established church, against Copenhagen itself. Neighbors turned hostile. His last years saw him on the streets handing out combative pamphlets." Kangas, *Errant Affirmations,* ix.

person oppressing and anxiety producing "leaven" of the established order. Kierkegaard writes,

> It is the same with Christianity or with becoming a Christian as it is with all radical cures. One postpones it as long as possible.[28]

So, at this point we will merely present a few pertinent excerpts from C. Stephen Evans that demonstrate a bit of Kierkegaard's "radical cure" of *pastoral* and explicitly *psychological* upbuilding against the easy "quack cure" propagandized by the established order. We will also see that this was no merely individualistic cure but was upbuilding of the truly *Christian* community as God's new order.

> If people in "modern" or "post-modern" society have trouble developing Christian faith, the reason may not be at all that we are too intelligent or learned to believe as people of past ages did. The problem may lie in our constricted understanding of what our essential task is as human beings and our impoverished attempts to become selves . . . Following Kierkegaard's lead, we can say that mental health is the state of the person who is receiving new life from God and learning to be the self God has created him to be. The aesthete would consider mental health a matter of satisfying as many immediate desires as possible. The legalist ethicist would consider it a matter of abiding by a certain ideal of behavior. But the Christian holds to a new scale of values in which pleasure is not the highest good . . . For Kierkegaard, the goal of selfhood is to make true community possible. Because of his polemics against the crowd and the evils of mass society, Kierkegaard is often stereotyped as someone who glorified a type of radical individualism. Nothing could be further from the truth . . . It follows from this that Christian therapy must also be placed in the context of community. The goal is not to build solitary individuals, but individuals in community.[29]

In sum, Kierkegaard's "pastoral schooling" remedial to that of "the established order" is the personal and communal formation that saves us from "the philistine bourgeoise mentality" and its "secular mother tongue" that we tried to picture through Brueggemann's "dominant script" and Peterson's "replacement trinity." Those are the "pedagogical" results of the "teaching" (or leaven) of the established order. Jesus' warning to *"beware the leaven"* represents the perennial temptation and danger to all individuals, to be indoctrinated/enculturated into *"the perpetual revolt, the continual mutiny*

---

28. Kierkegaard, JP 1, 415.
29. Evans, *Soren Kierkegaard's Christian Psychology*, 119, 124, 128–29.

against God" by the self-deifying "established order." Jesus was the ultimate gadfly for the "thoroughbred" established order. But God has periodically sent gadflies after the pattern of Christ (even if, like Socrates, they appeared before Christ did) throughout history. Thus, Soren Kierkegaard, prepared by God from his youth as "the fork" for his ability to verbally spear things, became a vastly influential and *self-conscious* gadfly against the leavening in Christendom. And Kierkegaard continues to "school" others to follow him in that role against leavening tendencies that continue in today's established order.

BEWARE THE LEAVEN . . . WELCOME THE GADFLY, AND MARK AS GADFLY

Every established order *requires* a divinely sent gadfly. Its host never perceives or receives the gadfly as an "expected one" just as Jesus was not received by the world or even by God's "chosen nation" of Israel (John 1:9–11). The established order provides God's servants and humankind in general with divinely ordered necessities and comforts. This is at least one aspect of what is pictured in the "gourd" providentially appointed for Jonah.[30] But God also appointed the gadfly worm to wither the gourd plant when Jonah "settled" himself beneath it while waiting to see what his limited "established order" view hoped for. The gadfly worm message to Jonah pictured what Jesus' "beware the leaven" message was meant to tell the disciples:

Beware, lest the leaven of self-seeking and comfort in "establishment" annul the view of those "poor" conveniently hidden from sight within, to whom the Established Order simply says "Corban." Beware, lest the view of the "border" of the established order becomes an exclusionary wall of indifference to all beyond its comforts for the few, those that "do not know their right hand from their left, and also many cattle" (Jonah 4:11). Beware, lest you miss *these signs* to *this generation* in the prophet Jonah.[31] Beware, lest the leaven of the established order replaces the true leaven of God's kingdom meant to leaven the whole world with God's true community.[32] Beware, lest the prophetic and pastoral schooling of the gospel becomes leavened by an established order which is suspicious of everything except itself. Most of all, beware, lest you who think you are the "brethren" of Jesus become infected by the leaven's seduction and seek to "seize" (arrest) Jesus (or at least assent

---

30. See Jonah 4:1–11.
31. See Matt 12:38–39. Also see Christman, *Gospel*, 78–80.
32. See Matt 13:33.

to it) in solidarity with the established order, and thus remain "outside" the true family of God (Mark 3:21; 31–35).[33]

Those individuals, communities, societies, and established orders that would follow Christ must always *beware the leaven* and *welcome the gadfly*. And Mark's explicit account which we have here attempted to throw light upon, along with his development of the leavening motif, demonstrate that Mark—explicating Jesus' ultimate gadfly work against the established order—was himself "schooled" in the "gadfly academy" of Jesus that Kierkegaard himself explicated and attempted to exemplify. Eliseo Perez-Alvarez rightly calls Soren Kierkegaard "A Vexing Gadfly" but Mark ultimately shows that the gadfly is not merely obnoxious but quite necessary for both individual salvation and the larger outworking of the gospel's redemption of humanity.[34]

---

33. See Burdon, *Stumbling on God*, 34–35. Burdon writes "The word for 'seize' (*kratesai*)is the same word that is used five times in chapter 14 of the conspirators and soldiers: here is the irony that the first people who try to arrest Jesus are those 'of his own house.'"

34. See Perez-Alvarez, *A Vexing Gadfly*, in which that designation, as much more than mere label, explicates Kierkegaard's gadfly activity in relation to the "economic matters" of Gospel appropriation.

12

"I See Men as Trees, Walking"

The "Radical Cure" of the Second Touch

Mark 8:22–26 (21st Century King James Version)

22 And He came to Bethsaida, and they brought a blind man unto Him, and besought Him to touch him.

23 And He took the blind man by the hand, and led him out of the town. And when He had spit on his eyes and put His hands upon him, He asked him if he saw anything.

24 And he looked up and said, "I see men as trees, walking."

25 After that He put His hands again upon his eyes and made him look up; and he was restored, and saw every man clearly.

26 And He sent him away to his house, saying, "Neither go into the town, nor tell it to any in the town."

But where danger is, grows / The saving power also.[1]—Friedrich Holderlin

It is the same with Christianity or with becoming a Christian as it is with all radical cures. One postpones it as long as possible.[2]—Soren Kierkegaard

---

1. As cited in Barnett, *Bob Dylan and the Spheres*, 153.
2. Kierkegaard, JP 1, 415.

In other words, sinners are afraid of being healed, for at least sin is familiar and comfortable compared to the disorienting prospect of a new life.[3]
—Lee C. Barrett

Fundamentally all understanding depends upon how one is disposed toward something. If a misfortune happens on a day one is really trusting and full of faith—well, even if it were utterly calamitous—if he is trusting and full of faith, he can explain it in various ways in the context of his joy—that God is letting something happen to him simply because now he has the strength to bear it, that now he is to use the occasion to learn to know himself in surmounting it, etc. –If a person is despondent, broken-hearted, melancholy— the most insignificant matter is enough to make him suspect bad luck, the law of fatality, in what happens. From this we see that a person's whole view of life actually is a confession of the state of his inner being.[4]—Soren Kierkegaard

Faith is seeing and hearing aright, an understanding of oneself formed by the narrative in which life emerges from death. Finding one's life by losing it gives freedom from the self and openness to the neighbor. Faith so understood defines the character of the disciple in Mark. This character or being is enabled by the Kingdom's coming, and out of it flow acts of love, which in turn shape character.[5]—Dan O. Via

At this point in Mark's gospel, we find ourselves at a juncture in many ways. As has been discussed in the last several chapters we are at a climactic midpoint of his narrative. We are thus also, as we near the end of this volume of our reading, at the climactic point of its "I see men as trees, walking" theme. But this mid-point is twofold, with a positive and negative view of the theme. Mark 8:22–26 provides the positive answer to the theme Mark has developed regarding the lack of understanding and faith in the disciples themselves. For Mark here portrays the positive healing of the blind man who signifies the disciples in need of a "second touch" from the very one they are already following. And Mark 8:27–38 provides the negative picture of the ongoing problem of lack of understanding and faith in the disciples as they are encapsulated in Peter. Of course, the answer to that problem is woven into the whole narrative of Mark 9–16. Therefore, 8:27–38 and

---

3. Barrett, *Kierkegaard*, 55.
4. Kierkegaard, JP 4, 4554.
5. Via, *Ethics of Mark's Gospel*, 190–91.

chapters 9–16 do not portray the positive answer 8:22–26 does with its two-stage healing of the blind man. Taking all these things together, this means that the present chapter on 8:22–26 is *prospective* of the "healing" Peter and all disciples viewed "in him" need to receive, which healing is held in an unresolved tension to the very end of Mark.

That said, this chapter will include a *retrospective* of all that has led to Mark's preview of the answer to the discipleship problem that is in many ways the primary theme of his gospel, penned to upbuild faith in "the follower at second hand." To present this retrospective, we will first consider the healing of 8:22–26 to further delineate its solution to the discipleship problem, and then try to relate how the contents of Mark 1–8 lead up to this timely preview of the full healing of a disciple "touched by the master's hand" yet still seeing "men as trees, walking." Throughout the reading of this chapter, we presuppose the "spiritual sense" we assume Mark intends from the beginning for "the follower at second hand," the would-be disciple who, like the original disciples, is "following" Jesus but is also, for reason of lingering "blindness," or perhaps better, vacillating between two options, putting off "the radical cure" as long as possible.

MARK'S PROSPECTIVE HEALING OF THE DISCIPLES' BLINDNESS

8:22 And He came to Bethsaida, and they brought a blind man unto Him, and besought Him to touch him.

The first verse in this mini-narrative that pictures the "full healing" of the blind disciples could be taken to signify that Mark's narrative has "brought" them to Christ. All disciples begin in helpless passivity as fully blind and in need of the touch of the only one who can heal blindness. What that total blindness is has been "recently" filled in quite wonderfully by Mark 8:1–21 as discussed in our previous chapter. Thus, the passivity of the blind man who is "brought" by "some people" to Jesus (ESV) may signify human inability to overcome spiritual blindness in general. But that may be further specified as in relation to the difficulty of accepting the gospel of the kingdom of God Jesus is bringing, the inexplicable paradox of the God-man, and the attractive "rationality" of the alternative "gospel" of the established order. Therefore, blindness is exacerbated by temptation to the "gospel of leaven" that creates the pseudo-divine established order. The human problem of faith and understanding inevitably leads to a "temptation" crisis of apocalyptic proportions for individuals and societies, given the powers of humankind for destruction.

The passivity could also signify, if Mark intended by literary technique to qualify his spiritual meanings, that the narrative has led its readers, sympathetic to the life-and-death struggle that would-be disciples face, to be "on board" with the desire that "beseeches" Jesus to "touch" the blind man (the disciples). Thus, we hope to further demonstrate how Mark has *literally* brought the disciples to this point and created readers who passionately *root* for them because they are essentially *rooting* for themselves. If this is indeed the case, Mark is a master of the parabolic narrative that invites his readers to *imagine themselves* into the story just as Jesus invited the Syrophoenician woman into the redemptive parable he told her. Of course, to suppose that the author of Mark might follow the method of the master storyteller is probably a given, given that writing the gospel was undoubtedly a large, if not the largest part, of his own vocation in discipleship. We also add that this would make the author of Mark quite Kierkegaardian, or perhaps, vice-versa.

8:23 And He took the blind man by the hand, and led him out of the town. And when He had spit on his eyes and put His hands upon him, He asked him if he saw anything.

Taking the blind man "by the hand" and leading him "out of the town" certainly reverberates with Mark's theme depicting persons emerging from "the crowd" to become "the single individual." This action of Jesus essentially pictures faith in Christ versus faith in the established order as delineated just above on 8:22. Jesus' almost violent process of spitting on the man's eyes, putting his hands upon him, and asking him what he saw, can, with a little imagination, be easily seen as a transposition of the boat scene in 8:14–21 which is certainly quite rough and interrogative! Of course, that scene ends, only to be immediately followed by this one. It must surely be possible that Mark intended the reading we are pursuing, and that the historical outworking of the "Do you not yet understand" in 8:21 is repeated in the "He asked him if he saw anything" of 8:23.

8:24 And he looked up and said, "I see men as trees, walking."

Therefore, the answer of the blind man in 8:24 is the unspoken answer of the disciples in the boat. They saw *something* in Jesus and his gospel, but at best, saw him as clearly as the blind man saw the men near him: "as trees" milling about.

This raises the interesting topic of what previously blind eyes of disciples should now see. Paul provides a brief statement that helps, writing, *"So from now on we regard no one from a worldly point of view. Though we once regarded Christ in this way, we do so no longer"* (2 Cor 5:16, NIV). We could seek comprehensiveness regarding what disciples ought to see. But we will seek it in the expansive specificity Paul has provided: disciples should see Christ and others with new eyes, regarding them according to how God sees them. This can be expanded to also include keeping God's great commandments of seeing and loving both God and man (Matt 22:37–39). The statement of Dan Via, which served as a chapter epigram above, poignantly portrays the full healing from blindness the gospel brings:

> Faith is seeing and hearing aright, an understanding of oneself formed by the narrative in which life emerges from death. Finding one's life by losing it gives freedom from the self and openness to the neighbor. Faith so understood defines the character of the disciple in Mark. This character or being is enabled by the Kingdom's coming, and out of it flow acts of love, which in turn shape character.[6]

Of course, the obstinate reluctance to receive this great liberation was provided in another chapter epigram above by Lee Barret:

> In other words, sinners are afraid of being healed, for at least sin is familiar and comfortable compared to the disorienting prospect of a new life.[7]

But note in that statement the proximity of comfortable "blindness" and disorienting "healing."

The blindness of disciples as intimately related to the "danger" of the leaven temptation need not overlook the real proximity of danger and salvation. We think this proximity is narrated in the epigram of Friedrich Holderlin, "But where danger is, grows / The saving power also."[8] His poetic statement encapsulates the entire situation of blind disciples in need of the second touch of Jesus. We can summarize that disciples in the "blindness" of temptation to the world's leaven, and therefore "in the valley of decision," are at the same time that much closer to full salvation (Joel 3:14). We could say that the first touch reveals both the necessity and proximity of the second touch.

---

6. Via, *Ethics of Mark's Gospel*, 190–91.
7. Barrett, *Kierkegaard*, 55.
8. Barnett, *Bob Dylan and the Spheres*, 153.

For until "disciples" are more wholly and positively disposed to Jesus and his gospel, they remain in a place where their subjectivity gravitates to what they already know. They judge everything outside their present subjectivity as suspect regarding "throwing in the towel" with Jesus and his way of the cross. The "prospect of a new life" following a "radical cure" simply does not yet convincingly outweigh the present comforts of home. One of the sentences in the lengthy epigram from Kierkegaard above makes the matter clear: "Fundamentally all understanding depends upon how one is disposed toward something." Kierkegaard goes on to demonstrate how a person's subjectivity colors their view of life itself, which certainly includes one's view of God. Thus, until the disciple is positively disposed toward the gospel, he or she remains in a substantially blinded subjectivity.[9] Kierkegaard added "*a person's whole view of life actually is a confession of the state of his inner being.*" And therefore, the discipleship problem: "blind" disciples need the radical cure of the second touch, the very thing they fear the most. We add that this is no new problem for the expansive covenantal relationship between God and his people, as Isaiah 42:16–20 makes clear.

8:25 After that He put His hands again upon his eyes and made him look up; and he was restored, and saw every man clearly.

Jesus is of course, ready, willing, and able to provide the radical cure. He makes the disciple "look up," perhaps signifying that faith will not succeed when looking at the fearful waves of life rather than at Jesus walking on those very waves (Matt 14:28–32). Looking up to Christ is the way, the way that is how. For thus sight is restored, the sight that no longer sees men as trees walking as was discussed just above. We may also surmise that this second touch is painful to eyes already sore from the previous treatment. In our spiritual reading, the second touch, or at least the "history" that leads up to it is the difficult journey narrated through the whole of Mark 8:27 to 16:7 for Peter. That preparation is in essence, God's "prescribed" providential governance that "squeezes" first touch disciples like Peter out from their "familiar and comfortable" way.

8:26 And He sent him away to his house, saying, "Neither go into the town, nor tell it to any in the town.

---

9. We note in passing that this mirroring of subjectivity back on oneself is essentially based in Kierkegaard's understanding of God's "like for like" as discussed in chapter 8.

This instruction is difficult to harmonize with our "spiritual" reading. We obviously think it is a spiritually evocative account that is meant to convey much if not all of what we have "seen" in it. But it is a historical account that may have in the nature of the case been another prohibition to circumvent publicity that would completely identify Jesus with the popular accounts of the Jewish messiah. So, at this point, perhaps the spiritual significance must give way to the history which hosts it and nevertheless provides a revelation from heaven regarding the second touch that provides spiritual sight for the followers at second hand.

A RETROSPECTIVE LOOK AT THE JOURNEY OF THE BLIND DISCIPLES

In this retrospection of Mark and our reading, for the most part we will not encumber the text with source references. Our reading will aim to portray how the "discipleship problem" is narratively embedded to climax *in* this parabolic preview of the second touch of Jesus which is, strictly speaking, still to come in the narrative of Mark 16. We will thus summarily narrate the parabolic picture in which Mark has placed the disciples. Of course, that also means that Mark places all would-be disciples in the boat with Jesus, or sometimes in the boat with only the disciples, but in any case, always "out over 70,000 fathoms" of the deep. Mark was a master of the imagination, and therefore, we attempt to employ as best we can his method whereby imagination provides the world-picture necessary for anything more than abstract ideas. Thus, we will attempt to follow his lead which evokes "gospel" responses from within the situations portrayed. Therefore, we also try to write in a way applicable to our point regarding Mark's narrative and to us today. That is undoubtedly difficult to pull off, but someone (possibly Chesterton) once said, anything worth doing is worth doing badly. Hopefully, we will speak meaningfully to both "horizons" of meaning.

The beginning of the gospel of Jesus Christ the Son of God.

Mark's "beginning of the gospel" is of course a narrative of the good news of Christ that he was writing for those of the following generation(s) from Christ, for all "followers at second hand." Mark was penning a story, a true "parable" if you will, in which his hearers and readers were meant to see themselves. They were meant to place themselves into the story, just as the Syrophoenician woman placed herself and her demon-possessed daughter into Jesus' parable of the Israelite children at supper. By accepting Jesus' invitation to do so, she and her daughter received the fragments of bread falling from the table that were sufficient for their needs. The "sacred history" is not walled off to humankind but has doors facing every side for those disciples coming in and of whom Jesus says "Behold, my mother and my brethren!" They have become, and can now see themselves as, new selves in a new world changed by the good news of Christ. And seeing themselves in the sacred history will also enable them to rightly see their neighbors, seeing them as true others rather than "as trees, walking." The beginning of the gospel is a new world created by the Son of God, a new "Genesis" of "existence communication" making humans new in Christ the God-Man, one by one. Mark's gospel presents this new world as a viable *imaginary* to his hearers and readers so they can receive it as new selves.[10] Mark's incremental scenes serve as "creation-day accounts" depicting that "everything (God had made) was very good." Mark's new creation reveals the "functions" for restored human life in this "imaginary" of the kingdom of God brought through Jesus (Gen 1:31).[11]

The voice of one crying in the wilderness...

Of course, those who are willing to enter the new gospel world and inhabit a new story are those who desire one. For many or most are happy in the present "social imaginary" provided by the established order. People therein are too easily enamored by their present lives or too fearful of a new one, or both at the same time. But God, knowing the true poverty of man's false utopias and the calamities inevitably coming upon the "status quo" of the established order, calls all people to come out of diversion from what is actually humankind's wilderness existence gone "East of Eden." He therefore sends voices crying in that wilderness to rise from the easy chair of despair that doesn't know it rocks back and forth in and over despair. God's prophets call us to "baptism in 70,000 fathoms," recognizing the death of

---

10. Our use of "imaginary," as a noun, essentially signifies what Wittgenstein called a world-picture. See our use of the term in the third reading of Mark 5:1–20. The term itself was given prominence by Charles Taylor and carries this meaning, as explained by James K. A. Smith with reference to Taylor: "Different than an intellectual system or framework, 'broader and deeper than the intellectual schemes people may entertain when they *think* about social reality in a disengaged mode,' a social imaginary is the way ordinary people "imagine" their social surroundings, and this is often not expressed in theoretical terms, it is carried in images, stories, legends, etc.' (pp. 171–72)." Smith, *How (Not) to be Secular*, 143.

11. We consciously allude to John Walton's view of ancient cosmology as "function oriented." See Walton, *The Lost World*, 23–46.

wilderness existence, dying to it by drowning, and rising to new existence in the kingdom of God. Fear makes our natural despair too easy to ignore. But God calls us to the wilderness of despair, to thereby enter the promised land through faith. Most would-be-disciples are already seeking something. But God knows they need direction, and so provides the voice calling in the wilderness. The counter-call is the priestly "gospel-choir" of the established order that sings of the wilderness paved over and made a virtual paradise. The voice in the wilderness cries against it, to overcome its fabrication.

You are my beloved Son; with you I am well pleased.

God's earnestness drives God, not as the unmoved mover but as the most-moved mover. But lack of earnestness has taken up residence in us. And the relationship to God is as easy as putting on one's socks. The way of faith is the easy chair of cheap grace in which "we are all Christians." So, earnestness drove God to become human in Jesus to bring earnestness back to people in the frivolous crowd called humanity. And God's earnestness declares that everyone, even in the crowd, shall have an opinion about the offensive earnestness named Jesus. Risking this possibility of offense signifies the ultimate love that is more willing to be rejected than to receive and "give" false love based in misconceptions regarding God's person. But we can be sure that though men see God as clearly as trees walking, God does not see men as trees walking, but as they truly are and in the redemptive need that can only be provided by God's Christ, the pleasing God-man who would even endure the darkness of the cross by faith in the joy set before him.

The Spirit immediately drove him out into the wilderness . . . The time is fulfilled.

Temptation is our problem, the proclivity to pursue life according to our own "sense" of what seems good and comfortable to us. And the established order hands out tracts of dominant scripts and slogans to encourage us to have faith in what "good" it promises. But it can't deliver the ultimate good. It promises the moon but delivers moonshine, the true opiate of the masses, even in wholly secularized states. But Christ is our prototype who has not only said "beware of the leaven" but has overcome it, albeit through the way of the cross. But we can either take up our cross, like that of Christ's, or receive the leaven of the established order that promises cross-less life to humans but takes away their humanity in their attempt. One "established order" says "go to heaven" as though this world means nothing. A rival order says "don't look down" because its "liberation" from heaven has lost earth in the process. But Jesus, the God-man bridged heaven and earth and the polarities of human beings that live and move and have their being in two worlds at the same time. For time and eternity meet and do so in a moment called "the fulness of time." We can stake our time and eternity on the one who brought that moment by being the God-man, the ladder connecting the two worlds in faithfulness to both. The established order can only bring time, such as that served when "doing time" within its fortified walls that seek to keep man in and the true God out.

And immediately they left their nets and followed him . . . And immediately he left the synagogue.

The followers of Christ, presently live in two worlds and thereby transcend normal understandings of life. They live now but are contemporaneous with the historical life of Jesus. The "middle term" of their life is "death" that brings life that does not die in death. They receive spirit within them, an earnestness in and for life that responds to God's Spirit. They live a paradoxical life, as does Jesus, the God-man. Such a life can live *in* the established order, albeit quite differently though often appearing quite the same, because it is not *of* the established order. For the true heir of all things, Jesus, has given them his kingdom, much to the chagrin of the former tenants. They may kill the Son and *his* rightful heirs, but they cannot inherit the vineyard itself, populated by the "fishing for men" enterprise of the disciples. When Jesus heals the blind and fearful disciples, they see all these things clearly, and their place therein.

He . . . departed into a solitary place . . . All men seek for thee . . . And a leper came to him.

Jesus knew the glory of being human. He knew the glory of the moment with eternal God, being strengthened there to not lose the glory in the fray, that the glory of being human is made manifest. For the glory of being human is "found" in solitude with God its giver and manifested in the totality of life that flows from that place. Solitude is not given for isolation, whether self-isolation or enforced social isolation. There is glory in solitude with God, but perpetual isolation can infect all solitude and rob its glory. The fortunate ones of the world enforce isolation on the unfortunate ones it ostracizes for falling short of their view of fortunateness. The leper's isolation from society pictures this, and disciples are often ostracized as if lepers. Disciples easily succumb to the worldly values that create such oppressions, especially if isolated from one another.

Jesus became the unfortunate one par-excellence to invert these human, all-too-human values, and the inhumane practices they justify. Thus, Jesus says "Behold *my* mother and *my* brethren." This means they are in solidarity to his "unfortunateness." For they have received compassion from the unfortunate one as themselves also unfortunate. In God's new world, the "unfortunate" ones have compassion on the "fortunate" who had shown no such compassion to them. All this helps disciples to see the mercilessness of the established order and become "better disposed" to Jesus and his gospel for the poor, the lepers, the unfortunate. They can see that God has ordained "like for like": those who show compassion to the unfortunate receive compassion from God; those who do not show compassion to others do not receive it from God. When disciples receive the second touch of Jesus, they see all things clearly and live accordingly, counting it joy to be unfortunate like Jesus.

Your sins are forgiven . . . I have not come to call the righteous, but sinners.

The mission of Jesus to sinners is the revolution the human revolutions cannot tolerate. If Jesus had only said "get up and walk" rather than "your sins are forgiven," all would be well for the human revolution which uses God as means to its ends. Of course, that revolution is always based on the sinfulness of others and the great abilities of man that merely need help from whatever it considers to be God. The human revolution is willing to despair, but only as victim, never as perpetrator or over its own sin. And ironically, the self-exalting way of the human revolution destroys humanity through war, because it forgets what God most desires in the true revolution, one new humanity made one because the sins of each are forgiven by God and one another. The leaven of the established order is mere power, rather than true justice which must be founded on mercy since all are sinners. This is the continual crossroads humanity faces, and Jesus leads the way in the true revolution ultimately founded on the love of God duplicated *in* the love of neighbor and even of enemy. The merely human revolution needs an enemy, but not to forgive. Disciples are always tempted at the crossroads between man's "righteous" wars and God's forgiving mercies. Only the radical cure of the second touch enables them to see the right path, following Jesus the only

Christ whose kingdom is built from sinners declared righteous, not from the sins of the "righteous."

Can the guests of the bridegroom fast? . . . Is it lawful on the Sabbath . . . to save life or to kill?

The disciple of Jesus find joy in their bridegroom and the liberation in God's commands. The religious of the established orders find austerity and rigor in their new laws and traditions that miss and void the life in God's commands. Thus, Jesus and the disciples following him in joy come into conflict with the "better way" of the leavened established orders which eventually and literally do not save life but kill. The second touch of Christ helps his disciples to see that following the joyous Jesus in the Sabbath made for man leads them into conflict with the new laws of the established order that enslaves men to its "Sabbath" rules that do not provide rest or bring shalom. They are enabled to endure the cross the established order cruelly lifts them upon, trusting in the joy set before them, God's Sabbath rest for all humanity come in the Christ.

And he told his disciples to have a boat ready for him because of the crowd, lest they crush him.

The crowd is as restless sheep without a shepherd, the divine Shepherd who loves them and gives his life for them. The crowd is also subject to propaganda and false publicity regarding the true Shepherd that is propagated by the principalities and powers, "the powers that be." They would paint Christ according to the human, all-too-human desires of man's *social imaginary*. Therefore, the crowd, and would-be disciples therein, would like to be part of that power that is. Of course, the powers only see the crowd as means to *its* end and do not truly care for the sheep. And as itself a means to its own falsely conceived end, the needy crowd can by turns become the "accepting" or dangerous mob when properly propagandized. The desperate crowd can as easily cry "Crucify!" as sing "Hosanna!". Its clamor, though ultimately caused by its true need of life, makes the crowd a perpetual danger to all would-be deliverers, the established order itself, and even to the true Son of God. And catering to the raw nerve of the crowd that does not know what it truly needs is but playing with fire. Disciples tempted to join the established order that would so use the crowd (or form their own such order) need to beware of playing with the leaven that promises power but reaps the mob's destructive rage. In contrast, Jesus did not propagandize or use the crowd as means to selfish ends. He healed with the very words of the way, the truth, and the life, for the way, truth, and life of each person therein. Ultimately, the "crush" of the stirred-up crowd can never overwhelm the one set above the vain crushing waves of the nations raging against God's Anointed.

He is out of his mind . . . Here are my mother and my brothers!

Persons inhabiting and thinking with the "social imaginary" of either the established order or of God's kingdom will at many points consider those in the other to be "out of their minds." Jesus, in relation to his nation, hometown, and family is therefore seen as "mad." Doing the acts of God's kingdom by following God's will does not coincide with the scruples, values, and expectations of the home crowd. Thus, Jesus drew from the crowd the beginnings of a new family that did the will of God, an alternative city "placed on a hill as the light of the world" by living and being a new social imaginary. Naturally, Christ's family in every era faces great difficulties in relation to the patriotic fervor of their hometown. They are usually considered to be out of their minds, especially if any nation exalts its nationalism as ultimate in God's multi-ethnic kingdom. But the true family of God may discern in such savior-states the leaven of the Pharisees, of Herod, and of the established order. The established order ultimately excludes and includes through coercion. God's kingdom includes by first binding the strong man of false power (leaven), showing it as evil, and liberating the children from it to enter the family of God. They do God's will, leaving the criterion of false patriotism in allegiance to the established order. To the leavened Jesus appears to be "out of his mind," simply for saying "beware the leaven" and do not become domesticated to the established order by it. Jesus is only domesticated to his Father's house, a "house of prayer for all nations," as are his mother and his brethren.

To you has been given the mystery of the kingdom of God.

The second touch of Jesus provides the ability to understand the mysteries of God's parables and learn how to inhabit them rightly as beneficiaries of the kingdom of God. Before being given (to fully understand) the mystery of *their situation*, in the valley of decision between the Pharisees' leaven and Jesus' gospel, the disciples are living in a parabolic boat of mystery out over 70,000 fathoms. The disciples "in the boat" were already the beneficiaries of the kingdom's miraculous provisions of bread and fish multiplied from meager means and providing multiple baskets of leftover fragments. They were already living amid God's full provisions, but Jesus needed to ask, "Do you not yet understand?" They needed the radical second touch by which they are "given (to understand) the mystery of the kingdom of God." When that touch is given, they will be able to see the leaven they are told to be wary of and follow the *unleavened* way of Jesus, the way of fragments that provide fullness rather than the way of the *leavened* "full loaf" that promises all but delivers futility.

They were terrified and asked each other, "Who is this?"

Witnessing Jesus calm the storm, while in the human, all-too-human boat with us "out over 70,000 fathoms" of the depths of the mysteries of life, terrifies us. How? Who is this? What does this mean? What does this mean for me? The ultimate paradox, the God-man, has us just where he wants us, out over 70,000 fathoms. But he is with us in the boat of human fragility and openness to mystery. He is not in the boat of the established order, precisely because their rationality has fully "divined" who God is. They carve and set some "divine" figurehead at the prow of their vessel, but it is the divinization of their own spirit, and because so-leavened eventually leads to the more usual sorts of human, all-too-human terrors. But disciples ask, "who is this" and don't themselves answer their own question. That is why it is "given" to them, especially in the second touch.

Come out of the man you unclean spirit!

Jesus did not endorse the spirits of the age. He exorcised them. If he had baptized them as "Christians" he would have been accepted. For "we are all Christians" is the spirit of our age. Our collective spirit determines what sort of "Christians" we are. Therefore, Jesus comes to exorcises the legion, the military of the leaven of the principalities and powers. The worldly leaven tempts the blindness of "holy war," no matter the unholy legion necessary for its battles. So, Jesus commands the unclean spirit to depart. The exorcised are then found "sitting there clothed," peacefully in their "right mind." The hometown crowd again says, "he is out of his mind" and begs him to leave their region. But exorcised disciples receiving the second touch will know he is the sane one. Being clothed with chains attached to tombstones and practicing the self-harm of war only speaks of uncleanness and bondage. If warning against the leaven does not prevent it, its unclean spirit must be cast out from those possessed by it. In every case, Jesus does not baptize the unclean spirit and exorcises it to restore the right spirit that sees everything clearly. The man demonized by the militaristic *legion*, whose only hope of deliverance was Jesus' exorcism of that demonic *leaven*, foreshadows the blind man needing the second touch and demonized leaven-tempted Peter needing the same. Like the blind man of Mark 8, the demoniac of Mark 5 previews Peter's coming exorcism.

Do not fear, only believe . . . Who touched my garments?

There is much fear in trusting the way of Jesus, in touching mere hems of peaceful flowing garments when we would rather be grasping the latest hard weaponry to overcome whatever has rendered life unbearable. Like Peter, we think the sword that swipes the ear mightier than Jesus who restores the hearing, our knee-jerk militia mightier than a Rome, the established order mighty to overcome all creation for its own benefit. But a ruler of the synagogue found that the touch and word of a synagogue-rejected Jesus could raise the dead the synagogue surely could not. A daughter of Israel found that even touching the hem of his garment could free from years-long oppression. Indeed, the radical second touch of Jesus provides the vision disciples need to see past the immediate fears that all too easily incite us to take matters into our own hands, and oftentimes violently so, though, of course, trusting God to bless us. Contrarily, the earnest hopeful touching of the one who said "go in peace and be healed of your disease" heals us of all the dis-eases of man that only give birth and find death in a cauldron of self-reliance. There we can easily forge a sword. We cannot so easily found peace. But Jesus has founded peace as the basis of the reconciliation of God's kingdom. Disciples follow that way of peace, so much as lieth in their powers.

And they took offense at him . . . Take nothing for the journey except a staff.

But the "normal" way of human kingdoms takes offense at the way of God's kingdom. When Jesus sent out his disciples, their lack of "equipment" other than a shepherd's staff, was to embody God's way of peace. They went out to holy war armed with the war of peace. Humankind's offense at that way brings judgment. For what else can the rejection of the gospel of peace bring? Thus, the judgment is enacted ahead of time in the shaking of the dust from the sandals of the bearers of peace. They were never there. This conversation never happened. Ironically, the disciples who *enacted* this way did not yet understand it's parabolic lesson. Peter, and all disciples embodied in him, rejected the way of the cross that they had previously lived in the two-by-two peaceful mission. Only after the cross of Christ did they come to realize that God's peace-bringing Messiah *must* die to bring reconciliation to humankind. Thus, the radical second touch of Jesus awaited the disciples and Peter in Galilee, until the very end of Mark's gospel. There is no way around the cross, to the second touch, for the cross of Christ to be taken up by his followers *is* the discipleship problem that must receive the radical second touch that affects the truth that the cross is the way.

"What shall I ask for? . . . I want . . . the head of John the Baptist on a platter."

The cross for Jesus and his followers was prefigured by the very head of the Baptist "served" on the festive platter in Herod's palace. Herod did not understand that his own leaven, the power he played with, would become uncontrollable and "ask" (demand) the execution of the one he rightly feared but also enjoyed listening to. For the leaven of the established order will not even tolerate faithful members thereof to "enjoy" a Baptist or a Jesus who witness to God's alternative way. In the end it demands all, more than its followers wanted to give. For the selfish one that pursues power is ultimately absorbed by that power. It leaves only the shelled ill-formed self that grasped its power. This reveals the anti-Christ who ultimately reaps the void opposite the self-emptying way of God in Christ that inherits all creation. Jesus tells the disciples to "beware the leaven of the Pharisees and Herod" because it will demand more than they are willing to give.

Even dancing-daughter Herodias of the established order must inquire what she should desire, showing that the powers that be do not provide true human autonomy. Rather, they procure servile obedience. Both Herod and Herodias found this out, though Herod even more so, frivolous as he was. Mark here provides the grisly details that do not lie, regarding the evil heart lying beneath even the festivities of the established order. The only alternative to partaking in such "feasts" served on a silver platter is, ironically, the willingness to be the meal, which doubly ironically in the case of Christ, provided the real "bread" that was *given* for the life of the world. And his followers can also *be given* to "fill up what is lacking in Christ's afflictions."

Later that night, the boat was in the middle of the lake, and he was alone on land.

The followers of Jesus at second hand are in the boat in the middle of history while Jesus is apart from them on the land beyond their present. But "leftover" fragments of his life with them, such as Mark's gospel, are provided. Christ sees them from heaven and passes by them in a theophany they perceive as a "ghost." They are already provided for, but still without understanding of their parabolic situation. Their hearts are still "hardened." The hem of Jesus' life-giving garment can still be touched and still provides healing, but they do not understand these things. They need the radical second touch to see. Only that will help them overcome the leaven that tempts toward means other than those provided in the gospel of Christ: the tempting "Christian" bourgeoise settlement that would crown them captains of their ship, masters of their fate, with God's blessing of course. That's always a "given" with God on our side. They don't realize the true peril out over 70,000 fathoms, namely the leaven that can infect a mere band of disciples in a boat, or a camp of the saints threatened by the leaven of "Gog and Magog" a "millennium" later in history.

All the Jews do not eat unless they wash their hands properly . . . Let the children be fed first.

The "Christian" bourgeoise settlement in pompous and hypocritical geniality prescribes new understandings of God's commands *while* plotting murder of God's Christ and his prophets. It "washes its hands" of their evil, saying, "let the children be fed first" *while* the hungry poor beg beneath the lofty table set only for the fortunate. It only knows a "God" of rigor without leniency and so gives "like for like" to others and receives therefrom the same "like" from God's immediate judgment. If would-be followers of Jesus succumb to their likeness, they will receive the same "like for like." "Beware the leaven of the Pharisees" warns disciples against the rigorousness of human judgment that boomerangs back upon itself, but now infinitized as divine judgment. Better situated are those that mercifully feed the unfortunate dogs and do so because they were "given to understand" that God has had mercy on them, the unfortunate, and on all unfortunate humanity. Through Christ's mercy he has freed them from the "instant karma" of judgment.

194   I SEE MEN AS TREES, WALKING

He has done all things well . . . Do you not yet understand?

As we come back to the present section of Mark, hopefully our snapshot survey of what has led up to his climactic mid-point has provided a greater idea of how his hearers and readers could become better disposed toward the gospel of Christ as against the real danger of the leaven of the Pharisees and of Herod. Mark does not dogmatically or theoretically present doctrines or arguments for this. Instead, he portrays, through manifold parabolic pictures of life as impacted by the kingdom of God in Christ, the inner motivations, and outer consequences of what we could call the two ways, the way of Christ or the way of power. As said earlier, he presents a world-picture, a social imaginary, depicting the life of the new creation of the kingdom of God, whereof God says, "it is very good." He has done all things well. Hopefully, disciples can now understand.

MARK'S PARABOLIC METHOD

The total world-picture Mark presents works "*affectively*" by presenting the *gospel imaginary* that viscerally touches his readers just as Jesus touched the blind man with his hands.[12] Mark's is no mere rationalistic philosophy. Anachronism notwithstanding, he could almost be considered as post-critical for seemingly leaping the obstacles Cartesian philosophy set for humans between his day and ours.[13] Thus, his method was much like Kierkegaard's own recognition of the value of *imagination* which calls for *the media of*

---

12. "Affect . . . is the name we give to those forces—visceral forces beneath, alongside, or generally *other than* conscious knowing, vital forces insisting beyond emotion—that can drive us to inward movement, toward thought and extension." Seigworth and Gregg, "An Inventory of Shimmers," 1; as cited in Smith, *Imagining the Kingdom,* 31. Smith's entire book presents the centrality of imagination which we have here posited as the spirit-inducing literary method of both Mark and Kierkegaard.

13. We allude to Michael Polanyi's "post-critical philosophy" which simply defined signifies holistic human knowledge. See Polanyi, *Personal Knowledge.* A comment by Drusilla Scott may help to convey the non-Cartesian approach of Polanyi that we see as previewed in Mark: "He embarked on a long search for understanding '*how we know*', and in his book *Personal Knowledge* he worked to free our minds from distorting assumptions about the impersonality and certainty of scientific knowledge, and the belief that anything outside the framework is unreal. These assumptions devalue man's moral values, spiritual powers, affections, responsibilities and judgments." Scott, *Everyman Revived,* 7. We consider the Polanyian "moral values, spiritual powers, affections and judgments" as capacities that Mark's gospel and Kierkegaard's writings continually cultivate to foster persons "fitted" to follow the gospel. We detect in the chapter epigram from Dan Via above his same observation of how the narrative method of Mark "works" in and for his readers.

words to foster and *affect* the proper gospel response which in the case of discipleship means acceptance, love, and obedience, to the gospel.[14] *That* new subjectivity *signifies* "a person's whole view of life" which "actually is a confession of the state of his inner being," in fact, providing for a new confession of "seeing every man clearly."[15]

In sum, Mark well-nigh accomplishes for the attuned reader what Mark 8:22–26 portrays: the radical second touch of Jesus that enables the disciple to follow the cruciform way of Jesus, albeit with fear and trembling. By linking the disciple's need of cruciform faith to Jesus when facing his own cross, it seems that the vital ingredient provided in the second touch emerges as "the joy." The author of *Hebrews* narrates "the joy" as *the imagination* that enabled Christ to overcome the shame and darkness of the cross.[16] In other words, Mark's gospel narrative, in sum, narrates "the joy" that overcomes the "blindness" of the disciple. The disciple's present subjectivity prevents them seeing: *the joy* beyond the cross and leaves them susceptible to the leaven of the Pharisees and Herod—which is essentially the *non-cruciform way of power*. In short, the gospel of joy *enables* the gospel of the cross. Of course, the joy is *resurrection*.

> Therefore, since we are surrounded by so great a cloud of witnesses, let us also lay aside every weight, and sin which clings so closely, and let us run with endurance the race that is set before us, looking to Jesus, the founder and perfecter of our faith, who for the joy that was set before him endured the cross,

---

14. For example, David Possen sees the logic and rhetoric of Kierkegaard's discourse "On the Occasion of a Confession" as not only portraying "a confessional occasion" but as aiming to "*foster* such occasions in its audience: to prompt its reader to *confess*." See Possen, "The Logic," 225. We believe that this method of Kierkegaard's was not merely occasional but runs through his entire authorship albeit in quite inconspicuous and clandestine ways. That imagination was of vital importance to Kierkegaard's method as can be seen from the following comment of Chris Barnett: "Kierkegaard makes hundreds of references to 'imagination' . . . albeit with a variety of intentions and meanings. Perhaps the most important reference turns up in *The Sickness Unto Death* (1849), in which Kierkegaard's pseudonym Anti-Climacus observes that imagination is interconnected with emotion, knowledge and will. The imagination is, in other words, "the capacity *instar omnium*." Barnett, *Bob Dylan and the Spheres*, 135. Barnett footnotes the reference as SD, 30–31, and provides the translation of the phrase: "for all capacities" on p147, n93.

15. Kierkegaard, JP 4, 4554.

16. The imaginary provides the objective content for the subjective imagination that overcomes the "blindness" of Mark's "discipleship problem." Barnett explains, "The will to change in reality depends on the ability to model images that are not currently available to sense experience. Without imagination, then, the self cannot develop, much less reach its full potential." Barnett, *Bob Dylan and the Spheres*, 135.

> despising the shame, and is seated at the right hand of the throne of God (Hebrews 12:1–2, ESV).

Mark's narrative in whole, and incrementally through each step of the way, demonstrates that Jesus, ultimately exemplifying the way to "the joy set before him" and thus before all of us, "has done all things well." Hopefully, the reader's imagination has become subjectively well-disposed toward Jesus and his gospel of joy and will receive his radical second touch to then go forth seeing Christ and all people rightly, rather than "as trees, walking," and living according to the liberties and responsibilities that such spiritual sight provides.

13

The "Disciple" Who Rejected the Way of Jesus' Death

The Crowd in Untruth, "The Single Individual," and Becoming a Self

Mark 8:27–38 (ESV)

27 And Jesus went on with his disciples to the villages of Caesarea Philippi. And on the way he asked his disciples, "Who do people say that I am?" 28 And they told him, "John the Baptist; and others say, Elijah; and others, one of the prophets." 29 And he asked them, "But who do you say that I am?" Peter answered him, "You are the Christ." 30 And he strictly charged them to tell no one about him.

31 And he began to teach them that the Son of Man must suffer many things and be rejected by the elders and the chief priests and the scribes and be killed, and after three days rise again. 32 And he said this plainly. And Peter took him aside and began to rebuke him. 33 But turning and seeing his disciples, he rebuked Peter and said, "Get behind me, Satan! For you are not setting your mind on the things of God, but on the things of man."

34 And calling the crowd to him with his disciples, he said to them, "If anyone would come after me, let him deny himself and take up his cross and follow me. 35 For whoever would save his life will lose it, but whoever loses his life

for my sake and the gospel's will save it. 36 For what does it profit a man to gain the whole world and forfeit his soul? 37 For what can a man give in return for his soul? 38 For whoever is ashamed of me and of my words in this adulterous and sinful generation, of him will the Son of Man also be ashamed when he comes in the glory of his Father with the holy angels."

Mark's Gospel is the book of secret epiphanies.[1]—Helmut Thielicke

The single individual is the category of spirit, of spiritual awakening, as diametrically opposite to politics as possible.[2]—S. Kierkegaard

It is impossible . . . to "fall in love *en quatre* [in fours] or *en masse*" . . . erotic love, pertains to the single individual.[3]—S. Kierkegaard

So, as we have mentioned, Mark's gospel narrative comes to a mid-point here. What is most interesting about this is that the mid-point is more precisely anti-climactic. This is because the outworking and inworking of the cumulative event of Jesus' collision with demons, disciples, his family, Israel's religious leaders, the crowds, and a variety of individuals, comes to a focal point. Mark narrates that point as the crisis wherein faith coexists with unbelief. A Nathan-like Mark puts Peter at the center of the crisis, saying "Thou art the man," the blind man of 8:22–26 who has experienced the "first touch" from Jesus, but not the second. Peter's personal crisis of faith/unbelief is microcosmic of the "cosmic" collision of "the gospel of the kingdom" with "the gospel of the established order," and therefore also, the focal point of Mark's gospel. Mark's narrative is onion-like so that peeled layers of blindness reveal deeper layers of blindness. Beginning from the one blind man in 8:22, the blindness is expansively revealed in: Peter, Israel, Rome, and ultimately, the world.

The title and subtitle of this chapter parallel those of chapter three, to frame the focal point of the whole narrative which we explicitly introduced there, namely "the single individual." This also helps demonstrate Mark's "Kierkegaardian" motif of "the individual."

We therefore compare the chapter titles and subtitles:

- Chapter 3: The "Daughter" Who Touched the Hem of Jesus' Garment
- Chapter 13: The "Disciple" Who Rejected the Way of Jesus' Death

1. Thielicke, *Modern Faith & Thought*, 508.
2. Kierkegaard, PV, 121.
3. Kierkegaard, PV, 117.

- Chapter 13: *The Crowd in Untruth, "The Single Individual," and Becoming a Self*
- Chapter 3: *"The Single Individual" as the Category through which the Human Race Must Go*

We point out some of the correlations we may now draw in light of the account of the blind man of 8:22 who required a second touch from Jesus for full healing:

- In chapter 3 a daughter of Israel becomes healed through faith that nevertheless needed to be "sharpened" by Jesus who pressed her toward a second and more direct "touch" than her *anonymous* hem-touching provided. After the "second touch" Jesus proclaims her healed and at peace.
- In chapter 13 a disciple becomes "healed" by faith in Jesus but remains a "fallible follower" for the rest of Mark's narrative wherein his coexisting faith/unbelief requires the "second touch" of Jesus for full healing.[4] Peter awaits the "second touch," before which he is certainly not at peace, from 8:33 to at least 16:7 or 16:14, 20 (depending on which ending, if any we have, is the authentic ending of Mark).
- In chapters 13 and 3 the crowd in untruth, the Human Race, must "go through the category of the single individual" in order for each person thereof to *become a self.*

Our reading in this chapter will consist of a reading of Mark's gospel which is largely informed by an important posthumous writing of Soren Kierkegaard called "The Single Individual." It is fitting that this second volume of our reading, subtitled "The Crowd in Untruth, the Single Individual, and Becoming a Self," will conclude at Mark's climactic point with attention given to Kierkegaard's *The Single Individual.*

MARK'S GOSPEL OF SECRET EPIPHANES AND "THE SECRET INDIVIDUAL"

Mark's gospel contains many secrets including up to this point: secret difficult journeys (1:12–13), secret demons in the synagogue (1:23), secret thoughts (2:8), secret conspiracies (3:6), secret exorcisms (3:12), secret binding and plundering (3:27), a secret family (3:33–34), the secret of the

---

4. "Fallible Followers" is how Elizabeth Struthers Malbon characterizes the "women and men" following Jesus in the Gospel of Mark. Malbon, *In the Company*, 41–69.

kingdom of God "told" in secret parables (4:11), seed growing secretly (4:27–32), a secret legion of demons (5:9), secret touches (5:30), secret healings (5:40), secret resurrections (5:41), secret praying (6:46), secret hypocrisy and defilement (7:6–23), secret negotiations (7:26–29), secret leaven (8:15), a secret Christ (8:27–30), and a secret Satan (8:33). This abundance of *secrets*, matched by as many *revelations*, led theologian Helmut Thielicke to call Mark's gospel "the book of secret epiphanies."

Perhaps the greatest of Mark's secrets would be that the ones leaving the crowd to become "the single individual" experience the greatest epiphany possible *in salvation*. At this point in Mark, Peter is faced with the problem of becoming the "secret individual" by leaving the crowd which entailed a rejection of the leaven of the Pharisees and of Herod who desired their own established order(s). In his book *The Single Individual* Kierkegaard demonstrates the salvation Peter needed:

> The single individual, not the single individual in the sense of the outstanding and the especially gifted, but the individual in the sense in which every human being, unconditionally every human being, can be and should be an individual, should place his honor—*but will also find his salvation—in being an individual*.[5]

This of course sounds more than amenable to our modern individualistic ears. But we must nevertheless ask whether Kierkegaard has replaced salvation with sheer "individualism." As we proceed, we will see that he has not, for his "single individual" is not born through the merely human and autonomous will. His conception is contextually descriptive of the "shape" or "appearance" of salvation. The context is the individual's life-course in relation to the crowd's, which in Kierkegaard's thought had no life itself nor life for its numerical members. He saw the crowd, also called "the public," as "a chimera . . . a sum of negative ones . . . a package of envelopes."[6]

Kierkegaard's contextual gospel seems wholly biblical when one remembers Abraham, the one Paul considers the "father" of faith (Rom 4:11–16). Paul recounts the narrative of the "uncircumcised" Abraham, which simply means that Abraham's faith was in answer to God's call to him as merely Abram:

> Go from your country and your kindred and your father's house
> to the land that I will show you (Gen 12:1, ESV).

---

5. Kierkegaard, PV, 117 (emphasis mine).
6. Moore, PSW, 236–37. (JP 3, 2952.)

In other words, "Abram" left the "uncircumcised" crowd, becoming "the single individual," and thus a self—becoming "Abraham." According to the meaning of his before and after names, he moved from "exalted father" to "father of many nations." This perhaps signifies, or at the least illustrates, the change that transpires when a person leaves the crowd and the merely human values of an established order to become "the single individual." In other words, to move from "exalted father" (in, or of, one nation) to "father of many nations" is not loss, but gain. Of course, what ultimately stood between those two states of fatherhood was the way of the cross. Likewise, the movement from the crowd to the individual by way of the cross is no mere feat. This will be seen more clearly as we proceed.

At this point we will consider a few more reasons that Kierkegaard's view of salvation by becoming an individual is no form of self-salvation.

First, becoming an individual is no naturally human achievement. Kierkegaard writes that "According to the supreme criterion *the single individual* is beyond a human being's powers."[7] Nevertheless, Kierkegaard is adamant that this incapability does not remove human responsibility:

> *The single individual* is the category through which, in a religious sense, the age, history, the human race must go.[8]

Kierkegaard is very clearly delineating the difference between God's "Abrahamic" call and our "Abramic" inability to answer that call *by a faith* that leaves the crowd and thus becomes *the single individual*. Kierkegaard could not be more Pauline than Paul's *Romans* as he writes of God's call and the *justifying faith* that answers.

Second, the overall biblical dynamic of love, which "works by faith," also mitigates against any "works righteousness" in Kierkegaard's conception of becoming a self. Below we will consider the biblical dynamic of love *in Christ*. At this point we merely note what Kierkegaard writes in the third chapter epigram above, that love is only possible, and only "pertains to the single individual" as such. We do not, and cannot, "fall in love ... *en masse*." In other words, the single individual only responds to God's love and participates in the body of Christ's love as an individual in community. For there is no such community of individuals in the crowd of the established order. And Kierkegaard's "single individual" does not prevent community and in fact both individual and community cohere therein:

> Only the single individual guarantees community ... in community the single individual is a microcosm who qualitatively

7. Kierkegaard, PV, 118.
8. Kierkegaard, PV, 118.

reproduces the cosmos. Community is certainly more than a sum, but yet it is truly a sum of ones.⁹

Third, the love of God *in us* is, to Kierkegaard, only real when it overflows in love of one's neighbor. And this love cannot be exercised *en masse* by loving the crowd. One can only fulfill the dynamic of faith, which is love, by leaving the crowd and loving the neighbor, albeit therein expressing:

> human equality unconditionally; . . . I have never read in Holy Scriptures this commandment: You shall love the crowd . . . but to love the neighbor is, of course, self-denial.¹⁰

Thus, all the most important aspects of faith, according to Kierkegaard, presuppose the impossibility of antonymous human fulfillment by human persons remaining in the crowd. Altogether, Kierkegaard demonstrates in these ways that becoming a self is "beyond a human being's powers." All this considered, we should probably posit another "secret" in Mark, the secret source of love in the person who truly loves, the source that is "the lake" of God's love. Kierkegaard writes:

> Just as the quiet lake originates darkly in the deep spring, so a human being's love originates mysteriously in God's love.¹¹

If love is indeed a major theme in Mark it is most certainly "secret," given the fact that love is only mentioned once in action, when Jesus loved the rich young man (10:21). Love as an imperative is only mentioned four times, all in one passage wherein Jesus answers one scribe's question regarding which commandment is the greatest (12:30–33). The other two mentions of love depict the self-love of the scribes as a group or, in Kierkegaardian language, as a "crowd" (12:38–40). Perhaps the "singular" scribe reveals that love, other than self-love, was of no major concern to the scribes of Israel, and that Mark presents love not through words but through imperative and practice. And it should probably be understood that everything Mark depicted of Jesus demonstrated that he "lived out" the love-imperative fully. Taken together, all these observations seem to demonstrate that God's love and the love of God are indeed depicted as the "secret source" of Jesus' love that flowed forth freely from his very being. Once again, Mark proves to be a gospel of "secret epiphanies."

We also add that "the joy set before him," that we previously saw as the key ingredient that enabled Jesus to endure the cross, does not stand

---

9. Moore, PSW, 236. (JP 3, 2952.)
10. Kierkegaard, PV, 111.
11. Kierkegaard, WL, 10.

alone. For "the joy," as the end or 'telos' set before Jesus, certainly signifies the joyous unity of "the single individual" and God's community at which Jesus joyfully declares "Behold, my mother and my brethren." And most importantly, *love* was the inner dynamic and motivation that enabled the enduring pursuit of "the joy set before him." In short, the second touch of Jesus is now further revealed as conveying not only faith in "the joy" set before disciples that helps *them* endure *their* cross, but also the *love* in and by which God, through the gospel of Christ, "has done all things well." Mark's gospel of secret epiphanies is therefore *crowned* with God's "secret love" in Christ and reduplicated in his new family.

THE ESTABLISHED ORDER'S "GOSPEL" OF SECRET LEAVEN

We have been looking at the positive side of Mark's "secret epiphanies," namely salvation itself as leaving the crowd through God's gospel-helps of faith, joy, and love to become *the secret* single individual. But Mark's secrets include a "dark epiphany," the false gospel of a *secret leaven* at work in the established order. This deadly contagion "overflows" from its secret spring in the fallen human heart to infect Peter, any and all would-be disciples, and even the crowd which had previously "followed" Jesus.

As Jesus and his disciples moved on from the blind man and Bethsaida to other villages, he asked them "Who do people say that I am?" (8:27). They answered that people said he was "John the Baptist or Elijah" (8:28). Jesus then asked them "But who do you say that I am?" to which Peter answered, "You are the Christ" (8:29). At this Jesus "strictly charged them to tell no one about him" (8:30). More secrecy. It can be supposed that Peter and the others who may have said the same, were having, or at least so they thought, an epiphany moment. Matthew's account gives stronger credence to the idea that it was, given an exuberant response by Jesus to Peter's confession (Matt 16:17–19). Nevertheless, as both Mark and Matthew record, Peter's epiphany was but a "first touch" that was nearly immediately revealed as leaving Peter seeing "men as trees, walking" because his mind was still set "on the things of men" (8:33).

Jesus undoubtedly knew that God's "first touch" that brought "epiphany" to Peter regarding Jesus being *the Christ* would immediately fall prey to the "dark epiphany" of the Jewish established order's secret leaven. That was the reason for the "strict charge" of Jesus for secrecy (8:30). For the "gospel" of the "Christ" of the Jewish established order was no "mustard seed" of the true kingdom-gospel (4:30–32). It was in fact Jewish/Roman leaven which

Jesus had earlier warned them against: "the leaven of the Pharisees and the leaven of Herod" (8:15). Their leaven signified "the things of (collective) man." It is thus epitomized by the non-singular crowd of Kierkegaard's "negative ones," the established order, the age, and the human race. Unfortunately, being "common to man," it was the leaven that Peter and the disciples were *highly* susceptible to.

At this point we must understand the crisis this presented. For as Jesus *immediately* attempts to *counter* the "dark epiphany" by proclaiming the inevitable cross standing ahead, Peter *immediately* "rebukes" Jesus. It is quite a crisis when Peter, representing all future disciples, rebukes Jesus. The significance of the crisis is fully revealed when Jesus rebukes Peter and says" Get behind me Satan!" (8:33). In Kierkegaardian terms, the "human thinking" leaven is *Satanic* and meant to thwart *"the single individual"*—including Jesus as "the category through which, in a religious sense, the age, history, the human race must go." Everything in redemptive history hung in the balance. For in essence, the reception of the secret leaven amounts to a Satanic baptism into the anti-gospel way of man. The Satanic leaven that had influenced Peter was the ethos of the established order—not only of the Jews—but also of Rome. The very power the Jewish nation and Peter sought deliverance from was the power they were bowing to by following their own "will-to-power" way. The "secret leaven" was and is the "perennial" false gospel of man's established order(s).

Of course, accepting and following the secret leaven to the end means *death,* as the Jews would tragically find out in the Jewish war with Rome from 66–70 AD. The secret leaven, the minding of the things of men, is essentially a capitulation to the Hobbesian "war as is of every man against every man" in a life that becomes "poor, nasty, brutish, and short."[12] There are no equal outcomes assured for those participating in the will to power party. It begins with the Hobbesian war and ends with the Darwinian survival of the fittest. The paradox is deep and tragic when men succumb to the secret leaven's "gospel" only to eventually reap self-destruction. This is the way man's way leads (Prov 14:12). But the better way, paradoxical to man's way, is the way of faith and the cross.[13]

---

12. Hobbes, *Leviathan,* 77.

13. See Christman, *Gospel,* for what is in essence a book-long meditation on the way of the will to power vs the way of faith.

MARK'S GOSPEL OF THE CROSS

Jesus not only teaches his disciples his way of the cross, but he also "calls the crowd to him with his disciples" to the way of the cross (8:34–37). Though Peter, and by implication the other disciples have received the "first touch" of "epiphany," they are essentially no different than the crowd, and are called along with the crowd to the cross.[14] The Jewish disciples and crowd are nearly succumbing to the established order *of Rome* which will crucify Jesus. Rome will at least control if not destroy them, unless, paradoxically, they become *the single individual* that answers the call to the cross:

> For whoever would save his life will lose it, but whoever loses his life for my sake and the gospel's will save it. For what does it profit a man to gain the whole world and forfeit his soul? (8:35–36, ESV).

Now we must note that Jesus' preaching of the way of the cross, while certainly and explicitly pertaining to the real-world consequences of seeking to "live by the sword" only to "die thereby" in wartime periods of history, also pertains to "normal" peacetime periods of history in which the loss of self is simply the consequence of remaining in the crowd rather than being saved by becoming *the single individual.* For the established order is itself in times of war or peace. (The peace is often only that which follows surrender to the established order in whatever way it coerces its servile subjects.) In his book *The Sickness Unto Death* Kierkegaard talked about this loss of life in the crowds, the mortgaging of oneself to the "secular mentality" of the established order, as a way of despair. He says,

> But . . . thus to be in despair does not mean . . . that a person cannot go on living fairly well, seem to be a man, be occupied with temporal matters, marry, have children, be honored and esteemed—and it may not be detected that in a deeper sense he lacks a self. Such things do not create much of a stir in the world, for a self is the last thing the world cares about and the most dangerous thing of all is for a person to show signs of having. The greatest hazard of all, losing the self, can occur very quietly in the world, as if it were nothing at all. No other loss can occur so quietly; any other loss—an arm, a leg, five dollars, a wife, etc.—is sure to be noticed . . . Surrounded by hordes of men,

---

14. Of course, salvation only begins for those willing to be in solidarity with the crowd Jesus died for as Kierkegaard notes: "Christ indeed died for all men, also for me, but this 'for me' must nevertheless be interpreted in such a way that he has died for me only insofar as I belong to the many." Kierkegaard, JP 2, 1976. This solidarity therefore means the solidarity with "the many," in other words, sinful humanity.

> absorbed in all sorts of secular matters, more and more shrewd about the ways of the world—such a person forgets himself, forgets his name divinely understood, does not dare to believe in himself, finds it too hazardous to be himself and far easier and safer to be like the others, to become a copy, a number, as mass man.[15]

An excerpt from Kierkegaard's *Works of Love* can expand our understanding of several important things:

> In the divine sense, he was Love; he loved by virtue of the divine conception of what love is, loved the whole human race. Out of love he did not dare to give up this conception, because that would mean to deceive the human race. For this reason his whole life was a horrible collision with the merely human conception of what love is.[16]

This excerpt helps us to not misconstrue the cross as a backwards way of engaging in a power struggle. For the cross was essentially the battle of love against our self-destroying grasping after power, even if that power is merely to procure comfort and security. For in truth, none of these things are found apart from "resting" in God (Matt 6:25–34; 7:24–27). "Love" cannot complicitly sit by this futile endeavor without being "deceptive" and thereby losing the battle by surrendering others to Satan's way. Kierkegaard continues from the above excerpt to describe the battle of the "love-rebukes" between Peter and Jesus. Kierkegaard tenderly portrays the patient love of Jesus for Peter, and for all of us "in him" so to speak, who have received his "first touch" and are thus "well-intentioned" and "burning with love" but nevertheless need Jesus' "second touch" that lovingly loves us further than we think we can go, to the loving way of the cross. In this way Kierkegaard shows that God's love lies at the heart of the cross, for that alone can win would-be disciples to the way of the cross which is the way of love. Any way of power would "deceive the human race" regarding God's essential love. Kierkegaard writes:

> It was the ungodly world that crucified him; but even the disciples did not understand him and continually seemed to be trying to win him over to their conception of what love is, so that he even had to say to Peter, "Get behind me Satan! The unfathomable suffering of this terrible collision: that the most honest

---

15. Kierkegaard, SD, 32–34.

16. Kierkegaard, WL, 109–10. Noting in Kierkegaard's words the dynamic of love in the endurance of the collision for the sake of "the joy set before him."

and most faithful disciple, when he, not only well-intentioned, no, but burning with love, wishes to give the best advice, wishes only to express how deeply he loves the master, that the disciple, because of his conception of love is false speaks in such a way that the master must say to him: You do not know it, but to me your words sound as if you were Satan who was speaking![17]

In Mark's gospel of the cross, colliding with the false gospel of the secret leaven, we can see the following ways that God's love resides therein and can overcome the temptation to mind the things of man and achieve them through the will to power.

- First, we see that Christ's love *for* the entire human race is categorically different and superior to the "love" that might be *supposed* to be operative in the crowd existing (we hesitate to say *living*) under the established order. For the love of Christ, exhibited in the cross "does not interest the world, because to make sacrifices, to be sacrificed—which must indeed become the consequence of not seeking to become a power in the external world—does not interest the world."[18]

- Second, Christ's *singular* self-giving for the sworn enemies of self-sacrifice demonstrates the impossibility of crowd-humans to reduplicate that divine love in and of themselves for reason, again, of their remaining within that "crowd-order." As members of the crowd, they reject the way of *the single individual*, Christ, and therefore also *the single individual* they are called to become through him, by following the call to "leave your people" as Abram did. Jesus the true forerunner of all "leaving" did. For he left the crowd's epiphany over *their* "Christ" to become the true Christ by the only way compatible to the cross, becoming *the single individual*.

- Third, Christ's way of love demonstrates the gain wherein an Abram, as "exalted father" in the crowd with the *accent on the one*, is transcended by an Abraham, as "father of many"—a multitude of "single individuals" through the faith of Abraham, with *the accent on the many*.

- Fourth, all these things flow from and reveal the deepest reality of the triune God wherein the self-giving of God for the world, exhibited in the Father giving the Son for the world and the Son giving himself for the world in obedience to the Father, and the Spirit united and uniting both in that willing death for the other and all others, results in the

---

17. Kierkegaard, WL, 110.
18. Kierkegaard, PV, 121.

Abrahamic "father of many"—the salvation of the world. That self-giving for the gain of life for the other(s) is impossible in the crowd united only externally and numerically as the crowd-sum where there are no single individuals nor any community of love.

MARK'S GOSPEL OF SALVATION

Mark's mid-point climax ends with a look to the future coming of Christ "in the glory of his Father" when he will be "ashamed" of all those of "this adulterous and sinful generation" who were ashamed of him and his words.[19] In essence they were ashamed of the singular words and singular way of the single individual. In Kierkegaard's unpublished book *The Single Individual* we see a similar eschatological look forward as he presses further his basic thesis: "*The single individual*—from the Christian point of view, this is the decisive category, and it will also become decisive for the future of Christianity."[20] At the end of his short book, Kierkegaard adds a mysterious "prophecy." He writes,

> When he, *the missionary*, comes. He will use this category. If the age is waiting for a hero, it surely waits in vain; instead there will more likely come one who in divine-weakness will teach people obedience—by means of their slaying him in impious rebellion, him, the one obedient to God, who would still use this category on an even greater scale, but also with *authority*.[21]

Kierkegaard does not seem to be claiming that he will be this missionary. This seems to be the necessary inference from his "prediction" that the coming missionary will be "with authority." Kierkegaard always wrote that he was "without authority."[22] He may have seen himself as, through his writings, becoming a "forerunner" of some coming "reformer" or "missionary" who uses the category of the single individual.[23] Kierkegaard's point may be that this person will essentially reenact the singular work of Jesus, authoritatively bringing a crisis wherein those who don't learn "obedience" from his "divine weakness" willingly participate in "slaying him in impious rebellion."

19. Another "like for like."
20. Kierkegaard, PV, 123.
21. Kierkegaard, PV, 123–24.
22. "*Without authority* **to make aware** of the religious, the essentially Christian, is the category for my whole work as an author regarded as a totality." Kierkegaard, PV, 12, (emphasis his).
23. See Kirkpatrick, *Attacks on Christendom*, 219–20.

The important thing in Kierkegaard's "prediction" is that God's will is to "still use this category (of the single individual) on an even greater scale, but also with (greater) authority" than Kierkegaard saw as accompanying his "without authority" efforts to "use this category." It seems that Kierkegaard's "vision" was of a coming day when *the gospel of the single individual* will be proclaimed authoritatively and more universally, perhaps as precursor to the return of Christ narrated in Mark 13:24–27.

Perhaps Kierkegaard's "missionary" was some sort of Moses/Elijah (John the Baptist) figure who will provide a climactic gospel witness before the coming of Christ (see Rev 11:3–14; Mark 9:11–13). We would love to entertain the idea that Kierkegaard saw the "two witnesses" of Rev 11:3–14 as alluded to in his "prophecy" and that he interpreted them as signifying the corporate witness of the "martyr" community of "the category of the single individual."[24] Whatever the idea, his point was that he saw the recovery of "the decisive category" of "the single individual" as necessary for the gospel to "become decisive for the future of Christianity" and that "the martyr" would play a significant role in that future, a form of witness that is probably implied in Mark 8:34–38, certainly present in Mark 13:9–13, and in Revelation 11:3–14 made into a corporate symbol of the Christian community, biblical over-literalists notwithstanding.

It seems that Jesus' prediction at this climactic midpoint serves to press the weight of the future upon those hearing him then. (Perhaps Kierkegaard's non-authoritative "prediction" served a similar function for his readers.) The important thing is that both declarations "would" bring an immediate crisis. Both "would still use this category on an even greater scale."

> For whoever is ashamed of me and of my words in this adulterous and sinful generation, of him will the Son of Man also be ashamed when he comes in the glory of his Father with the holy angels.

This declaration of "singularity," in its *authoritative* and *decisive* "whoever," *immediately* places the crowd and the disciples, who were specifically "called to him" to hear its judgment, in a place of decision. This is a warning of a future like for like that "fulfills" the present "like for like" seen in the discussion of 7:1–23. The judgment follows *the imperative* in 8:34–35 of Jesus' way of the cross which must be *taken up* by all followers. For "whoever is ashamed of *me*" (the crucified Christ), "and *my words*" (the cruciform life that follows all he has taught), "*of him will the Son of Man also be ashamed.*" Simply put, humans, in the *Abram/pagan* place of mass-man solidarity, are

---

24. See Bauckham, *Theology*, 84–88; Peterson, *Reversed Thunder*, 112–16. For more from Kierkegaard on this "missionary" see PV, 280–93; JP 3, 2649.

called to find salvation in and through allegiance to Jesus and his way of the cross and thereby become *the single individual*. Peter and the disciples are so called. All are called to solidarity with *the missionary* who in divine weakness but also "with authority" may "teach people obedience" through being slain "in impious rebellion."[25] Kierkegaard writes,

> The martyr is the suffering single individual who in his love of mankind educated others in Christianity, converting the mass into single individuals—and there is joy in heaven for every single individual he rescues from [*deleted*: what even the apostle calls the "animal category"]: the mass.[26]

We can certainly see in Kierkegaard's "martyr" the positive outcome of "joy in heaven" that Peter and the disciples so feared as they "awaited" the second touch of Jesus.

Both Mark and Kierkegaard surely know that the cross does not merely signify self-denial of "the easy life" during peacetime, but self-sacrifice during the wartime of the church militant. They mince no words. Mark has revealed another secret, that goes unresolved right through to 16:7–8 and even in 16:9–20 unresolved until 16:20. That secret is the secret individual and apart from "obedience" to that secret people will only know the Son of Man's shame at them because in the leavened crowd they only knew the "shameful" Son of Man.

Mark's gospel certainly seems to have been designed to leave the disciples and his readers (in them) in tension, waiting for the "second touch" of Jesus. Both Mark and Kierkegaard, knowing and using the power of narrative, told their respective "stories" in a way that their readers find themselves therein, whether as disciple or in the crowd, in leaven or in faith, in love or in selfishness, or in the in-betweens of all these in faith and unbelief. Both writers, because of Jesus the single individual par excellence, posited *the single individual* as the category through which "the age, history, the human race must go" for salvation. The shame of Jesus at the end, over those ashamed of him during their life in the middle-time of history, is at this point, the paradoxical promise that warns all against falling short of the gospel of the cross of Christ. Once again, we meet paradox: the way to avoid final shame is to embrace the shame of Jesus and his cross. Kierkegaard summarized that,

---

25. Or possibly *as "the missionary"* according to our hopeful thoughts on Kierkegaard's martyr-missionary "prophecy" in relation to Rev 11:3–14, as discussed above.

26. Kierkegaard, PV, 282.

Every human being, unconditionally every human being, can and should be an individual, should place his *honor*—but will also truly find his *salvation*—in being an individual.[27]

"CHRISTIANITY" AND THE LEAVEN OF ESTABLISHMENT

E. Stanley Jones, the great modern missionary to India, wrote of his struggle with Western evangelism's "Christian-establishment" *leaven* and the terrible struggle he went through to be able to evangelize for the sake of Christ alone:

> Christianity must be defined as Christ, not the Old Testament, not Western Civilization, not even the system built around him in the West, but Christ himself and to be Christian is to follow him . . . I have dropped out the term "Christianity" from my announcements (it isn't found in the Scriptures, is it?), for it had *connotations that confused,* and instead I have used the name of Christ in subjects announced and in the address itself . . . It must be the Christ of the Indian road . . . I have come to the conclusion that the right way was just to be a Christian with all the *fearless* implications of the term. But who was sufficient for these things? For it meant *standing down* amid the currents of thought and national movements sweeping over India and interpreting Christ to the situation. I was painfully conscious that I was not intellectually prepared for it. I was the more painfully conscious that I was *not Christian enough* to do what the situation demanded. And most depressing of all, I was physically broken.[28]

We briefly point out the following things for an "application" of Mark 8 to Christianity today.

---

27. Kierkegaard, PV, 117 (emphasis mine).

28. Jones, *Christ of the Indian Road*, 22–23; 18, (emphasis mine). We note that Kierkegaard also, though not predominantly so, indicted the term "Christianity." At times he used the term to convey the core truth of Christianity, that, *"truth is Christ."* Hong & Hong, in "Notes" to *Journals and Papers,* JP 1, 514. He also used the term as discussed above: "Christianity, becoming and being a Christian, is accompanied by suffering to such a degree that in order to endure these sufferings they are promised a 'Spirit' which shall make the whole conversion easy for them, since otherwise, according to the New Testament's own teaching, it could not be endured." Kierkegaard, JP 1, 541. Another usage was to contrast "Earlier Christianity" with "Contemporary Christianity," JP 1, 543; 560. And as his "attack on Christendom" developed, he used the term "Christianity" as "abolished by" or even synonymous with "Christendom." See JP 1, 383; 560.

- *First*, his reference to Western Civilization and "the system built around him" (Christ) point to the "establishment" tendencies of Christendom/Christianity. This is a form of "leavening" with much the same impetus as that with which Peter was tempted.
- *Second*, he realized, through conversations with a Hindu leading Government official, that this leavened "gospel" innately contained "connotations that confused." Thus, although Jones seemed to be "fearful" of "selling" what would be the "less assured" results of the non-leavened gospel to the "missions-establishment" of "the British gospel," he was already more fearful of misrepresenting the gospel of Christ to a nation that needed Christ's gospel, not the West's leavened "gospel."
- *Third*, He knew that to be a Christian was the "fearless" way but sorely felt himself wholly insufficient to follow such fearlessness. He was "painfully conscious" that he "was not Christian enough"—as himself still "a man of unclean establishment-leavened lips of a people of unclean establishment-leavened lips"—to follow and proclaim the *establishment-unleavened* gospel of Christ alone.[29]
- *Fourth*, Jones continues from his "not Christian enough" confession to narrate what we must consider a veritable "second touch" of Jesus given him, in his words, "in one of my darkest hours":

> While in prayer, not particularly thinking about myself, a Voice seemed to say, "Are you ready for this work to which I have called you?" I replied: "No, Lord, I am at the end of my rope." The Voice replied, "If you will turn that over to me and not worry about it, I will take care of it." I quickly answered, Lord, I close the bargain right here." A great peace settled into my heart and pervaded me. I knew it was done! Life—abundant Life—had taken possession of me . . . Christ to me had become *Life*.[30]

Thus, we end on a *positive* note, albeit at the anti-climactic midpoint of Mark's own narrative of faltering followers with Peter as chief. Jones is a modern-day illustration of the perennial leaven-crisis all would-be disciples/evangelists of the gospel inevitably face. Meditation on this evangelistic temptation, which Mark has poignantly and powerfully revealed, must

---

29. We allude to Isa 6:5 and the crisis of individual and collective "unclean lips" in relation to commissioning from God that follows in Isa 6:8. We admit that E. Stanley Jones is not an "exact fit" for illustrating Peter's *triumphalist* establishment-leavening and see his applicability as of an already self-sacrificial disciple struggling to break out of the mold of the easier tried-and-true way of *colonialist* "establishment-missions."

30. Jones, *Christ of the Indian Road*, 19–20, 21, (emphasis his).

THE "DISCIPLE" WHO REJECTED THE WAY OF JESUS' DEATH 213

certainly be considered as designed to help enable the proper faith-response to Jesus' warning to "beware the leaven." Mark reveals the ultimately humbling temptation disciples face, at least in God's intent which is to be the liberating, the "second touch" of Jesus. That touch enables disciples to follow Christ in the *Christian suffering* that Kierkegaard held to be "essentially a danger to every Established Order."[31] In a sense the crisis between Christ and established order leaven is dangerous to both.

Regarding "disciples" such as leavened *Peter*, the danger to the gospel is evangelizing as the mouthpiece and representative of Satan for a leavened established order.[32] And therefore, the warning of Jesus to "beware the leaven" means that disciples should only preach *Christ crucified* as the gospel (Mark 15:39; 1 Cor 2:2). For to preach *Christianity* is to proclaim a leavened gospel. For the gospel is Christ, the Single Individual, "who suffered under Pontius Pilate," under the established order.

Regarding *the disciple as sufferer*, he or she is the ultimate danger to the established order. This is because the disciple's God-given cross leads to what C. S. Lewis called the surprise of joy:

> The Prodigal Son at least walked home on his own feet. But who can duly adore that Love which will open the high gates to a prodigal who is brought in kicking, struggling, resentful, and darting his eyes in every direction for a chance of escape? The words *compelle intrare,* compel them to come in, have been so abused by wicked men that we shudder to use them; but properly understood, they plumb the depth of the Divine mercy. The

---

31. Westphal, "Kierkegaard's Teleological Suspension," 114. We also add that E. Stanley Jones realized the danger the unleavened gospel presented to the "Christianity" he had sought to proclaim.

32. Amy-Jill Levine seems to us to present a common contemporary establishment-leaven in which it is ironically "revolution" against the "established order." This seems to demonstrate that the leaven Jesus warned against has the power of shape-shifting to appease most any "revolutionary" self-constructed desire. This is especially tempting for modern pseudo-religious "revolutions" although we have already seen in Mark that it has universal appeal for good old-fashioned "religious" revolutions (holy wars). Levine writes, "Revolutionary comes to mean, especially to sectors of the academy as well as the popular imagination, what 'we' want. In this setting, 'change' is good, and the status quo is dreadful (no subtlety here, even if via colonial mimicry the 'new' is a replication of the old, just with different players). My students, most of them studying to be Christian ministers and religious educators, and almost all of them invested in counter-cultural expressions, with the 'culture' defined variously as late global capitalism, colonialism, heteronormativity and anything to do with Donald Trump, require Jesus to be a revolutionary. They need him for their own ideological agendas.' Levine, "Jesus the Storyteller," 52–53.

hardness of God is kinder than the softness of men, and His compulsion is our liberation.[33]

For the disciple is and remains a prodigal until lifted by the cross, receiving the second touch from the crucified, and finally becoming a self. But that disciple, when become a self, signifies the ultimate danger to the established order and the crowd in untruth. Thus, Peter, the "blind disciple" *par excellence* will ultimately be intimated by Mark's narrative as "good soil." A "secret Peter" thereby emerges as *the secret epiphany* of Mark's gospel of discipleship largely penned for "the follower at second hand." And thus, Mark's gospel is that God's "hardness," that *requires* and *makes* cruciform shaped disciples, is the liberation of all humankind from the easy-chair "softness" of the established order and its pacified, rather than passionate, mass-men. Of course, the dark side of that easy chair is that it brings death in many guises. But Jesus promises that "whoever loses his life for my sake and the gospel's will save it (8:35).

---

33. Lewis, *Surprised by Joy,* 229.

Conclusion to Volume 2

Mark has brought us from "the beginning of the gospel," where the tempted Jesus first overcame Satan in the wilderness, to the *anti-climactic* crisis, the Satanic temptation in Peter wherein for this disciple par excellence overcoming seems precarious if not *impossible*. In this second volume of our reading, we began with the demoniac Satanized by the legion, likely an allusion to the Roman unit of soldiers. Now Peter, seemingly infected by the will-to-power leaven of the Pharisees and Herod, may be possessed by a Satanic legion such that he would lead God's "new Israel" in Holy war against Rome's physical legions. This presents quite the cliff-hanger as we prepare, Lord-willing, the third and fourth volumes wherein we can see how Mark further develops what seems to be the main concern of his gospel: authentic faith of disciples who desperately need a "second touch" from Jesus. For the time being, they "see men, as trees walking."

Mark has provided a "preview" of the second touch in the account of the blind man which we, following Mark's "imaginary" of the kingdom of God, drew out to deepen the spiritual nature of the second touch and demonstrate *how* Peter (and all disciples "in him") *can* thereby escape the Satanic leaven of the worldly order to become Kierkegaard's and Mark's *single individual*. Of course, the way was also previewed in several single individuals who Mark has shown "emerging" from the crowd. The crowd itself has not yet become "leavened," as it eventually will in support of the crucifixion of Jesus, but nevertheless demonstrates that even in less acute political circumstances complicity with the crowd prevents becoming a self. Thus, at Mark's mid-point of *crisis*, the seemingly *impossible* way of the cross and the "category of the single individual" have been explicitly introduced as *the way* all those emerging from the crowd must pass. That passage may be from the shallow socially leavened *bourgeoise* crowd that Kierkegaard and would-be disciples of his day faced, or from the dangerous politically leavened *revolutionary* crowd that Jesus and would-be disciples of his day faced.

Along the way we have seen how Mark's gospel "works" in the lives of disciples. At this point we will provide a simple conclusion via theologian John Sanders which succinctly narrates how the aspects of Mark's "media" methods we have seen work in tandem with the entire Bible narrative and especially provide what we have called the "second touch" vitally necessary for discipleship.

> The Bible provides an overarching narrative about who God is, the situation we find ourselves in, and what God has done to help us. It is a love story... The Bible provides examples of how to live out the journey of faith. The stories and reflections shape our own spiritual narratives.[34]

Looking ahead, we will see that Mark and Kierkegaard both demonstrate the impossible challenge disciples face as both possibility and promise since God provides what is impossible for men (Mark 10:27). Altogether, what is provided through Christ is the first-touch that sees "men, as trees walking," and the second-touch faith that sees and receives his way of the cross as one's own. Yet this way is fraught with the terror of what is impossible, humanly speaking. Kierkegaard wrote,

> really and truly, anyone who has the remotest idea of what it is to die to the world also knows that this does not take place without frightful agonies.[35]

The next volumes will therefore follow Mark's ever-descending dive into the frightful agonies of the disciples as they face their own complicity with the "leaven" of the established order while also knowing that the "powers that be" seem to hold the powers of life and death. Mark therefore proceeds toward the coming generation-long conflagration in Jerusalem, in which the disciples and those reading Mark will need to "live and move and have their being" (Mark 13). Thereby, Mark "deconstructs" the established order as "home," and reconstructs home as Jesus' new family, the titular focus of our first volume. We can now conclude the titular focus of this second volume by saying that God's new family consists of Abrahamic *single individuals* who, like Abram, left their pagan home-crowd. This volume has delineated the ironic way of the cross that only portends death yet through God's possibility brings the salvation-life the crowd does not live, namely the life of *becoming a self*. Jamie Lorentzen defines and portrays this graphically:

---

34. Sanders, *Embracing Prodigals*, 68.
35. Kierkegaard, JP 2, 1410.

> To become fully human means to unlearn duplicitous cultural norms and values . . . Not choosing the true self . . . [leaves one] "in the congregation of the dead."[36]

The necessity of the "second touch" is even more acutely seen in the second half of Mark's gospel and thus also the subsequent volumes of our reading. We will see that this necessity *unveils* human impossibility. The conflict with the leaven of the established order reveals the sheer *nakedness* of fallen humans before God. But the gospel also discloses another secret—its *secret possibility* of what is possible *with* God—made possible *because* on the cross Jesus *was forsaken by* God (Mark 10:28; 15:34). This reveals Mark's ultimate secret epiphany, the *secret of the cross* as the way for disciples.[37]

Thus, we look forward to Mark's further developments, ultimate secrets, and puzzling "endings" regarding all these things, along with the Kierkegaardian "philosophical fragments" to be gathered along the way that truly provide Christ as our full provision for life.[38] At the final climax, we will hopefully find ourselves at one with the women disciples at the empty tomb, in their secret epiphany of *fear and trembling*.[39]

---

36. Lorentzen, *Sober Cannibals, Drunken Christians*, 16–17. The quoted words are the words of Ishmael in Melville's *Moby Dick*. But we note that several of the writings of "A" in *Either/Or 1*, are "Delivered before the . . . [Fellowship of the Dead]." See Kierkegaard, EO1, 137, 165, 217.

37. Perhaps the ultimate paradox of Mark's gospel is the "secret paradox" of the mystery of the God-forsaken faithful Jesus dying on the cross so that all God's possibilities for humanity could be provided in the presently unseen resurrection life to follow.

38. Remembering the "secret" behind Kierkegaard's "Philosophical Fragments" was that they were *secretly* biblical truths.

39. "The fear and silence of the women belong to the structure of epiphany." Malbon, *In the Company*, 64.

Bibliography

Andic, Martin. "Love's Redoubling and the Eternal Like for Like" in *Works of Love*. International Kierkegaard Commentary, Volume 16, edited by Robert L. Perkins, 9–38. Macon: Mercer University Press, 1999.
Auden, W. H. *The Living Thoughts of Kierkegaard: Presented by W. H. Auden*. Bloomington: Indiana University Press, 1971.
Backhouse, Stephen. *Kierkegaard: A Single Life*. Grand Rapids: Zondervan, 2016.
———. "Politics as Indirect Communication in *The Moment* and the *Attack upon "Christendom."* In *Kierkegaard and Political Theology*, edited by Roberto Sirvent et al., 43–62. Eugene: Pickwick, 2018.
Baggett, John F. *Seeing Through the Eyes of Jesus: His Revolutionary View of Reality & His Transcendent Significance for Faith*. Grand Rapids: Eerdmans, 2008.
Barnett, Christopher B. *Bob Dylan and the Spheres of Existence*. Theology, Religion, and Pop Culture, edited by Matthew Brake. Lanham, MD: Fortress Academic, 2023.
———. *From Despair to Faith: The Spirituality of Soren Kierkegaard*. Minneapolis: Fortress, 2014.
Barrett, Lee C. *Kierkegaard*. Abingdon Pillars of Theology. Nashville: Abingdon, 2010.
Bauckham Richard. "Kierkegaard and the Epistle of James." In *Kierkegaard and the Christian Faith*, edited by Paul Martens, et al., 39–54. Waco: Baylor, 2016.
———. *The Theology of the Book of Revelation*. New Testament Theology, edited by James D. G. Dunn. Cambridge: Cambridge University Press, 1993.
Bonhoeffer, Dietrich. *Discipleship*, Translated by Barbra Green et al. Dietrich Bonhoeffer Works, Volume 4. Minneapolis: Fortress, 2001.
———. *Ethics*, Translated by Reinhard Krauss et al. Dietrich Bonhoeffer Works, Volume 6. Minneapolis: Fortress, 2005.
———. *Letters and Papers from Prison*, Translated by Isabel Best et al. Dietrich Bonhoeffer Works, Volume 8. Minneapolis: Fortress, 2010.
———. *Letters and Papers from Prison published originally as Prisoner for God*, Translated by Reginald H. Fuller, edited by Eberhard Bethge. New York: Macmillan, 1953.
———. *Life Together - Prayerbook of the Bible*, Translated by Daniel W. Bloesch et al. Dietrich Bonhoeffer Works, Volume 5. Minneapolis: Fortress, 1996.
Boring, M. Eugene. *Mark - A Commentary*. The New Testament Library. Louisville: Westminster John Knox, 2012 Paperback/Kindle edition.
Brueggemann, Walter. *Mandate to Difference: An Invitation to the Contemporary Church*. Louisville: Westminster John Knox, 2007.

Burdon, Christopher. *Stumbling on God: Faith and Vision through Mark's Gospel.* Grand Rapids: Eerdmans, 1990.

Caputo, John D. "What is Merold Westphal's Critique of Ontotheology Criticizing?" in *Gazing Through a Prism Darkly: Reflections on Merold Westphal's Hermeneutical Epistemology,* edited by B. Keith Putt, 100–115. Perspectives in Continental Philosophy, edited by John D. Caputo. New York: Fordham University Press, 2009.

Cavanaugh, William T. *Being Consumed: Economics and Christian Desire.* Grand Rapids: Eerdmans, 2008.

Chesterton, G. K. *The Everlasting Man.* San Francisco: Ignatius, 1993.

———. *Heretics/Orthodoxy.* Nelson's Royal Classics. Nashville: Thomas Nelson, 2000.

Christman, Bryan M. *Behold, My Mother and My Brethren! The Beginning of the Gospel and Becoming a Christian in (Post) Christendom.* A Kierkegaardian Reading of the Gospel of Mark, Volume 1. Eugene: Resource Publications, 2022.

———. *The Gospel in the Dock: Is the Gospel of Jesus Christ Good for the Church, Humanity, and the World.* Eugene: Resource Publications, 2021.

———. "Lewis and Kierkegaard as Missionaries to Post-Christian Pagans" in Evangelical Review of Theology, 46:2 (2022) 123–136, Eugene: Wipf and Stock.

Cross, Terry L. *The People of God's Presence: An Introduction to Ecclesiology.* Grand Rapids: Baker Academic, 2019.

Cutting, Pat. "The Levels of Interpersonal Relationships in Kierkegaard's Two Ages." In *Two Ages.* International Kierkegaard Commentary, Volume 14, edited by Robert L. Perkins, 73–86. Macon: Mercer University Press, 1984.

Dalton, Stuart. *How to Misunderstand Kierkegaard: An Instruction Manual for Assistant Professors and Other Immoral and Disreputable Persons.* Eugene: Cascade, 2022.

Daniel-Rops. *Jesus and His Times: A New Life of Christ.* Translated by Ruby Millar. New York: E. P. Dutton & Co., 1954.

Dumbrell, William J. *The Faith of Israel: It's Expression in the Books of the Old Testament.* Grand Rapids: Baker, 1988.

Dru, Alexander. *The Soul of Kierkegaard: Selections from His Journals,* Mineola: Dover, 2003.

Edwards, Aaron P. *Taking Kierkegaard Back to Church: The Ecclesial Implications of the Gospel.* Eugene: Cascade, 2022.

Emmanuel, Steven M. *Kierkegaard's Concept of Revelation.* Albany: State University of New York Press, 1996.

Evans, C. Stephen. "Merold Westphal on the Sociopolitical Implications of Kierkegaard's Thought" in *Gazing Through a Prism Darkly: Reflections on Merold Westphal's Hermeneutical Epistemology,* edited by B. Keith Putt, 35–45. Perspectives in Continental Philosophy, edited by John D. Caputo. New York: Fordham University Press, 2009.

———. *Soren Kierkegaard's Christian Psychology - Insight for Counseling and Pastoral Care.* Vancouver: Regent College, 1990.

Farley, Lawrence R. *The Gospel of Mark: The Suffering Servant.* The Orthodox Bible Companion Series. Ancient Faith: Chesterton, IN, 2004.

Ferreira. M. Jamie. "Levinas and Kierkegaard on Triadic Relations with God" in *Gazing Through a Prism Darkly: Reflections on Merold Westphal's Hermeneutical Epistemology,* edited by B. Keith Putt, 46–60. Perspectives in Continental Philosophy, edited by John D. Caputo. New York: Fordham University Press, 2009.

———. *Love's Grateful Striving: A Commentary on Kierkegaard's Works of Love,* New York: Oxford University Press, 2001.

Garff, Joakim. *Soren Kierkegaard: A Biography*. Translated by Bruce Kirmmse. Princeton: Princeton University Press, 2000.

Garland, David E. "A Theology of Mark's Gospel." In *The Biblical Theology of the New Testament*, edited by Andreas J. Köstenberger. Grand Rapids: Zondervan, 2015.

———. "Mark." In *The NIV Application Commentary*, edited by Terry Muck. Grand Rapids: Zondervan, 1996.

Gorman, Michael J. *Reading Revelation Responsibly. Uncivil Worship and Witness: Following the Lamb into the New Creation*. Eugene: Cascade, 2011.

Groot, Tracy. *Madman*. Chicago: Moody, 2006.

Guardini, Romano. *The Death of Socrates - An Interpretation of the Platonic Dialogues: Euthyphro, Apology, Crito, and Phaedo*. Translated by Basil Wrighton. New York: Sheed & Ward, 1948.

Hall, Ronald L. "Spirit and Presence: A Kierkegaardian Analysis" in *Either/Or, 1*. International Kierkegaard Commentary, Volume 3, edited by Robert L. Perkins, 271–285. Macon: Mercer University Press, 1995.

———. *Word & Spirit: A Kierkegaardian Critique of the Modern Age*. The Indiana Series in the Philosophy of Religion, edited by Merold Westphal. Bloomington: Indiana University Press, 1993.

Hobbes, Thomas. *Leviathan or The Matter, Forme & Power of a Common-wealth Eccesiasticall and Civill*. The Barnes & Noble Library of Essential Reading. New York: Barnes & Noble, 2004 [1651].

Hoberman, John M. "Kierkegaard's Two Ages and Heidegger's Critique of Modernity" in *Two Ages*. International Kierkegaard Commentary, Volume 14, edited by Robert L. Perkins, 223–258. Macon: Mercer University Press, 1984.

Holland, Tom. *Revolutionary: Who Was Jesus? Why Does He Still Matter?* Edited by Tom Holland, London: SPCK, 2020.

Horne, Mark. *The Victory According to Mark: An Exposition of the Second Gospel*. Moscow: Canon, 2003.

Iersel, Bas van. *Reading Mark*. Translated by W. H. Bisscheroux. Collegeville, MN: Liturgical, 1988.

Janz, Denis R. *The Westminster Handbook of Martin Luther*. The Westminster Handbook to Christian Theology. Louisville: Westminster John Knox, 2010.

Jones, E. Stanley. *The Christ of the Indian Road*. New York: Abingdon, 1925.

Juel, Donald H. "Mark." In *Augsburg Commentary on the New Testament*, edited by Roy A. Harrisville, et al. Minneapolis: Augsburg Fortress, 1990.

Kangas, David J. *Errant Affirmations: On the Philosophical Meaning of Kierkegaard's Religious Discourses*. London: Bloomsbury, 2018.

Keller, Timothy. *King's Cross: The Story of the World in the Life of Jesus*. New York: Dutton, 2011.

———. *The Prodigal God: Recovering the Heart of the Christian Faith*. New York: Dutton, 2008.

Kierkegaard, Soren. *Christian Discourses and The Lilies of the Field and the Birds of the Air and Three discourses at the Communion on Fridays*. Translated by Walter Lowrie, London: Oxford University Press, 1940.

———. *The Concept of Anxiety: A Simple Psychologically Orienting Deliberation on the Dogmatic Issue of Hereditary Sin*. Translated by Reidar Thomte, Kierkegaard's Writings, VIII. Princeton: Princeton University Press, 1980.

BIBLIOGRAPHY

———. *Concluding Unscientific Postscript to Philosophical Fragments, Volume I.* Kierkegaard's Writings, XII.1. Translated by Howard V. Hong and Edna H. Hong, Princeton: Princeton University Press, 1992.

———. *The Corsair Affair and Articles Related to the Writings.* Kierkegaard's Writings XIII. Translated by Howard V. Hong and Edna H. Hong, Princeton: Princeton University Press, 1982.

———. *Eighteen Upbuilding Discourses.* Kierkegaard's Writings, V. Translated by Howard V. Hong and Edna H. Hong, Princeton: Princeton University Press, 1990.

———. *Either/Or Part I,* Kierkegaard's Writings, III. Translated by Howard V. Hong and Edna H. Hong, Princeton: Princeton University Press, 1987.

———. *Either/Or Volume II.* Translated by Walter Lowrie. Princeton: Princeton University Press, 1972.

———. *Fear and Trembling/Repetition.* Kierkegaard's Writings, VI. Translated by Howard V. Hong and Edna H. Hong, Princeton: Princeton University Press, 1983.

———. *For Self-Examination/Judge for Yourself!* Kierkegaard's Writings XXI. Translated by Howard V. Hong and Edna H. Hong, Princeton: Princeton University Press, 1990.

———. *Kierkegaard's Attack upon "Christendom" 1854–1855.* Translated by Walter Lowrie, Princeton: Princeton University Press, 1946.

———. *The Moment and Late Writings.* Kierkegaard's Writings, XXIII. Translated by Howard V. Hong and Edna H. Hong, Princeton: Princeton University Press, 1998.

———. *The Point of View.* Kierkegaard's Writings, XXII. Translated by Howard V. Hong and Edna H. Hong, Princeton: Princeton University Press, 1998.

———. *Practice in Christianity.* Kierkegaard's Writings, XX. Translated by Howard V. Hong and Edna H. Hong, Princeton: Princeton University Press, 1991.

———. *Provocations: Spiritual Writings of Kierkegaard.* Edited by Charles E. Moore. Walden NY: Plough, 2002.

———. *Purity of Heart is to Will One Thing: Spiritual Preparation for the Office of Confession.* Harper Torchlight. Translated by Douglas V. Steere, New York: Harper & Brothers, 1956.

———. *The Sickness unto Death: A Christian Psychological Exposition for Upbuilding and Awakening.* Kierkegaard's Writings, XIX. Translated by Howard V. Hong and Edna H. Hong, Princeton: Princeton University Press, 1980.

———. *Soren Kierkegaard's Journals and Papers,* 7 Volumes. Translated by Howard V. Hong and Edna H. Hong, Bloomington: Indiana University Press, 1967–1978.

———. *Spiritual Writings - Gift, Creation, Love: Selections from the Upbuilding Discourses.* Translated by George Pattison. Harper Perennial Modern Thought. New York: HarperPerennial, 2010.

———. *Stages on Life's Way.* Kierkegaard's Writings, XI. Translated by Howard V. Hong and Edna H. Hong, Princeton: Princeton University Press, 1988.

———. *Three Discourses on Imagined Occasions.* Kierkegaard's Writings, X. Translated by Howard V. Hong and Edna H. Hong, Princeton: Princeton University Press, 1993.

———. *Upbuilding Discourses in Various Spirits.* Kierkegaard's Writings, XV. Translated by Howard V. Hong and Edna H. Hong, Princeton: Princeton University Press, 1993.

———. *Works of Love.* Translated by Howard V. Hong and Edna H. Hong, Harper Perennial Modern Thought. New York: HarperPerennial, 2009.

———. *Works of Love*. Kierkegaard's Writings, XVI. Translated by Howard V. Hong and Edna H. Hong. Princeton: Princeton University Press, 1995.

Kirkpatrick, Matthew D. *Attacks on Christendom in a World Come of Age - Kierkegaard, Bonhoeffer, and the Question of "Religionless Christianity."* Princeton Theological Monographs Series. Eugene OR: Pickwick, 2011.

———. "Kierkegaard and the End of the Danish Golden Age" in *The Oxford Handbook of Kierkegaard*, edited by John Lippitt et al., 28–43. Oxford: Oxford University Press, 2013.

Leithart, Peter J. *Solomon Among the Postmoderns*. Grand Rapids: Brazos, 2008.

———. *Traces of the Trinity: Signs of God in Creation and Human Experience*. Grand Rapids: Brazos, 2015.

Levine, Amy Jill. "Jesus the Storyteller: The Revolutionary Power of Parables" in *Revolutionary: Who Was Jesus? Why Does He Still Matter?* edited by Tom Holland, 52–76. London: SPCK, 2020.

Lewis. C. S. *The Abolition of Man: How Education Develops Man's Sense of Morality*. New York: Macmillan, 1943.

———. *Letters to Malcom: Chiefly on Prayer*. San Diego: Harcourt Brace, 1964, 1963.

———. *Mere Christianity*. New York: Macmillan. 1978.

———. *Surprised by Joy: The Shape of My Early Life*. San Diego: Harcourt Brace, 1955.

———. *The Weight of Glory and Other Addresses*, Revised and Expanded Edition, edited by Walter Hooper, New York: Collier, 1980.

Lorentzen, Jamie. *Sober Cannibals, Drunken Christians: Melville, Kierkegaard, & Tragic Optimism in Polarized Worlds*. Macon: Mercer University Press, 2010.

Lynch, William F. *Images of Faith: An Exploration of the Ironic Imagination*. Notre Dame: University of Notre Dame, 1973.

———. *Images of Hope: Imagination as Healer of the Hopeless*. Notre Dame: University of Notre Dame Press, 1965.

Malbon, Elizabeth Struthers. *In the Company of Jesus: Characters in Mark's Gospel of Jesus*. Louisville: Westminster John Knox, 2000.

Malina, Bruce J. and Jerome H Neyrey. *Portraits of Paul: An Archaeology of Ancient Personality*. Louisville: Westminster John Knox, 1996.

Martens, Paul. "The Emergence of the Holy Spirit in Kierkegaard's Thought" Critical Theological Developments in For Self-Examination and Judge for Yourself!" in *For Self Examination and Judge for Yourself!* International Kierkegaard Commentary, Volume 21, edited by Robert L. Perkins, 199–222. Macon: Mercer University Press, 2002.

———. "The Pharisee" Kierkegaard's Polyphonic Personification of a Univocal Idea" in *Kierkegaard and the Bible: Tome II: The New Testament*. Kierkegaard Research: Sources, Reception and Resources, Volume 1, edited by Lee C. Barrett and Jon Stewart, 93–105. Farnham, Surrey: Ashgate, 2010.

Matusik, Martin Beck. "The God Who Refuses to Appear on Philosophy's Terms" in *Gazing Through a Prism Darkly: Reflections on Merold Westphal's Hermeneutical Epistemology*, edited by B. Keith Putt, 100–115. Perspectives in Continental Philosophy, edited by John D. Caputo. New York: Fordham University Press, 2009.

McSwain, Jeff. *Movements of Grace: The Dynamic Christo-realism of Barth, Bonhoeffer, and the Torrances*. Eugene: Wipf and Stock, 2010.

Moo, Douglas. "The Epistle to the Romans." In *The New International Commentary on the New Testament*, edited by Gordon D. Fee. Grand Rapids: Eerdmans, 1996.

Moore, Scott H. *The Limits of Liberal Democracy: Politics and Religion at the End of Modernity.* Downers Grove: IVP Academic, 2009.

Mulder, Jack. "Governance/Providence" in *Kierkegaard's Concepts Tome III: Envy to Incognito.* Kierkegaard Research: Sources, Reception and Resources, Volume 15, edited by Steven M. Emmanuel et al, 113–18. London: Routledge, 2016.

Newbigin, Lesslie. *Lesslie Newbigin: Missionary Theologian, A Reader.* Complied & introduced by Paul Weston. Grand Rapids: Eerdmans, 2006.

Oden, Thomas C., and Christopher A. Hall. "Mark." In *Ancient Christian Commentary on Scripture*, New Testament II. Edited by Thomas C. Oden. Downers Grove: IVP, 1998.

Pascal, Blaise. *Pascal's Pensees.* New York: E. P. Dutton & Co., 1958.

Perez, Eliseo Perez. *A Vexing Gadfly: The Late Kierkegaard on Economic Matters.* Princeton Theological Monographs. Eugene: Pickwick, 2009.

Perkins, Robert L. "Envy as Personal Phenomenon and as Politics" in *Two Ages.* International Kierkegaard Commentary, Volume 14, edited by Robert L. Perkins, 107–132. Macon: Mercer University Press, 1984.

———. *Two Ages.* International Kierkegaard Commentary, Volume 14, edited by Robert L. Perkins. Macon: Mercer University Press, 1984.

———. *Works of Love.* International Kierkegaard Commentary, Volume 16, edited by Robert L. Perkins. Macon: Mercer University Press, 1999.

Peterson, Eugene H. *Eat This Book: A Conversation on the Art of Spiritual Reading.* Grand Rapids: Eerdmans, 2006.

———. *Reversed Thunder: The Revelation of John & the Praying Imagination.* New York: HarperOne, 1988.

Plekon, Michael. "Towards Apocalypse: Kierkegaard's Two Ages in Golden Age Denmark" in *Two Ages.* International Kierkegaard Commentary, Volume 14, edited by Robert L. Perkins, 19–52. Macon: Mercer University Press, 1984.

Podmore, Simon D. "To Die and Yet Not Die: Kierkegaard's Theophany of Death" in *Kierkegaard and Death,* edited by Patrick Stokes et al., 44–64. Indiana Series in the Philosophy of Religion, Bloomington: Indiana University Press, 2011.

Polk, Timothy H. "The Tax Collector: Model of Inwardness" in *Kierkegaard and the Bible: Tome II: The New Testament.* Kierkegaard Research: Sources, Reception and Resources, Volume 1, edited by Lee C. Barrett and Jon Stewart, 107–122. Farnham, Surrey: Ashgate, 2010.

Polanyi, Michael. *Personal Knowledge" Towards a Post-Critical Philosophy.* Chicago: University of Chicago Press, 1958.

———. *The Tacit Dimension.* Chicago: University of Chicago Press, 1966.

Possen, David D. "On Kierkegaard's Copenhagen Pagans" in *Christian Discourses and The Crisis and a Crisis in the Life of an Actress.* International Kierkegaard Commentary, Volume 17, edited by Robert L. Perkins, 35–60. Macon: Mercer University Press, 2007.

———. "The Logic of 'On the Occasion of a Confession'" in *Three Discourses on Imagined Occasions.* International Kierkegaard Commentary, Volume 10, edited by Robert L. Perkins, 225–243. Macon: Mercer University Press, 2006.

Putt, B. Keith and Merold Westphal. "Talking to Balaam's Ass: A Concluding Conversation" in *Gazing Through a Prism Darkly: Reflections on Merold Westphal's Hermeneutical Epistemology,* edited by B. Keith Putt, 181–205. Perspectives in Continental Philosophy, edited by John D. Caputo. New York: Fordham University Press, 2009.

Rae, Murray. *Kierkegaard and Theology*. Philosophy and Theology. New York: T & T. Clark, 2010.

Rhoads, David et al., *Mark as Story: An Introduction to the Narrative of a Gospel*. Third Edition. Minneapolis: Fortress, 2012.

Roberts, Kyle. *Emerging Prophet: Kierkegaard and the Postmodern People of God*. Eugene: Cascade, 2013.

Roberts, Robert C. *Faith, Reason, and History: Rethinking Kierkegaard's Philosophical Fragments*. Macon: Mercer University Press, 1986.

———. "Passion and Reflection" in *Two Ages*. International Kierkegaard Commentary, Volume 14, edited by Robert L. Perkins, 87–106. Macon: Mercer University Press, 1984.

———. *Recovering Christian Character: The Psychological Wisdom of Soren Kierkegaard*. Kierkegaard as a Christian Thinker, edited by C. Stephen Evans et al. Grand Rapids: Eerdmans, 2022.

Rosenstock-Huessy, Eugen. *The Christian Future or The Modern Mind Outrun*. Eugene: Wipf and Stock, 2013.

Sanders, John. *Embracing Prodigals: Overcoming Authoritative Religion by Embodying Jesus' Nurturing Grace*. Eugene: Cascade, 2020.

Scott, Drusilla. *Everyman Revived: The Common Sense of Michael Polanyi*. Grand Rapids: Eerdmans, 1985.

Seigworth, Gregory J. and Melissa Gregg. "An Inventory of Shimmers," in *The Affect Theory Reader*, ed. Melissa Gregg and Gregory J. Seigworth. Durham, NC: Duke University Press, 2010.

Smith, James K. A. *Desiring the Kingdom: Worship, Worldview, and Cultural Formation*. Cultural Liturgies Volume 1. Grand Rapids: Baker Academic, 2009.

———. *How (Not) to be Secular: Reading Charles Taylor*. Grand Rapids: Eerdmans, 2014.

———. *Imagining the Kingdom: How Worship Works*. Cultural Liturgies Volume 2, Grand Rapids: Eerdmans, 2013.

———. *You Are What You Love: The Spiritual Power of Habit*. Grand Rapids: Brazos, 2016.

Stroup, George W. *Before God*. Grand Rapids: Eerdmans, 2004.

Talbert, Charles H. *Matthew*. Paideia Commentaries on the New Testament. Grand Rapids: Baker Academic, 2010.

Tanner, John S. *Anxiety in Eden: A Kierkegaardian Reading of Paradise Lost*. New York: Oxford University Press, 1992.

Taylor, Charles. *A Secular Age*. Cambridge: Harvard University Press, Belknap, 2007.

Thielicke, Helmut. *Modern Faith and Thought*. Translated by Geoffrey W. Bromiley. Grand Rapids: Eerdmans, 1990.

———. *The Silence of God*. Translated by Geoffrey W. Bromiley. Grand Rapids: Eerdmans, 1962.

Tietjen, Mark A. *Kierkegaard - A Christian Missionary to Christians*. Downers Grove: IVP Academic, 2016.

———. *Kierkegaard, Communication, and Virtue: Authorship as Edification*. Indiana Series in the Philosophy of Religion, edited by Merold Westphal. Bloomington: Indiana University Press, 2013.

Torrance, Thomas F. *Incarnation: The Person and Life of Christ*. Downers Grove: IVP Academic, 2008.

Trueblood, Elton. *The Humor of Christ: A Significant But Often Unrecognized Aspect of Christ's Teaching.* New York: Harper & Row, 1964.

Turlington, Henry. "Commentary on Mark." In *The Broadman Bible Commentary*, Volume 8, edited by Clifton J. Allen. Nashville: Broadman, 1969.

Tyson, Paul. *Kierkegaard's Theological Sociology: Prophetic Fire for the Present Age.* Eugene: Cascade, 2019.

Via, Dan O. Jr. *The Ethics of Mark's Gospel in the Middle of Time.* Philadelphia: Fortress, 1985.

Walsh, Sylvia. *Living Christianly: Kierkegaard's Dialectic of Christian Existence.* University Park: Pennsylvania State University Press, 2005.

Walton, John H. *The Lost World of Genesis One: Ancient Cosmology and the Origins Debate.* Downers Grove: IVP Academic

Ward, Michael. "Imagine There's No Heaven?: C. S. Lewis on Making Space for Faith." In *The Story of the Cosmos: How the Heavens Declare the Glory of God*, edited by Paul M. Gould et al., 149–166. Eugene: Harvest House, 2019.

Watkin, Julia. *Historical Dictionary of Kierkegaard's Philosophy.* Historical Dictionaries of Religions, Philosophies, and Movements, No. 33. Lanham: Scarecrow, 2001.

Westphal, Merold. *Kierkegaard's Concept of Faith.* Kierkegaard as a Christian Thinker, edited by C. Stephen Evans et al. Grand Rapids: Eerdmans, 2014.

———. *Kierkegaard's Critique of Reason and Society.* University Park: Pennsylvania State University Press, 1987.

———. *Levinas and Kierkegaard in Dialogue.* Indiana Series in the Philosophy of Religion, edited by Merold Westphal. Bloomington: Indiana University Press, 2008.

———. "Kierkegaard's Teleological Suspension of Religiousness B" in *Foundations of Kierkegaard's Vision of Community: Religion, Ethics, and Politics in Kierkegaard*, edited by George B. Connell et al., 110–29. New Jersey: Humanities, 1992.

Williams, Bernard. *In the Beginning Was the Deed: Realism and Moralism in Political Argument*, edited by Geoffrey Hawthorne. Princeton: Princeton University Press, 2005.

Williamson, Lamar, Jr. "Mark." In *Interpretation - A Bible Commentary for Preaching and Teaching*, edited by James Luther Mays. Louisville: John Knox, 1983.

Witherington, Ben III. *The Gospel of Mark: A Socio-Rhetorical Commentary*, Kindle edition. Grand Rapids: Eerdmans, 2001.

Wodehouse, P. G. *Enter Jeeves – 15 Early Stories.* Mineola NY: Dover, 1997.

Zimmermann, Jens. *Incarnational Humanism: A Philosophy of Culture for the Church in the World.* Strategic Initiatives in Evangelical Theology. Downers Grove: IVP Academic, 2012.

Ziolkowski, Eric J. "Don Quixote and Kierkegaard's Understanding of the Single Individual in Society" in *Foundations of Kierkegaard's Vision of Community: Religion, Ethics, and Politics in Kierkegaard*, edited by George B. Connell et al., 130–43. New Jersey: Humanities, 1992.

Index

Abram/Abraham, 41n17, 136, 200–201, 207–8, 216
ages/eras 13, 21–32, 42–43, 48, 55, 60–69, 90–91, 94–99, 126, 172–73, 189–90, 201, 204, 208, 210
Agrippa, 96
Andic, Martin, 119, 126, 126n21, 131n7
apologetics, 79, 142
asceticism, 74, 160
anti-theism, 25
Atlantis, 97
atonement, 99, 144
Auden, W. H., 134
authority, 68, 75, 78, 85, 171, 208–10

baptism, 44n27, 184, 204
Backhouse, Stephen, 62, 120n10,
Baggett, John F., 137, 139
Barnett, Christopher B., 42, 195n14, 195n16
Barrett, Lee C., 178, 181
Bauckham, Richard, 149n7, 209n24
beauty, 7–8, 90, 93
begging, 1–2, 12, 15, 28, 31–32, 38, 102, 113, 114, 130–31, 135–36, 158
benediction, 161
blessing, 103–4, 136, 140, 161, 193
Bonhoeffer, Dietrich, 68, 160, 169
Boring, M. Eugene, 3n5, 44n29, 49n11, 54n22
Browne, Sir Thomas, 131
Brueggemann, Walter, 173

Burdon, Christopher, 29n71, 176n33

Caputo, John, 171
Cartesian, 15n28, 194
Cavanaugh, William T., 74n4
Chesterton, G. K., xi, 44, 126, 183
Christendom, 5, 52, 68n26, 89, 91, 117, 124, 149, 164, 168–71, 175, 211n28, 212
Christian atheism (Christian humanism), 126
Christianity, 22–24, 29, 32, 37, 39, 44, 48, 51–53, 55, 59n35, 73, 75n3, 75, 91, 97, 120, 124, 126, 128–29, 149, 150–51, 154, 155, 168–69, 174, 177, 208–13
Church, the, 62, 78n11, 137, 169, 173n27, 210
community, 5, 15, 26, 170, 174–75, 201–3, 208–9
compassion, 17, 36, 38, 76, 101, 187
confession, 18, 42, 57, 178, 182, 195, 203, 212
consumerism, 74
Corban, 116, 121–23, 125, 131, 142, 175
creation, 27n60, 44, 83, 99, 159–61
creaturehood, 5, 8, 89, 109
critique, 21, 22, 32n79, 57, 94, 96, 116–18, 120–22, 124, 170–73
Cross, Terry L., 137n19
crossroads, 187

INDEX

Cruysberghs, Paul, 13–14
Cutting, Patricia, 94–96

Dabhar, 26–28, 30–32, 122
Dalton, Stuart, 109n14, n16
Daniel-Rops, 37
Darwinian, 204
Day, Dorothy, 80
death, 7, 23, 25n54, 29, 32, 37, 44, 77, 83–86, 92, 94, 103, 114, 151–54, 157, 159, 178, 181, 186, 197–214, 216
Demoniac, the, 3–33, 37, 131, 191, 215
demonic,
    boredom/pandemonium, 9–12
    defiance/despair, 4–9, 11, 14, 16, 20, 40, 49–50
    spirituality, 22, 25, 27–29, 31
demons, 9–14, 16–21, 26, 134, 173, 199, 200
Descartes, Rene, 30n77
desire, 10, 12, 13, 15, 18, 28, 31, 42, 57, 127–28, 152, 180, 184, 213n32
dialectic, 53, 88, 150–51, 157
discipleship, 68n26, 150, 160, 179–80, 182–83, 192, 195, 195n16, 214, 216
diversion, 48–49, 173, 184
Don Quixote, 89–91
Dylan, Bob, 125

Ecclesiastes, 43–44
Eden, 6, 106n8, 184
Edwards, Aaron P., 169n13
Edwards, James, 137, 141–42
Emmanuel, Steven M., 107, 111–12
Enlightenment, the, 96
Evangelicalism, 171
Evans, C. Stephen, 174
Eve, 7
exclusivism, 142–44
existential, 6, 7, 13, 39, 83, 89, 149
exorcism, 11, 21, 23, 30, 32, 191

Farley, Lawrence R., 72n38, 86n12, 116

Faust, 24–25, 28, 30n77
fellowship, 57, 217n36
Ferreira, M. Jamie, 129n27, 145n41
forgiveness, 50, 77, 127, 128, 153n16
fortunate/unfortunate, 186–87
freedom, 4, 8, 18, 23, 27, 31, 148, 172, 178, 181
Frost, Robert, 138
Fundamentalism, 170, 171
future, the, 35, 44, 55, 58, 69, 94, 148, 204, 208–9

Garland, David E., 5n7, 86n12, 105n6, 134–35, 142n33, 164n4, 166n6
generation, 64, 106, 140
    of Jesus/Mark, 103, 115, 159, 163, 165, 175, 198, 208–9, 216
    of today, 54, 183
Gentiles (nations), 3, 118, 130–38, 140–41, 143–44, 148, 158, 165
Gnosticism, 15n28, 79
gospel
    affect, 194n12, 195
    ambassadors, 110–12
    dying to self, 150–51, 157
    historical fragments, 105, 109–10, 112–14
    invitation, 51–52, 55–56, 118, 129, 130–45, 184
    mission, 22, 32, 74–75, 78, 90, 103, 113, 118, 133, 142, 173, 187, 192
    narrow way, 77, 159
Groot, Tracy, 19n35

Hall, Ronald L., 21–30
happiness, 63, 91, 107, 111–12, 115
heaven, 10, 15, 16–18, 51, 56, 69, 79, 102–3, 105–6, 108, 110, 113, 114, 140, 146, 158–61
Heidegger, Martin, 15n28, 95, 98n42
hell, 2, 3, 10–11, 49, 116, 118–20
Herod, 81–97, 100, 164–67, 189, 192, 194–95, 200, 204, 215

Herodias, 81–82, 85–86, 89, 131, 145, 192
history, 55, 75, 83, 88, 90, 98, 98n42, 99, 99n46, 101–15, 160, 168, 175, 183, 193, 204, 205, 210
Hobbesian, 15n28, 204
Hoberman, John M. 98n42, 99n46
Holderlin, Friedrich, 177, 181
Holland, Tom, 126n20
Holy Spirit, 111n22, 112, 115, 153–54, 157, 159
home, xi-xii, 15–16, 20, 31, 62, 70, 79, 182, 189, 213, 216
honor, 41n17, 70, 92, 122, 123, 200, 211
Horne, Mark, 165n5, 166
humanity, 5n7, 15n28, 17–18, 20–21, 27–28, 31–32, 55, 56n27, 74–76, 78–79, 94–95, 105, 106n8, 119, 144, 160, 167, 176, 185, 187–88, 193, 205n14, 217n37

Iersel, Bas van., 148n4, n5
imagination, 110, 127, 135, 139n27, 183, 194–96, 213n32
Instant Karma, 119, 120, 193
inversion, 73–80
Isaac, 41n17
Israel, 57, 61, 70, 72, 116, 118–19, 136, 141, 158, 166–67, 175, 215

James, 43, 124, 149
Jeremiad, 172
Jesus
    ascension, 110
    ashamed, 208–10
    authority, 75, 78
    cross, 77, 110, 185, 192, 195, 202, 205–7
    humor, 132–33, 133n12, 137–38
    life as collision, 117, 198, 206, 206n16
    love, 137, 144, 202, 206
    messianic secret, 200, 217, 217n37
    resurrection, 44, 44n27, 110, 148
    return, 114, 209
    Servant, 103, 115
    Son of God, 15, 22, 183, 184, 188
    Son of Man, 17, 100, 114, 209–10
    sighing, 146, 150, 158–59, 165–66
    spitting, 146, 147, 160–61, 180
    subversiveness, 136, 142–45
    temptation, 215
    touches, xiii, 177–196, 198–99, 203, 205–6, 210, 212–14, 215–17
Jewish War, 204
Job, 39–42, 44
Jonah, 175
John the Baptist, 81–82, 84n10, 90–91, 94, 173, 194, 209
Jones, E, Stanley, 211–12, 213n31
judgment, 42, 68, 79, 93, 114, 117, 117n4, 118–20, 125, 191, 193, 209
justification, 20–21
justice/social justice, 93, 119, 187

Kangas, David J., 173n27
Keller, Timothy, 143n35, 144
Kierkegaard, Soren,
    concepts,
        absurd, the, 38, 49, 112, 150
        admirers of Christ, 57–58
        aestheticism, 22, 24, 26n59, 27, 89–90, 95–96
        anxiety, age of, 172–73
        becoming a self, xi, xiii, 66, 84, 152, 199, 201–2, 214, 215–16
        Blatherskite, 48, 48n7
        boredom, 9, 11
        certainty, 36n5, 68, 112, 115, 166, 194n13
        contemporaneity with Christ, 106–7, 112, 149
        Christian bourgeoise, 32, 116–18, 120–26, 129, 193
        criterion, 14, 36n5, 119, 201

Kierkegaard, Soren (*continued*)
concepts (*continued*)
crowd/herd/public, xi–xiii, 11–13, 28, 32–33, 47, 65, 85, 89, 95, 98, 103, 105, 122–26, 157–58, 174, 180, 185, 188–89, 199–214, 215–17
crudeness (societal), 88–89
decision, xii, 67, 77, 181, 189, 209
despair, 5–15, 21, 40–42, 44, 48–50, 79, 96, 172–73, 184–85, 187, 205
dizziness of freedom, 18
double mindedness/duplicity, 14
dying to, 150–55, 157, 185
earnestness, 87, 133–35, 139–40, 185, 186
established order, xii-xiii, 162–76, 179–80, 184–89, 192, 198, 201, 203–14, 216–17
existence communication, 39, 149, 184
Eternal, the 35, 39, 40–45, 49, 53–54, 103, 105, 107, 109, 172–73
festivity, 93
follower at second hand, 104–11, 142, 179, 183, 193, 214
freedom, 8, 18, 27, 31, 148, 172
frivolity, 83–88
gadfly, 162–76
governance, 39, 43–44, 47–48, 49n9, 51–52, 56, 56n30, 127, 152, 169, 182
glory of being human, 186
God-man, 62, 142
highest passion, 63, 133, 139–40
highest perfection, 34–45, 126n21, 156
humans, as a synthesis, 8, 75n5
humor, 131–33, 137–38
idea, 81–88, 89, 98n43
impossibility/possibility, 19, 20, 30, 49, 83, 107, 142, 152, 200, 202, 207
inclosing reserve, 6–8, 13, 49

indirect communication, 84, 137, 155–56
infinite qualitative distinction, the, 32, 156
inviter, 51–52, 130–45, 184
irresolution, 51
jolt, 105, 107, 108, 110, 112
knight of faith, 96
leap of faith, xii, 18, 58, 98, 104
leveling, societal, 67–68, 71, 98
like for like, 116–29, 131, 170, 182n9, 187, 193, 208n19, 209
loftiness/lowliness, 62, 65, 73–80, 97, 108n12
love command, 121–23, 126, 137, 202
martyrdom, 69 209–10
middle term of death, 151, 186
mirror, God's word as, 118, 139
moment, 18n34, 24, 30, 54, 99, 108, 120, 129, 147, 186
objectivity/subjectivity, 36, 38, 42, 87, 149, 182, 195
offense, 5, 14, 62, 75–76, 78–79, 107–8, 110, 133, 139, 185, 191
opinion, 2, 139, 185
out on 70,000 fathoms, xii, xiin3, 103, 106–7, 110, 113, 115, 183, 184, 189, 190, 193
power that established the self, 13, 172
prototype, 70, 74, 149, 152, 155, 185
radical cure, 173–74, 177, 179, 182, 187
reflection, 60–67, 69, 71, 95–97
reflective envy, 60–69, 71–72
sacred history, 99, 104, 115, 184
secular mother tongue, 36, 156–57, 174
silence, 155
single individual, xi–xiii, 12, 12n21, 19, 32, 46, 55–56, 59n35, 66, 67, 69, 71, 79, 99, 123, 180, 197–213, 215

INDEX 231

situation, xii, 15n30, 38–39, 54, 104, 106, 108, 110, 189
spiritlessness, 23, 27–28, 52–53, 89, 122
stages of existence, xiii, 87–89, 94, 96
tyrants, 69
uncertainty, 36, 103, 106, 110, 134
venturing, 18, 54–55, 58, 133, 135, 145
without authority, 208–9
person,
   forerunner, 208
   gadfly, 164, 168–69, 171–76
   missionary, 168–69
   pastor, 169, 169n13
   prophet, 168, 169, 169n13
   revolutionary theologian, 100
   readers, xii, 36, 76, 209, 210
pseudonyms,
   A, 2n4, 26n59, 217n36
   Anti-Climacus, 2, 2n3, 13, 16n30, 35, 36n5, 47, 74, 76, 88, 108, 130, 152n15, 163, 172, 195n14
   Johannes Climacus, 89, 103, 105, 106–11, 115, 171
   Johannes the Seducer, 24, 24n49
   Vigilius Haufniensis, 15n30
writings,
   "The Anxieties of the Heathen," 135
   Attack on Christendom, 5, 164, 171, 211n28,
   "Blessed is He Who is Not Offended at Me," 108
   Concluding Unscientific Postscript, 87, 89, 90
   The Concept of Anxiety, 15n30, 18n33
   Either/Or, 2n4, 22, 24n49, 27n59, 143, 217n36
   "The Expectancy of Faith," 45
   Fear and Trembling, 56n29
   For Self-Examination/Judge For Yourself, 154
   "He Must Increase; I Must Decrease," 85, 91
   Journals and Papers, 211n28
   "Joyful Notes in the Strife of Suffering," 58
   "A Leper's Self-Contemplation," 6n14
   Philosophical Fragments, 104, 106, 108n12, 109, 109n16, 217n37
   Practice in Christianity, 108n12
   "The Publican," 15, 16n32
   Repetition, 41n17
   "The Seducer's Diary," 24n49
   The Sickness Unto Death, 6, 13, 14, 152, 172, 195, 205
   "The Single Individual," 200, 208
   "To Need God is the Highest Perfection," 35, 44
   Two Ages, 68, 69, 71, 94, 95, 97, 98, 98n42, 98n43, 99, 100n46
   Three Upbuilding Discourses, 91
   "Ultimatum," 143, 144
   Upbuilding Discourses, 35
   Works of Love, 13, 68, 78, 119, 120, 120n10, 129, 152, 157, 206
Kingdom of God, 13, 15, 78, 165, 179 184–85, 189–90, 194, 200, 215

Leithart, Peter J., 15n28, 43
Lennon, John, 119
Lessing's Ditch, 99n44, 104n5, 108
Levinas, Emmanuel, 144n38
Levine, Amy Jill, 213n32
Lewis, C. S., 4–5, 18n34, 88–89, 96, 110, 213
Lorentzen, Jamie, xiii, 216–17, 217n36
longing, 17, 47, 52–53, 128
Lynch, William F. 110, 139n27

Malbon, Elisabeth Struthers, 199n4, 217n39

232 INDEX

Mark,
    family motif, 32, 56–58, 132n9, 142, 176, 189, 199, 203, 216
    fellowship, 57
    foreshadowing/motifs, 61, 85–86, 191
    gospel of the cross, 205–7, 209–10, 213–14
    parabolic method, 4, 142, 180, 183, 194
    readers, xii, 5, 44, 180, 183, 184, 194, 194n13, 210
Mark as Story (Rhoads/Dewey/Michie), 132n9
Martens, Paul, 16n32, 154n19, 157
Marx, Karl, 170
masters of suspicion, xii, 170
McSwain, Jeff, 159
mediation, 112
Melville, Herman, 113, 115, 217n36
Milton, John, 2n2, 6–7, 10–12
Moby Dick, 102n1, 217n36
Modern age, Modernism, 13, 21–32, 48, 54, 64, 66, 69, 83, 90, 100, 124–26, 174
Mosaic law, 49–50, 116–22, 129
Mother Teresa, 80, 134
movements of grace, 159–60
Mulder, Jack, 43n24

name, 4, 13, 27, 28n65, 131, 145, 173, 194n12, 206, 211
nature, natural world, 7, 159
Nazi Germany, 160
New Testament, 24, 43, 87
new creation, 44, 160–61, 184, 194
Newbigin, Lesslie, 138
Nietzsche, Friedrich, 170
nihilism, 25n54, 28n66, 29, 31

Old Testament, 39, 211
Olsen, Regine, 41
ontotheology, 171

pagan, paganism, 23, 35, 44, 209, 216
parables, 136–37, 140, 189, 200
paradox, 55, 74, 107, 179, 190

Pascal, Blaise, 133–34
Paul, xiii, 37, 39, 45n30, 55–56, 67, 111–12, 118, 136, 143–44, 151, 161, 181, 200–201
peace, 57–59, 79, 172–73, 191–92, 199, 205, 212
pedagogy, 109–10, 112
Perez-Alvarez, Eliseo, 71, 74n3, 176
Perkins, Robert L., 87–89, 94n32, 99n44, 117, 119, 121, 126
persecution, 58, 91, 100
Peterson, Eugene H., 173
Pharisees/Scribes, 16n32, 20–21, 37, 55, 117–18, 127, 129, 131, 136, 142, 164–68, 189, 192, 193, 194, 195, 200, 204, 215
philosophy, 171, 194, 194n13
Plekon, Michael, 95n34, 98n43, 99, 100n47
Polanyi, Michael, 194n13
politics, xi, 55, 198
Polk, Timothy Houston, 16n32
Possen, David D., 135n17, 195n14
post-Christendom/post-Christian, 78, 117, 126
post-critical Philosophy, 194, 194n13
poverty, 74–78, 80
power, 7–8, 13–15, 17, 21, 24, 28, 28n66, 29n72, 31, 35, 36, 39, 41, 45, 54–55, 67, 85, 86, 93, 96, 97, 100, 105, 114, 122, 131, 132, 140, 141, 146–47, 152, 155, 158, 164, 172–73, 181, 188, 189, 192, 194–95, 204, 206–7, 213n32, 215
prayer, 19, 161, 189, 212
prodigal son, 143, 213
promises, of God, 214
psychology/psychological, xiii, 15n30, 18, 71, 173–74
publicity, 52, 183, 188

Rae, Murray, 104n5, 153n16
rationalism/reason, 83, 99n44, 107–8, 108n12, 179, 190
reality, xiii, 7, 11, 15n28, 26, 39, 40, 58, 78, 83, 98n42, 113,

115n27, 124, 126, 172, 184n10, 195n16, 207
redemption, 21, 55–56, 127, 144n40, 159, 176
Reformation, Protestant, 149
repentance, 14, 75, 78, 93, 109, 153n16
resurrection, 44n27, 151, 195, 217n37
revelation, 36, 67, 106, 112, 115, 171, 183
Revelation, 110, 124, 209
revolution, 95, 98, 99, 163, 187, 213n32; *see* ages/eras
risk, xii, 54, 54n23, 132–34
Roberts, Kyle, 169n13
Roberts, Robert C., 36n4, 39n11, 56n27, 63–66, 71, 115n28
Roman Empire, 164, 166, 172, 215
Rosenstock-Huessy, Eugen, 44, 44n27

sabbath, 12, 13, 188
sacred canopy, xii
sacred history, 99, 104, 115, 184
salvation, xii, 10, 13–15, 20, 31, 42, 50, 53–54, 56–58, 69, 79–80, 107, 127, 152, 153n16, 172, 176, 181, 200–201, 203, 205, 208, 210–11, 216
Sanders, John, 129n26, 216
Satan, 6–7, 9–12, 20, 40
scapegoating, 123, 160
Scott, Drusilla, 142–43, 194n13
secular/secularism, 36, 90–91, 120, 124–25, 156–57, 170, 174, 205–6
sin, 5, 10, 13, 14, 16, 17–18, 49, 53, 77, 78, 88–89, 109, 122, 125, 160, 181, 187, 195
Smith, James K. A., 127–28, 184n10, 194n12
social ethos, 64–66
social imaginary, 184, 188–89, 194, 195n16, 215
Socrates/Socratic method, 163n1, 164, 168, 168n7, 175
solitude, 19, 93, 103, 186

speech, 26–29, 31–32, 36, 61, 61n2, 66, 122, 148, 155–56, 158, 165
spiritual blindness, xi–xiii, 148n5, 154, 179–81, 190, 195
spiritual trial, (*anfechtung*), 47, 91
Stroup, George W., 42n19
subversion, 86, 93, 136, 142, 143n35, 144
suffering, 4, 50, 58, 67–69, 77, 91, 99, 157, 160, 166, 171, 206, 210, 211n28, 213
suicide, xiii

Tanner, Kenneth, 6–13
Taylor, Charles, 184
telos, 203
temptation, 40–41, 49, 135, 170, 179, 181, 185, 207, 212–13, 215
theophany, 105, 105n6, 106, 108, 110, 113–15, 193
Thielicke, Helmut, 132, 139n28, 198n1, 200
Tietjen, Mark A., 140n30, 155, 168
Torrance, Thomas F., 144n40
Trueblood, Elton, 131n2, n3, 133n12, 137n21, 138
Turlington, Henry, 132n11
Tyre, 134
Tyson, Paul, 97

United States, 124
unity, 63, 203

Via, Dan O., 83n6, 178, 181, 194n13
victory, 45, 68, 85

Walsh, Sylvia, 151
Walton, John H., 184n11
Ward, Michael, 110
Watkin, Juila, 16n30, 38–39
Weil, Simone, 68
Westphal, Merold, 13, 77, 144n38, 170, 170n16
wilderness, 84, 92, 173, 184–85, 215
Williams, Bernard, 25n52

Williamson, Lamar, 61–62, 70n32, 84n9, 84n10, 105n6
Witherington, Ben, 70
Wittgenstein, Ludwig, 21n36, 184n10
Wodehouse, P. G., 85n11
world-picture, 21, 21n36
world-relation, 23–24, 30

Zimmermann, Jens, 126n20
Ziolkowski, Eric J., 89–91

www.ingramcontent.com/pod-product-compliance
Lightning Source LLC
Chambersburg PA
CBHW070310230426
43663CB00011B/2073